TALES FROM SCHOOL

You Can't Make This Sh*t Up!

CHUCK SCHMIDT

Tales From School:
You Can't Make This Sh*t Up

TABLE OF CONTENTS

Introduction 5

Prologue..7

1 – How I Got Here...9

2 – Rookie Teacher...21

3 – Teaching Again...37

4 – Coaching 53

5 – False Start 77

6 – Assistant Principal 83

7 – Principal 99

8 – Extracurricular Activities.................................. 117

9 – Superintendent 133

10 – The Superintendent and Students.................... 137

Photos 163

11 – The Superintendent and the Public 171

12 – The Superintendent and the Political Landscape................ 193

13 – The Superintendent and Staff 211

14 – The Job: The Toughest Job You Will Ever Love.................... 233

15 – Kids Say the Darnedest Things.......................... 243

16 – Difficult Students 253

17 – Back to School... 267

Epilogue 293

About the Author 299

INTRODUCTION

About halfway through my career in education, the idea of preserving the stories I had accumulated over the years occurred to me. However, my life was so busy with family and job that there was never time to sit down and begin writing. Some electronic files with notes about those stories were started, and over the years some files and correspondence from students, colleagues, parents, and staff were retained.

Only after finally retiring was I able to begin the process of writing these stories down in book form. However, after my first retirement I ended up taking several more interim jobs. Work on the book continued, but the jobs caused this process to take longer. Every educator can understand just not having time to write the book while working. However, once I retired for good, the motivation and time to maintain the writing was found.

These accounts have been written in chronological order of my career, but the messages and lessons are timeless. If I learned anything throughout my career, it is that establishing relationships is the key to education. Until your students know that you care about them, your impact on their lives will be minimal. Any young people who are preparing for a career in education should take this message to heart. It took me some years to learn this. Hopefully others can learn more quickly.

With the help of so many people, this book has finally been completed. My parents, who had little formal education, believed strongly in the value of an education and encouraged all seven of their children to pursue college and beyond. I thank them for their support and the pride they showed in my accomplishments while working my way through the hierarchy of the education establishment.

Thanks especially to my wife, Mary, who proofread so many of my chapters and put up with my single minded focus while I was hogging the computer. Please forgive me for all the housecleaning and cooking that I didn't do. And forgive me for the times when I woke you up in the middle of the night as I stumbled my way through the dark to the computer and recorded a new story that came to mind in my sleep.

Thanks to Linda, my editor, for her attention to detail. She helped groom this narrative into a smoother read and gave me great inspiration. And thanks to my mother-in-law, Mary Akin who also helped edit. Thanks to Ken Raney for his formatting and cover design.

Thank you to Christine who helped this dinosaur navigate the intricacies of formatting and other technical aspects of the writing. Thank you to my grandchildren for putting up with my absence while completing this project. Thanks especially to Adelyn for giving me a child's impression of my stories. And Adelyn and Anna Gwenyth drew illustrations and gave me concepts for the cover. All my children, Matthew, Nathan, Sarah, Christine, and Alexandra helped read and critique my many drafts.

Thanks to so many friends and family who read parts of this manuscript and gave advice. Thank you to so many colleagues who shared their stories with me and listened to my stories, sometimes more than once! Thank you to all the students who taught me so much about life and about myself. They so often inspired me to search for better ways to teach and learn and reach for the stars.

All of my inspiration came from the many mentors I have encountered throughout my career. I learned so much from so many of them. They helped me overcome my inexperience and develop confidence in my ability. Because of them, I can look back on my career and feel that I have made a difference.

And a special thanks to all of my former teachers. Their example of dedication helped a young boy open his eyes to the world and dream big. They truly made a difference in my life.

Many of the names in these stories have been changed to protect the privacy of individuals. I'm sure many of you will recognize yourselves, and you can remain anonymous if you wish. However, you will never be anonymous to me.

Chuck Schmidt

PROLOGUE

As I pulled my notes together on the fight and reviewed the disciplinary referral on Gary, I was dreading his dad's arrival for our meeting. Gary was a 16-year-old kid with a short temper who occasionally got into trouble because he couldn't control his emotions. If a teacher asked him to stop doing something distracting, Gary might pop back with some smart aleck remark. The teacher would then get angry, and Gary would behave in ways that escalated the encounter. Eventually he would end up in my office for insubordination.

Likewise, Gary might have an innocent encounter with another student, which left Gary feeling like he was being disrespected. Pretty soon words would fly and fists would follow. In such instances, both students ended up in my office to deal with the consequences. Both scenarios were typical for Gary. He was a likable boy and he could be very respectful at times. He could even be helpful when someone asked him (in the right way) to do something. He had a lively spirit. Unfortunately, Gary's temper frequently flared in response to some perceived or real slight.

As the new assistant principal in a Midwest urban school, it was my job to deal with such situations. So, I asked his dad to come to the school; it was time to do something about the root cause of Gary's outbursts. Gary's dad, a large man, arrived in the outer office announcing his purpose in a booming voice that scared the secretaries,

"I'm here to see that assistant principal, Schmidt," he proclaimed loudly.

It was obvious that he did not want to be there and was angry because he'd been summoned. I could hear his heavy footsteps traversing the hallway to my room after the anxious secretary directed him to my office. Before long, his large frame darkened my door.

"I had to leave work for this," he said loudly. What's the problem now?"

I invited him to have a seat and then explained the circumstances of Gary's latest incident. He glared at me with contempt as I spoke.

Upon hearing that Gary's consequence would be another suspension; he'd raised his huge frame from the chair and said menacingly,

"I ought to just come over this desk and kick your ass."

I didn't fear him physically because I felt I could defend myself. However, I do recall thinking,

"What have I gotten myself into?"

As I stared into Mr. Johnson's bulging eyes and red face, all I could think about were the wonderful days in the classroom when students were anxious to learn and when they accepted me as an authority figure. Why had I assumed anything would be better as an administrator? What had I been thinking? The conclusion to this story is in a later chapter.

By the time Gary came along, I had been a teacher and coach for thirteen years and enjoyed most of the experience. I had decided to try my hand at administration, thinking that a change in routine would both give me new enthusiasm for my vocation and a pay raise. I had kids attending college, which stretched a teacher's salary pretty thin. Early on in my applications for a position in administration, I was successful. As the saying goes, be careful what you wish for. Throughout my 13 years as a teacher and coach and 20 years as an administrator, I saw changes that I could never have imagined in my early years. This book recounts those experiences.

It is my hope that this book will help beginning teachers and administrators go into the profession with their eyes wide open to the realities of the job. It is a marvelous profession with great emotional rewards. You won't get rich in money, but you may get rich in emotional fulfillment. And it won't be without pain and soul searching as well as happy times.

By reading about my experiences as a teacher and administrator you may profit from my mistakes and successes. You may learn that you are ideally suited for the vocation or you may learn that this is not the job for you. Either way you will have a more realistic view of what it means to be an educator.

1

HOW I GOT HERE

I grew up on a farm in Western Kansas with parents who valued education highly, even though they had only one year of college between them. That my six siblings and I completed undergraduate, and in most cases, graduate degrees is a testament to the success with which our parents instilled similar values in their children. Despite my parents' emphasis on the importance of education, I did not seriously contemplate pursuing a career as a teacher until my college years.

Before Mom and Dad married, Mom taught for a year. At that time, one could get a teaching license without having a college degree. Mom taught in a one-room first through eighth grade country schoolhouse, which was affectionately known as Skunk Hollow. As a child, I remember Mom telling us stories about her teaching experiences. Her students were all farm kids who needed summers off to work on their farms. Many of them even stayed home to work during the school year when they were needed for farm work. All of her students came from two-parent families and most assumed they would go back to the farm when they graduated.

One of Mom's stories was about a sixteen-year-old third grader who drove himself to school. He was old enough to have a driver's license because he had gone to school intermittently, which was not uncommon in those days. Many students walked the legendary "country mile" and in some cases multiple miles to get to school. Some students brought hunting rifles to school so they could shoot dinner on the way home. These stories were amusing, but it never occurred to me that I would encounter similar absurdities in my modern-days career. Little did I know that I would one day have different, but just as remarkable stories of my own to tell.

The makeup of the student body has changed considerably from Mom's days at the one-room schoolhouse. It's even quite different than it was when I was in school. In the 1950s and 1960s, it was rare to have classmates who did not have both parents at home. I remember how scandalous it was when a friend's parents divorced while we were in grade school. It bothers me now that we treated him differently because his parents were divorced, but it seemed as though he were from another planet. I remember teachers making allowances for him because of his broken family. His situation was so uncommon that none of us knew how to deal with it.

Drugs were not an issue, but alcohol certainly was. It was normal in our German Catholic community to attend all day wedding ceremonies at which beer flowed freely. No one checked ages and it was common for children to join in the drinking. It was also common for teenagers to cruise Main Street while drinking beer. The police seldom enforced drinking laws. Looking back, it is clear that there were students who had drinking problems. Some of Mom's students began drinking while they were in grade school.

Although becoming a teacher wasn't on my radar in those early years, some incidents were predictors of my future vocation. I was always a good student, but had a few spells where I was also very ornery. In those days our parents were as much to fear as the teacher when we acted up in school. Children learned the social skills necessary to attend school from their parents; it was a given that parents were responsible for educating their children in this manner before they began attending school. Since two parent families were the norm and most valued education, this was a realistic expectation.

We were taught by Catholic nuns in the elementary grades. Whereas it's not uncommon for people to recall their experiences with nuns with fear and loathing, I liked the nuns and have mostly good memories from those days. Sr. Marita was my first-grade teacher. She was strict but caring. Like any first-grade teacher, she taught us many basics that were critical to our education. We learned to read and write and she conducted her classroom in an orderly fashion. Looking back, I realize Sr. Marita gave us a very strong foundation for future years in school.

Sr. Ann was my teacher in the second grade. This was the year when the first seeds about an education career may have been planted in my head. Sr. Ann was young and seemingly attractive, although only a small portion of her face was visible because of the black and white habit she wore. My friends and I found the nuns to be mysterious; to our childish minds, they didn't seem human. We could not imagine their going to the bathroom or having hair—no hair was visible under the habits. They seemed like creatures from outer space.

Nonetheless, I developed a crush on Sr. Ann. She was kind and soft-spoken and she took a liking to me. One day, she had to leave the room for a short time. Many years later, I deduced that she probably needed to go to the bathroom. At the time, that never occurred to me. She called me to her desk and asked me to watch the classroom while she was gone. I was totally flattered. She even had me sit in her chair at her desk. When she left, some of the students began to act up and I ordered them to be quiet. One of them asked me if he could go to the bathroom. I denied him the privilege; I was taking my position of power very seriously because I did not want to let Sr. Ann down.

While waiting for her to return, I felt an urgent need to pee myself. I was reluctant to leave the room and abdicate my responsibility lest chaos ensue in my absence. Instead, I squirmed around on Sr. Ann's chair for what seemed like an eternity. Finally, I could hold it no longer; I peed down my leg and all over her chair. Soon Sr. Ann returned and thanked me for watching the class. I got up and slunk back to my desk.

When Sr. Ann sat down on her chair, she realized something was seriously amiss. She stood up again and saw the puddle on the floor. I kept my head down and tried to avoid her glance. She made her way to my desk and whispered,

"Charles, did you go to the bathroom in my chair?"

Horrified and embarrassed, I denied it vehemently in spite of the fact that my jeans were soaking wet. However, we both knew what had happened. After she questioned me a while, I finally admitted that I didn't leave to go to the bathroom because I didn't want to shirk my responsibility. Mortified, I thought Sr. Ann would never speak to me again. My fear was unfounded. She soon got over the incident and treated me well throughout the rest of the school year. So it was that my first responsibility as an educational leader ended in an embarrassing failure.

Another interesting thing happened that year, which piqued my interest in education. One evening, while waiting for Mom to pick me up at school, the sixth grade teacher, Sr. Peter Damian, saw me sitting on a ledge in front of school. She noticed I was reading a rather advanced book for a second grader. The book was about Kansas history. She complimented me on reading at such a high level and invited me to come to her sixth-grade class the next day to demonstrate my reading to her students.

I was more than happy to do so. However, the sixth grade boys seemed to have felt they were being shamed for their poor reading habits. They did not take kindly to my demonstration. For some time I became the target of the jealous sixth grade boys when we were outside on the playground. At the time, it did not cross my eight-year-old mind that showing up the sixth graders might cause trouble. Regardless, I couldn't have turned the Sister down anyway.

Sr. Marcella was my teacher in third grade. Not only was she kind, but she was also a cousin, so she knew my family well. Sr. Marcella saw my academic talent and was encouraging. Once, on a day when she was absent, the substitute teacher directed us to write something of our choice. I wrote a story that involved a high school boy who was a good athlete and won over the girl of his dreams. The substitute thought it was a quality story and gave it to Sr. Marcella when she returned. Sr. Marcella was impressed. She encouraged me to continue writing and suggested I might someday be an author. Hmmm!

Unfortunately, there was an embarrassing incident in Sr. Marcella's class that, like the one in Sr. Ann's class, also involved peeing on myself. At the end of every school day, Sr. Marcella would have the class stand and say the "Our Father." On this day, I desperately needed to get to the bathroom. However, in my childish mind, it would have been sacrilegious to walk out during the "Our Father." While finishing the prayer, I could hold it no longer and peed down my leg. To my horror, there was apparently a slope to the floor. From the rear of the room, a stream of pee rolled from my back corner clear to the front and out the door. I discreetly left as the class was dismissed and waited on the playground for Mom to pick me up.

Suddenly, I noticed Sr. Marcella walking toward me. My first instinct was to run, but I did not. She asked if I had had an accident in the classroom. As I had to Sr. Ann, I denied it. She looked at my jeans, which were soaking wet, and told me to return to the room. I suggested that water from a flower pot must have spilled. There was just no way I was going to admit that I had peed in my pants. Sr. Marcella did not buy my story and had me clean up the mess, which required numerous rags. Finally, I was allowed to return to the playground where my mom was waiting. Sr. Marcella followed me to the playground and told my mom what had happened. Once again, I experienced total humiliation. There seemed to be a pattern developing.

By my sixth grade year, I was well on my way to becoming a delinquent. Sr. Peter Damien was my teacher, and several of we boys made it our purpose in life to aggravate her. We had a group called the Big Three. Drew, Steve and I thought we were pretty cool. We did things like spit sunflower seeds in the radiator, make rude noises and pester girls. Anything we could do to irritate our teacher was fair game. Poor Sister Peter Damian. She may have had a nervous breakdown that year; she was absent from school for a week on several occasions. I was terrible. As I got older and thought back to all that we'd done while in her class, I felt horrible for being such a jerk. My debt to her would be paid back to me in later years when I had to deal with students who behaved toward me as my friends and I did toward Sr. Peter Damian. Karma is a bitch.

By seventh grade, the principal knew about the Big Three and split us up. That was just as well because it was getting kind of tough for Drew to be a delinquent, since his dad was a teacher at the same school. When he got in trouble, the principal would just march him to Mr. Riedel's room and Drew would get a good scolding from his dad. Then he paid for it at home.

There were finally some male teachers at the seventh-grade level. I was placed in Mr. Hammer's class. His name was indicative of his disciplinary style. He used a paddle, which I received more than once. The other male teacher was Mr. Pfeifer who was 6'5" and weighed 290 pounds. He was a big Teddy Bear, but his size deterred any problematic behavior from the members of our club. Not long after the principal separated the Big Three, we officially disbanded and we all decided to go straight.

Junior High was our first opportunity to play organized sports. I was consumed with a love of football and basketball. At that level, we began to have relationships with coaches who had more influence than most of our teachers. Football, basketball and track were the sports we could play in junior high. Since I loved sports and had a lot of success playing them, sports became my primary reason to go to school.

Although we attended a public school, we frequently had a religion class in the morning before the school day started. Many of the boys served as altar boys in junior high. We served at regular school masses, on weekends and at the occasional wedding or funeral. To be a server you had to be trained. Sr. Paulina was the trainer for altar boys. She was one of the few Sisters who struck fear in my heart. She was very demanding and insisted that we do everything perfectly. In those days, we not only assisted the priest, but we also had to respond verbally in Latin to his Latin prayers. That took a lot of practice.

At the time, there was a popular Mafia movie with an evil character named "Stickface." We began to use that name for Sr. Paulina. Like I said, we were horrible. One day in seventh grade, the altar boys were supposed to go to server practice after school. Several of us who were on the football team decided we would not go and instead went to football practice. We were in the locker room dressing when we heard "Stickface" telling our coach that we had to come to practice. Suddenly, she walked into the locker room and confronted a bunch of teenaged boys standing around in their jockstraps. We were horrified that a nun was in our locker room and tried to cover ourselves. She firmly told us to get dressed and get to server practice immediately. As we re-dressed and walked out to go to the church, the coach looked at us and shrugged his shoulders as if to say,

"What am I gonna do?" Maybe Coach was afraid of "Stickface" too.

In high school I attended a Catholic Military Academy with both day students and boarding students. There were students from all over the United States and several foreign countries. The Catholic education and military training attracted many of the families. Many of our teachers were priests and we wore military uniforms and had a military class as part of the daily schedule. The military department was staffed by both regular military officers and non-commissioned officers. While sports remained my focus, a new world began to open to me. The priests were highly educated men who mostly came from the eastern part of the country; many of them were from Pennsylvania. They had advanced degrees in many subjects in addition to theology. Some of them had written books and were very accomplished in their fields of study.

But one of my most influential teachers was Mr. Traffas, a layman. He was a freshman English teacher, newly graduated from our local college. Mr. Traffas was unlike anyone I had ever met before. He introduced his students to classical literature. I remember reading the books of the Bronte Sisters, particularly Jane Eyre and Wuthering Heights. Charles Dickens' Great Expectations was another of the classics we studied. These books opened my mind to a fascinating world. The experience of reading these classics was probably the greatest of the influences that set me on a path to a career in education. I doubt if Mr. Traffas realized it, but he seemed mysterious and powerful to our young minds as he opened them to whole new worlds.

Thanks to Mr. Traffas' class, I developed a thirst for knowledge. Learning became exciting and entertaining. My focus was mostly in the social sciences. I began a love affair with history and government.

Throughout high school, besides my athletic interests, my thirst for knowledge of all kinds increased. I developed friendships with several boarding students who came from very different backgrounds. The diversity of lifestyles interested me. Coming from a rather sheltered farm background, I was fascinated by how differently other people lived and how the ways they lived affected their thoughts and dreams.

My senior year opened up yet another world for me. I developed friendships with classmates who were not involved in sports. I found it liberating to get away from athletics and athletes periodically. Little by little, my world was expanding.

During high school, I had my first encounter with ethnic diversity. Several boarding students were African American and Latino. I developed strong friendships with a number of them, which in some cases have lasted a lifetime. My friend Conrad was a middle-class African American and a brilliant musician. We maintained contact throughout our lives until his recent death. Rick was a close friend from New Mexico, and Bob was a doctor's son from Denver. Julio was Latino and John was from South Philadelphia. It was an eye-opening opportunity for this farm boy from Kansas.

In 1968, I started college at the University of Kansas, which would challenge my whole world view. I was a student-athlete playing football while taking classes. My schedule was exhausting as we would come home from practice tired, but with a lot of studying to complete. I took school seriously and was as focused on my education as I was on football.

1968 was a time of great turmoil in our country. Martin Luther King, Jr. had just been assassinated as had Robert Kennedy. It was the peak of the anti-Vietnam War movement, the civil rights movement and a general rejection of authority among my generation. While staying close to my core beliefs, the events of the era opened my mind to other beliefs, world views and worlds with which I had no previous experience.

The anti-Vietnam War movement was very active. In the spring of 1970 U.S. Troops invaded Cambodia. The invasion sent the anti-war movement to a fever pitch. There were demonstrations and some shootings near campus. At this time, National Guard troops shot three people at Kent State University, which created even more unrest at KU.

Eventually, the Chancellor shut down the school at the beginning of May to get people to leave campus in the hope of avoiding more turmoil. It was fascinating to watch the drama unfold around me. For the first time, I questioned my government. Although I stayed close to my core values, the world was changing, and my beliefs were in a state of flux.

By the fall of 1970, tensions were still high. When football players returned for early practice, the campus was on curfew and National Guard Troops surrounded the city. No one was supposed to be out after dark. There had been more shootings and someone had bombed the ROTC building and burned the Student Union. I remember dodging behind trees returning to my fraternity after football practice. It was a strange time and again exposed me to a world I had never seen.

There was one instance when I was walking to practice at Allen Fieldhouse with a group of football players. An anti-war demonstration was going on in front of the Fieldhouse. As we walked by, several of my teammates remarked that they just might go kick some hippy ass. Emery, an intimidating African American all-Big Eight linebacker looked at them and said,

"Why? I'm on their side."

That ended the discussion and we all went to practice.

When I began college, my interest was in getting a sociology degree and becoming a social worker. While pondering which major to choose in my sophomore year, I visited with the Academic Counselor for the athletic department. Mr. Novotny had been a high school social studies teacher before he became Academic Advisor. He told me that getting a teaching degree was a good option. With a teaching degree, he said, you could do a lot of different things. While pondering that option, I declared a major in Secondary Education with social studies emphasis.

The summer before my senior year was spent as a congressional intern for my home district congressman in Washington, D.C. A friend and I worked and lived together that summer and had a marvelous experience. We witnessed the House of Representatives at work and attended many educational opportunities provided to the interns. We toured all the government buildings and historical sites.

That summer heightened my interest in history and government and gave me even more incentive to teach.

After completing all my coursework, I was assigned a student teaching semester. My assignment included teaching American History and American Government at nearby Hayden Catholic High School. Each day I drove the 25 miles to Topeka with a football teammate, Steve, to arrive at our respective student teaching assignments. Steve and I drove in my broken down Mercury Comet with worn out shock absorbers. We bounced violently at each rut in the road and by the time we got to school we were wide awake.

I went into my teaching assignment with great excitement. My enthusiasm for inspiring young minds about the wonders of history and government was boundless. I was anxious to share the stories of my recent experience in Washington, D.C. Lucky for me, my cooperating teacher, Neal, was a coach who saw his teaching as secondary to coaching. He was anxious to turn the class over to me as soon as feasible. Very soon, I was conducting a class on my own. I also assisted with the class of another cooperating teacher named Joe. Joe was also a coach, but he was more serious than Neal about the value of the class with which I was helping. Joe was a great help in guiding this young, enthusiastic but inexperienced teacher. His guidance helped me learn how to manage a classroom. To my dismay, only a small percentage of the students shared my enthusiasm for history and government. Nevertheless, I approached each day full of optimism.

One of the few students who seemed interested was a senior girl who was very intelligent. She also had a wry sense of humor and a rebellious streak. She compulsively ate sunflower seeds in class and left a mess every day. When I saw her eating sunflower seeds, it reminded me of my days of throwing sunflower seeds in the radiator in Sr. Peter Damian's class. At first I battled her over the seeds. Finally, I conceded that this was a battle that may not be worth fighting. Eventually, we reached an agreement that it was OK to eat the seeds if she cleaned up her desk after class each day. This was my first realization that I needed to have some flexibility in my standards in order to keep students engaged.

Soon my student teaching semester was over. After twelve weeks of trying to inspire high school students, I was discouraged. Teaching was no longer attractive to me and I began looking for other jobs. I was getting married that summer and my wife-to-be, Melly, was still going to school, so anything that would earn me some money would be fine. I was offered a job at a lumber yard, which I accepted. The position would begin the following fall. Not long after I accepted the lumber yard position, Hayden High School offered me a full-time teaching and coaching position. My determination not to teach succumbed to pressure from my parents and my wife-to-be. They convinced me that I had to at least give it a try. Thus began my formal career in education.

I didn't know it then, but it was going to be quite a ride.

2

ROOKIE TEACHER

During my first year of teaching, I had an eye opening experience of just how public the life of a teacher can be.

In 1973, the Vietnam War was a serious source of conflict in the United States. A timetable had already been established for withdrawal of troops and it seemed there was no reason for more American soldiers to die. My concern about more American deaths led me to become involved with some anti-war activists who were planning a demonstration. That spring I attended several planning meetings and was selected by the group to speak at a demonstration. The original event planners had arranged to use the State Capitol grounds for a short march and rally. Some new people came to the meeting and were agitating for a march down the street.

We knew marching in the street would be unlawful and that we would probably be arrested. Therefore, the original organizers stuck to their plan, because they did not want to do anything illegal. Later, I learned that it was not unusual for outside agitators to push for an illegal march. We were told that they may be agents of the FBI who were trying to get us arrested. I don't know if that was true in our case, but it did happen in some cases.

A local funeral home owned by the parents of one of my students anonymously donated a coffin. The coffin was to be a graphic representation of the last soldier to be killed before the U.S. got out of Vietnam. My role was to clarify that since we were going to get out anyway, prolonging that withdrawal would result in the unnecessary deaths of more American soldiers. I was only 23 years old and could identify with the soldiers. Some of my friends from high school had been to Vietnam.

It was a bit intimidating standing on the steps of the Capitol looking out at a large audience of activists. During the speeches, individuals circulated throughout the crowd taking pictures. We later learned that it was common practice for the FBI to take pictures and create files on anti-war activists. I'm sure my picture is somewhere in a government file cabinet.

Several days later, I was called to the principal's office. He asked me about my participation in the anti-war rally. He said he had received complaints from some parents. He didn't chastise me for my participation, but it was clear that my involvement was concerning to the principal and some parents.

That's when it dawned on me that teachers are public figures. My students' parents were going to notice when a teacher became involved in political activism. My visit to the principal's office was my first awakening about the public role of a teacher. I would learn much more throughout my career about the public nature of an educator.

———————

In the fall of 1972, I began my first paid teaching job. My assignments were freshman World Geography, junior American History, and senior Government. Hayden High School in Topeka was the private Catholic high school where I had done my student teaching. The school had two campuses, so a fellow beginning teacher and I started our day at the freshman-sophomore building and then carpooled to the junior-senior building in the afternoon.

World Geography was not a strength of mine. Indeed, I was only marginally qualified to teach the subject. This was a big concern for me and I had to learn along with the students while staying a step ahead of them.

In the 1970s, teaching centered around the textbook. There was no prepared curriculum other than what was in the book. At my first job, they just handed me a book, a set of keys and my classroom assignments. Of course, education has changed tremendously since then. But in those days, you followed the textbook and whatever else you brought to the class.

As it turned out, World Geography became my favorite class to teach. The students were freshmen, and I enjoyed learning right along with them. As we studied different parts of the world, I had students write letters to the embassies of the countries we studied to ask for information. They received large packets with all kinds of interesting facts and pictures. The students used these packets to give reports on their assigned countries. Keep in mind there was no internet at the time, so this was the only way we could get information. Researching is so much easier today, but we had a lot of fun with those packets and reports. It was always exciting when these packets arrived in the mail. I never dreamed that I would end my educational career as I'd started it, again teaching world geography and world history.

Many years later, I met some of the students who had been freshmen in my World Geography class. Even as grown adults, they remembered the reports they gave on their assigned countries and indicated that they'd enjoyed the class. Fortunately, none of them remembered the time I had the Nile River flowing the wrong direction and a student corrected me!

Thirty years later as an administrator and a member of a professional educational organization, I made a call to that organization to get some information. The woman on the phone recognized my name. She was one of my former students in World Geography. We had a wonderful conversation about the research activities and presentations that students made in that class. This was one of many times I heard from previous students and realized that what I did made a difference. Throughout my career, one of the great joys of teaching was encountering former students who not only remembered me, but also what we did in class.

I often used movies to help students understand countries and their cultures. As we studied the Far East, we viewed a movie about Buddhism. It was an excellent portrayal of the dominant religion in some of these countries, and it showed the peacefulness and oneness with nature that was part of their culture. This movie made such an impression on me that I used it as the entertainment at a faculty social. That was a mistake.

It was the practice of some of the faculty members to get together for a monthly social gathering at the homes of teachers. The host provided refreshments and entertainment. Keep in mind that we taught at a very traditional Catholic School. In my first year, I joined with a new biology teacher and our wives to host one of those socials. We used the movie about Buddhism as the entertainment. There were a lot of quizzical looks as we showed the film to our veteran Catholic School colleagues. Several years later it occurred to me that the movie may not have been the best entertainment choice. Our colleagues probably thought we were trying to convert them to Buddhism.

My afternoon American History and Government classes were not as engaging as the World Geography class. The afternoon students were juniors and seniors and many didn't care about the subjects. I tried everything I could to engage them, from using simulation games to creating a constitution to bringing in speakers. Too often, their eyes glazed over and it was clear that they had no interest in the subject.

However, occasionally they would get involved in a topic. This was 1973 and Watergate was a dominant issue in the news. Even the students were interested in what was happening, though they didn't understand much about the issue. In the spring of 1974, I told my government students that when they returned in the fall of 1974 for the school year, Richard Nixon would no longer be president. They were shocked that my prediction came true when he resigned on August 9, 1974.

During that first couple of years of teaching, I began learning to deal with parents. Most of the parents were supportive of the school and were realistic about their children. Occasionally, you had the parent who thought their child could do no wrong. And there were a few parents who tried to influence the teacher to get favorable treatment for their child.

In my first year, there was a likable young man who was not a very good student. He didn't take school very seriously and received a D in my class. At the parent/teacher conference we had a cordial discussion. At the end of our meeting, the father mentioned that he knew I was very interested in history and gave me a brand new hardback biography of Harry Truman. At first, I was delighted and accepted the book without hesitation. However, it occurred to me later that the book might have been intended as a bribe. Not knowing what to do, I kept the book but still graded the student objectively. I never did find out if the parents intended their gift to affect my grading.

One activity that engaged my students was a discussion of the political spectrum from conservative to liberal. Again, keep in mind that this was in the early 1970s. I found some speakers to represent both extremes. There was a liberal state legislator who annually introduced a bill to legalize marijuana and a person from the far right who was a family friend of one of the students. I invited both to speak on consecutive days to show the students the range of difference in political beliefs.

The liberal legislator came to class and students were captivated by his ideas. In addition to his stand on marijuana legalization, he espoused all of the liberal causes of the time: anti-Vietnam War, pro-civil rights, and so on. By the end of the period, he was sitting in the lotus position on top of my desk and pontificating to the students. Many of them were probably pot users at the time and hung around to visit with him after the class. Still, it was great to see them so engaged.

The next day the conservative speakers came to class. They were introduced to me as John Birchers by the parent of a student. However, they quickly informed us that they no longer were in the John Birch Society because it was too liberal.

They believed that Jews were the cause of most of our problems in the United States and the world. The speakers also felt that the Rockefellers were behind almost everything that they, former John Birchers, opposed. They believed the government was controlled by Jews and the Rockefellers, and this was the source of all their conspiracy theories.

Once again, the students were captivated by what they heard, as was their teacher. I had never heard so many conspiracy theories before. I'm not sure the speakers were good representatives of the left or right, but they certainly displayed the massive gulf between the two extremes. This was years ago, but the same chasm in beliefs is present today.

Maybe the most moving activity in my classes was our project on the judicial system in government class. Our city had a minimum-security prison that conducted open discussions weekly. I encouraged my senior government students to attend these events with me for extra credit. Quite a few began attending on a weekly basis.

The discussions were captivating. Prisoners talked about their lives; what they had done to end up in prison, how the courts treated them and what they hoped to do when they got out. The students heard emotional stories from these convicts and became personally attached to them.

One prisoner, Kevin, an African American, was clearly the leader of the discussion. He was intelligent and articulate. He explained that he ran off with the white daughter of a prominent person in town. The girl's father had him charged with statutory rape. According to Kevin, the woman was an adult and went with him voluntarily. However, the father convinced her to claim that Kevin forced her to go with him, so he ended up in prison.

Many of the students openly sympathized with Kevin and were impressed with his eloquence. After almost five years in prison, he was within three months of being released. One week we went to the discussion and Kevin was gone. We were told by prison officials that he had escaped. The students and I were devastated. We couldn't understand why he would do that when he was so close to release. It was a cold, hard dose of reality for all of us.

Because the students were so enamored with the justice system and the prisoners they had met, they were hungry for more similar experiences. The local county jail had a program in which they allowed prisoners to come to schools to speak. Their message was basically, "Don't do what I did." That included drugs and other illegal activity.

One day, four county inmates came to our majority white school.

Three of the four inmates were black. They spoke in my classes and then had lunch with the students. Again, this was a real awakening for many of my middle and upper-class white students. They were interacting with people from cultures they had never before experienced.

During my first two years of teaching, I also coached. I was an assistant in football and track. Having just completed my career in Division I football, I had quite a bit of experience in that sport. The head coach, Leroy, had been my coach in high school. He knew me well and gave me a lot of freedom to coach. I was somewhat surprised that he was mellower than I remembered him from the days he coached me. As a young coach, he was intense and hard driving. Most of us feared him at that time.

That first year, we started football practices about two weeks before the beginning of school. I was able to get to know the athletes well in that time. They were impressed with the fact that I had played football at the college level and showed respect for my knowledge of the game.

A week before school started there was a welcome back dance for the students. My wife of two months, Melly and I attended. She was only 20 years old at the time and still attending college. I left her standing for a bit while I went to the bathroom. Upon returning a couple of the senior football players were chatting it up with her thinking she was a new student in the school. They were obviously hitting on the new girl. When I came back and introduced her as my wife, they about fainted. There was a lot of stuttering, and they quickly returned to the dance.

Part of my football assignment was coaching the freshman team. We had some good athletes and played several games at the freshman level. One of my freshman players was a huge, athletic kid who was new to the area. While getting to know him, I learned that his father was in prison and his mother had moved to the area so they could visit his father regularly. As a freshman, Andrew was already over six feet tall and weighed more than 200 pounds. He was a dominating football player in his class. I could envision him developing into an exceptional athlete.

Because they had just moved to the area, there was some question about his eligibility. I had checked with the state athletic association and they said he had to go through a hardship hearing to be eligible. I visited with his mother and she was adamant that he play sports to keep him out of trouble. However, when I asked the principal to support his hardship hearing, he would not support the action.

This made me angry, and I pleaded with the principal. I explained that the mother wanted him involved and feared that he would get in trouble if he couldn't play sports. The principal was unmoved.

Being a young, impetuous and idealistic coach, I tried to go around the principal and contacted the state association on Andrew's behalf. The principal found out what I was doing and warned me about insubordination. I realized that I had just risked my career by defying authority and eventually dropped the issue. This incident caused me to become disillusioned with administration. I had believed that they would be anxious to help the young man. I'm sure there were other considerations that my inexperienced mind did not comprehend. I filed this incident in the back of my mind and referred to it later as an administrator.

I have often wondered if my main concern was Andrew's welfare or the fact that he had the potential to be an outstanding athlete on my team. Later in the year, Andrew left school, and I never did hear from him again. I hope he was able to stay out of trouble and have a productive life.

Part of our job as coaches was taping ankles and checking out injuries. One day as we were getting ready for football practice one of my athletes came to me about a problem with his back. I asked one of the older assistant coaches what we could do for the boy. Jerry was a grizzled veteran who had seen a lot in his long career. He took me into the coach's office and explained that the boy was always complaining about mysterious injuries. He told me to watch what he did for this boy.

Jerry took the boy to the training room and asked him where it hurt. The boy pointed to a spot on his back. Jerry told him,

"There is a nerve that runs from that spot in your back to a place in your foot. You may have injured that nerve in the foot."

He then vigorously rubbed and manipulated the boy's foot for several minutes. Then he asked, "Does that ache in your back feel better now?"

"Oh yes, it is much better now," said the boy as he jumped up and ran out to practice.

Afterwards, I asked Jerry about what he had done. Jerry explained that this boy just needed attention. The boy thought that coaches knew everything, so when Jerry told him something, he believed it completely. He just needed a placebo to make him feel better. This was puzzling, but I learned that as a teacher and coach, students and athletes often looked up to you and attributed powers to you that you didn't really have.

Every year, our freshmen played a game against the Boys Industrial School. This was a reform school for delinquent boys. Some of them were outstanding athletes, but they had been in trouble with the law. They were encouraged to get involved in sports to keep them engaged in positive activities.

Our team was almost all white and the boys at BIS were nearly all black. This was a bit of a culture shock for my team. The coach at BIS was a legendary gentleman known as Chief Price. Chief Price was part Native American and part African American. He was a wonderful man who served as a father figure for most of the boys. He could be hard-nosed when necessary, but he was soft enough that his athletes knew he cared about them.

My boys were a bit afraid of the BIS team because they knew some of them had engaged in criminal activity and could be vicious. However, despite being talented, they were not very successful athletically because they didn't have great teamwork or conditioning.

Once when we played them, my boys complained about activity taking place in the pileup after a tackle. They said the BIS boys were grabbing our boys by their scrotums and squeezing. They also said one of the boys had a razor blade and had cut one of our boys on the leg. I immediately went over to Coach Price and told him what was happening. He had a talk with his team and the behavior stopped.

Chief Price was an inspiration to me. I once asked him how he managed to work with such difficult kids. He said,

"I can give them direction about what they need to do, but I can't make them do it. If they follow my direction, they might be able to overcome their difficult circumstances and have productive lives. If they don't, there is nothing I can do."

Chief Price was highly respected in the coaching fraternity. He never won a lot of games, but he probably did more to influence lives than any of us. His attitude inspired me throughout my coaching career.

One of my freshman athletes was a small, energetic boy who played with high energy. Jerry was five feet two inches tall and barely weighed 100 pounds. He wanted to play running back, but I felt he was too small to take that pounding, so he was positioned at defensive back. Occasionally I would let him run the ball late in a game just to give him the opportunity.

Jerry taught me a powerful lesson a few years later. I had looked at his size and denied him the opportunity he craved. I had neglected to look at his heart and see how badly he wanted to succeed. Jerry grew a little by his senior year, but he was still only five foot six and 130 pounds. The new head coach, showing more wisdom than me, gave him a chance to be a running back and he ended up leading the league in rushing. This taught me not to prejudge an athlete by his physical appearance.

One of our outstanding varsity athletes was Sherman. Sherman had incredible speed and jumping ability. He set a state record in the long jump and was a successful sprinter. However, Sherman was not particularly fond of getting hit while playing football. We used him as a running back. If he could get outside around the end, he was hard to catch. Coach Leroy was as frustrated with Sherman as I was. We could not inspire his desire to play and we couldn't keep him on the field as much as we would have liked. Sherman was often injured and sometimes just didn't want to play.

As I got to know Sherman, I found out he was an orphan who had been adopted by another family. He did not get along well with his adoptive family, but at least he had a home. While Sherman had a lot of success in track, he was always a frustration for me in football. I thought he could be a lot better, but he just didn't like the game that much. As coaches, we tried to guide him and keep him involved. There were a lot of after practice discussions with Sherman about problems he was having with family and life in general.

Many years later I ran into Sherman. He had a nice family and a responsible job. He seemed happy and successful. I realized that although he had frustrated us in football, our caring for him personally was much more important in his life. That was another lesson I learned from Chief Price.

Part of my coaching assignment was coaching the freshman track team. We had some talented athletes and competed successfully in the area. As in football, it was always an adventure to go to the meet hosted by Boys Industrial School. Some of those kids were incredible athletes, but often they did not train and condition themselves. In the middle distance and distance races especially, I told my athletes to never give up no matter how far the BIS boys might be ahead of them.

There was a 400-meter race in which one of the BIS boys went out full speed and was 50 meters ahead of the field at the 200-meter mark. Sure enough, he started to fade and one of my boys caught him on the straightaway and won the race. One of my 1600 meter runners was trailing the boy from BIS by almost 200 meters after the first two laps. By the time they finished the third lap the BIS runner was fading badly, and my runner was about to pass him. When my runner passed him on the curve, the BIS runner stepped off the track. He came over to the area where I was standing, and I heard him say "F... this shit" as he picked up his sweats, lit up a cigarette and walked away.

During these track meets, I spent a lot of time talking with Chief Price. He was always full of interesting stories. I asked him if it was frustrating coaching these talented athletes when he couldn't require them to work out and develop their talent.

He said, "My most important job is to help them develop as young men, not young athletes. I tell them what it takes and they can choose to do it or not." What an inspiring man he was.

Jim was our head coach in track. He was also an assistant in football with me. Jim was an energetic former athlete who loved the details of technique in the various track events. We would spend hours after practice talking about techniques. It seemed that almost every weekend Jim would go to another track clinic. Inevitably, he would bring home some new idea that would cause us to change our workout routines. Eventually, in frustration, I asked Jim if we couldn't just settle on one technique and stick with it. He laughed and said he would probably attend another clinic the next weekend. And he did and we changed again. In spite of how much this frustrated me, Jim and I continued a great friendship until the time of his death.

Early in my second year of teaching, I became disillusioned. It did not seem like the students cared about the subjects I was teaching and I was frustrated. I had burned some bridges with my principal over the issue of eligibility for the freshman football player. I began visiting with my parents about returning to the farm.

My colleague in social studies, Joe, tried to convince me to stick with teaching. Joe was a fellow coach and midway through the year, he became the head football coach when Leroy announced his retirement. Joe wanted me to stay and assist him.

As Joe and I discussed students' lack of interest, he tried to encourage me. He pointed out that we were reaching the students who were receptive and that was all we could expect. When I decided to go back to the family farm, Joe predicted that I would eventually return to teaching. I told him he was crazy and that I would never teach again.

Despite my unhappiness with teaching at that point, there had been some special relationships in those first two years. As a beginning teacher, I was only 4 years older than some of my students. I could relate to their lifestyles and concerns. Some saw me as an ally who understood them in contrast to their much older teachers.

Mary T., for example, was a student with whose family I became very close in my first years of teaching. She was the daughter of a man I had come to know well, and she and Melly and I hit it off immediately. We went to movies with her and even had picnics together. We were invited to her home by her parents and ran into each other frequently. Twenty-five years later we socialized with Mary T. and her husband. Unfortunately, we also mourned with her at the funerals of her husband and her father. Forty-five years later we are still friends, and we frequently communicate via social media.

Mike was another student with whose family I became close in my first few years of teaching. His parents were philanthropists in the community, and we participated with them in many causes. Years later, when his mother passed away, we mourned with him at the funeral.

That funeral was an interesting experience. Mike's mother was a wonderful lady who donated generously to many worthy causes, mostly artistic endeavors. She was well loved by many and a devout wife and mother. Unfortunately, she contracted cancer and died at a relatively early age.

There was a huge crowd at her funeral. This was when Fred Phelps and his notorious Westboro Baptist Church were active in demonstrating against gay rights. Mike's mother had no direct connection to any gay rights activities, but she was accepting of everyone and interested in the fine arts. That may have been why the Westboro group decided to demonstrate at her funeral.

When we arrived for the funeral, we passed the demonstrators with their repulsive signs. They made me so angry that I had to be restrained by Melly from going after them. Demonstrating at her funeral seemed the cruelest, most unchristian thing anyone could do to her family. Eventually, I went into the church but was filled with anger at the heartlessness of this group. That kind of demonstration became commonplace for this bigoted organization in future years.

Sometime later I experienced another encounter with this bigoted group. While riding the school bus with our football team, some of the players flipped off a group of Westboro Baptist protestors as we drove by. The next week our fax machine at school was inundated with repulsive images from the Westboro group. This was the way they harassed anyone who opposed them in the 1970's.

Danny was another young man with whom I hit it off immediately. He was in my class but also participated in football and track. Danny always had a smile and something positive to say. He was a good athlete, and we spent a lot of time just talking. Later he became a basketball referee, football official, and baseball umpire. I occasionally ran into him at games. Forty-five years later we still see each other from time to time.

In my early years of teaching, there was not as much suspicion when a teacher had a close relationship with a student, as there is today. In later years, after many scandals, people became much more cautious about having such friendships.

In the era of social media, such contacts are scrutinized even more closely. One of the staples of new teacher training is a discussion of the boundaries between teachers and students. Some beginning teachers want to become best friends with their students. There is a place to be friendly, but if the teacher doesn't maintain a respectful distance he could lose his authority or worse, become involved in a scandal. During my time in education, I have seen some careers ruined or almost ruined by not maintaining distance.

In my second year of teaching, I became friends with our male counselor who was in his 40s. Jim was a gentle man who had a wife and five children, some of whom attended our high school. He was well-liked by students and faculty and seemed to be a good counselor. The kids felt comfortable talking to him about anything. At the end of that year, we were all shocked when we found out that Jim had left his family and run off with an 18-year-old student who had recently graduated.

Incidents of that sort were relatively rare in the early 1970s, but they became more frequent in the later years of my career. As an administrator, I had to deal with inappropriate relationship issues several times.

So, in spite of some positive experiences and relationships in those first two years, I still decided to give up teaching. It was primarily my inability to handle the frustration of unmotivated students that killed my inspiration to teach. I was just too immature.

When I returned to the farm, I generally distanced myself from teaching. However, at that time Melly was teaching in our hometown, and that kept me somewhat connected to education. She was teaching at my alma mater, another private Catholic school that had very high academic standards. Despite leaving education, I maintained some interest through her experiences. Sometimes I was envious because she seemed to have students who were engaged and interested. I missed my personal relationships with students. At other times, I was just glad not to be teaching.

I spent nine years in the dairy and wheat business in partnership with my parents. We did quite well financially, but by that time we had three children. Melly and I were concerned that I was not spending enough time with them. Leaving in the dark and coming home in the dark did not make for good parenting. I also missed the interaction with others, especially young people. Finally, I made a decision to change careers, but not yet back to teaching.

After quitting the farm work, I spent two years doing drug and alcohol abuse counseling. A friend had started a private agency and needed help. Some of my education training was relevant, and I received further training to become certified as a drug and alcohol abuse counselor. For a time, I found the work meaningful and enjoyable, but after a couple of years, it began to wear me down. There were so many negative situations that it became depressing. There was also a financial strain. If we didn't get enough business or grants we weren't able to pay ourselves. That didn't work for a man with a wife and three children. However, the experience was invaluable when I later returned to education.

3

TEACHING AGAIN

In 1985 an opportunity came to get back into education. My private Catholic School alma mater, Thomas More Prep-Marian, offered me the position of Admissions Director and I enthusiastically accepted.

This position involved public relations and recruitment for the boarder program. My job was to develop promotional programs for the school and travel throughout several states to recruit boarder students. The school had changed considerably since I had attended. It was no longer a military school, but the academics had actually improved. Thus, it was attractive to people in the community who highly valued education.

When I took the job, I was 35 years old and full of energy. I had three children and knew this position involved travel. Melly was teaching at the school, so I knew the staff well. I loved this school and promoting its values came naturally to me.

Some interesting situations arose out of this job. It was exciting to meet so many people throughout the state and in other states. Because of the nature of this job it allowed me to establish some close relationships with the families of students. It also gave me a deeper level of interest in the success of these students that I had recruited. Sometimes things worked out and sometimes they didn't.

One time a parent called me in the middle of the school year to tell me that her daughter, Judy, would be transferring from the local public school to our Catholic School. I asked her if Judy was resistant. She said that Judy didn't know about the change of schools yet. Apparently, she was running with a bad crowd, and her mom wanted to get her away from that group. Mom had bought the uniforms, and she said that Judy would discover that her closet had turned blue on Monday.

I expressed my concern that the girl would be resistant and said I would try to work with her. Judy showed up with Mom the following Monday morning with a defiant attitude. I convinced her that she should give it a fair try while we got her enrolled in classes. After a couple of weeks of resistance, Judy began to make friends and lost the belligerence. To my surprise, she eventually did quite well and graduated on time. It didn't always work out that way.

One boy was required by his parents to attend our school. He was an outstanding athlete but struggled a bit academically. He also had some difficulty following the rules. After two years, he convinced his parents to let him transfer to the public school. He eventually became a star athlete and graduated from public school.

Andrew was the son of wealthy parents in a nearby city. He had gotten into drugs and had some encounters with the law. His father, a wealthy businessman, contacted me about enrolling his son. We discussed how it was going to be difficult for Andrew to adapt to the simple living quarters and a disciplined life. Dad was willing to give it a try. Unfortunately, Andrew could not adjust, and he lasted less than a year. Dad was grateful for our efforts to work with his son and donated generously to the school.

One father from out of state contacted us when his son was only in sixth grade. He desperately wanted a Catholic School experience for Chris. Finally, when Chris was ready for high school, he was enrolled and arrived in his freshman year. Homesickness soon set in and he struggled to get through that first year.

During Chris' high school years, Dad frequently made the trip to Kansas to help Chris cope with homesickness. Eventually, Chris graduated and went on to achieve a college degree. Dad was so thankful that, after becoming a widower and retiring, he came to work at the school supervising boarder students.

In this job, I traveled to Catholic grade schools and gave presentations to their students. One of my presentations was at St. Andrew's Catholic School in Independence. I remember thinking how far Independence was from Hays, which was in the opposite corner of the state. Ironically, 20 years later, I would serve as the Superintendent of Schools in Independence.

After three years in my position as Admissions Director, I was feeling very confident and bought a new pickup for my travels. At the time, I was deeply involved in local politics as the county Democratic Chairman and actively campaigned for Democratic Governor John Carlin. Governor Carlin implemented a severance tax on oil pumped in Kansas. A local oil company funded the Trust that paid for my position and was a significant donor to the school. Eventually, the school was notified that if I were not removed, the company would withdraw its funding.

I will always remember the meeting with the principal in which she terminated me from my position. It was apparent she was conflicted. She claimed they wanted to go with someone with more experience. It was clear to both of us that I was being dismissed because of my political activism, but the principal stuck to her story. My suspicions were confirmed when I later confronted some of the executors of the Trust. They made it clear that my political activism was the determining factor in their decision to press for my termination.

This blow to my employment was the impetus for my return to the classroom. The old saying that when one door closes, another one opens, proved to be true. I didn't look at it that way at the time, but losing my job opened the door to a great future for me.

After terminating me as Admissions Director, the principal offered me a part-time teaching job. I was bitter about what I considered to have been an unfair dismissal, but despite my initial resistance to taking the part-time job, I eventually accepted the position. It turned out that Joe, my friend from my first teaching assignment, was correct when he predicted that I would eventually return to teaching.

After a thirteen-year absence from teaching, thus began my journey back to what would become a lifelong career in education. When

I returned to the profession, I could not have imagined the amazing experiences that awaited me.

———

I returned to teaching still bitter about losing my previous job because of politics. However, the Trust that had funded my previous position also provided grants for tuition for teachers to continue their education. I decided to make use of those grants and work toward an administration degree. They may have had me fired, but I was going to use their resources anyway. So, while teaching, I also began taking masters level courses in administration at the local college, Fort Hays State University.

My assignment was teaching religion classes at the Catholic high school. Thomas More Prep-Marian was my former high school, but it had transitioned into a co-ed Catholic college prep school. I taught the Old Testament, New Testament, Christian Morality, Church History, and Sociology. The Church History and Sociology fit well with my history major. The other classes were outside my expertise, and I relied on textbooks and took some online courses from a Catholic College.

Initially, I resented being put in this teaching assignment because of what I perceived as unfair termination. However, I soon decided to motivate myself to be an outstanding teacher and get excited about the subject material. I poured my heart into the job.

One of my favorite lessons in Old Testament class was when I taught about the ten plagues visited on the Egyptians when the Pharaoh would not let Moses and the Jews leave Egypt. I simulated some of the plagues with symbolic objects. For the second plague of frogs, I threw out a stuffed frog that was a favorite of my young children. For the seventh plague of hail, students were surprised by getting hit with ice that I tossed from a bucket. For the eighth plague, I threw paper cutouts of locusts at the students. The ninth plague of darkness was easily replicated by simply turning out the lights. I don't know if this allowed students to assimilate the events better, but it sure did keep them awake and alert to the possibility of being hit by flying objects. Of course, the final plague, the killing of the firstborn child of the Egyptians could not be replicated.

Another notable activity in the Old Testament was the writing of Psalms. We studied the Book of Psalms extensively and learned about the different types. I had students write a modern-day psalm in their own words. There were some very touching and insightful submissions, and we had students judge the top ten psalms. The winner was Corey, a huge but sensitive football player who wrote a psalm titled "Spit on the Ceiling." He surprised me with the skillful articulation of his feelings.

There are several different types of psalms, but the most popular with the students was the Lament Psalm. This is primarily gloom and doom, but it ends with a statement of hope. For some reason, most of the students chose this style. Students could vote for the best psalms, and the two they selected are below.

Erebus

*My depression is the sun rising in the morning. It casts shadows over the buildings, stealing away their definition, their detail.
The buildings are my life.*

*I strain as I try to look deeper into the shadows,
hoping to find some familiar aspect.
To no avail, the more I probe, the more the excruciating light of the
sun burns its face into every surface of my wanting eye.*

*I close my eye only to find the image of the dominating sun
etched on the back of my eyelids.
As the tide ebbs from the shore, so will the depression from my life.
The blistering sun will drift with undetectable progress to the opposing horizon, this I know. But as I anticipate the relief from the glare, I
turn to God for the strength to look beyond the unforgiving sun.
And the skyline devours the smoldering sun. But still, I turn to God
for I know that the sun will rise again.*

~ Bobby
Spit from the Ceiling

Oh God! Why have you forsaken this day as you have?
The leaves of the trees have
Withered and died, and the flowers have lost their petals. You have
scorched the Earth with bitterness and made its people evil.

The rain has turned to blood, oozing down from the clouds
like spit from the ceiling.
Why have you done this Lord? You have thrown your people into
poverty and made them sinners and beggars.
The food on my table is that of molded bread and sour milk.

But you Lord, are all knowing and all loving
and I trust in your almighty judgment.
Do as you wish, and I will follow you.

~ Corey

I was pleased with how well so many of the students did with this assignment. They put some real creativity and poetry into the project. The opportunity to write their own psalms gave them a better understanding of the Biblical Psalms, and it gave them an opportunity to be creative.

In the course of reading the Old Testament, the students were frequently surprised by the violence in some of the verses. The students and I decided to use some of these Bible verses as we cheered for our athletic teams and against our opponents. At one basketball game, they chanted, "may your children be smashed against the rocks." (Psalm 137:9) The principal heard these chants and admonished me. I told her they were just quoting the Bible. She was not amused and ordered us to stop. I shouldn't have allowed them to do this, but it did reinforce their knowledge of Bible verses, and they paid more attention.

The Book of Proverbs was another opportunity for students to create their own narratives. Some of the students wrote very insightful proverbs. Their critical thinking led me to put up a poster board in the room called Profound Statements. Whenever a student wrote something or brought something up in the discussion that seemed steeped in wisdom, it was written on the Profound Statements poster board. It became a goal of students to be quoted on the Profound Statements board. Some of the better proverbs are listed below.

"You lie the loudest when you lie to yourself." ~ **Megan**
"A kind word soothes the anger." ~ **Burt**
"A wise person writes with a pencil and corrects their mistakes and learns from them, while a fool uses a pen and embeds his mistakes in the paper of mankind." ~ **Mark and Jason**

Once again, I was surprised and pleased by the wisdom and creativity of my students. They had internalized the lesson and became engaged in the topic. I was learning that when students are allowed to create something that has meaning to them, they develop a greater understanding of the topic.

New Testament class involved becoming more familiar with the Gospels and the other books. To bring the class alive, I had the students form parishes. Students were allowed to elect their pastor, and we conducted activities as a parish. In a few cases, the students elected girls to be the pastors. This, of course, went against Catholic doctrine and I checked with the principal if that would be alright. She approved that bit of progressiveness.

Our parishes enacted an early centuries Christian Mass. Masses in those days were performed in homes and were very intimate affairs just like the first Mass, what we now call The Last Supper. Students brought bread along with a few other snacks, and we used grape juice for the wine. The pastor conducted the Mass including a symbolic consecration of the bread and wine. The pastor then gave a sermon. This activity was quite well received by students, and it gave them a better picture of how the church began. It was enlightening to hear the sermons by our student pastors. In some cases, they were better than the ones I heard in church.

Their sermons touched on subjects that were part of the students' lives. The pastors applied doctrines of faith to issues that directly affected their classmates, bringing relevance to the sermons. Sometimes our real pastors talk in vague terms that are not directly applicable to our daily lives. These students made the connection.

The leaders were also responsible for developing some service or informational activities for the parish. Surprisingly, one of the more popular activities was a visit to a mortuary to learn about the funeral process. We had a parent who owned a funeral home and was always willing to give us a tour and explanation. I always gave the students a choice to opt out of this activity if they did not want to attend.

Another activity was to tour a cemetery and allow students to talk about loved ones who might be there. In one instance, there was a student, Julie, who had recently lost her father. I asked this girl if she would rather not participate. She was insistent that she attend. While in the cemetery, several students talked about the lives of relatives or friends who had passed on. When it was Julie's turn, she gave an emotional account of her father's life. There was not a dry eye after that tribute.

The point of these activities was to understand the process of death and dying and how it applied to our current lives. A good friend of mine, Gerry, was a professor in the local college who taught classes on death and dying. I had attended some of his classes, and we had discussed his research. The poignant message he left us with is that we should live our lives, so we don't have regrets at the time of our death. He also helped us to understand death better so as not to have an unhealthy fear of our own death.

We also did a lot of other things that were not as morbid. One of our activities was cleaning a homeless shelter. This was interesting for us all as we were instructed to use rubber gloves at all times. This was at a time when there was great fear and little knowledge about AIDS and other sexually transmitted diseases. There was definitely some squeamishness among the students during this activity.

Another activity was to do a random act of kindness for a needy person. There was a disabled homeless individual who lived in our town who was referred to as "Walking Bob." Bob was recognized all over town and was often seen collecting aluminum cans. It was gratifying to me that the students suggested we treat Walking Bob to a good breakfast.

When we did these activities, I drove a school bus to take the class to the site of our activity. One student made the arrangements about where to pick up Bob. He got on the bus, and his choice for breakfast was McDonald's. Students clamored to speak with Bob during the bus ride. We paid for Bob's meal with the money we had raised for our projects. The students were excited about doing something meaningful for such a needy individual. They also learned something about his life, which gave them some insight into this homeless man as an individual. It was fascinating to watch the students interact with Bob.

Another activity was a trip to a homeless shelter in Denver. Students had to raise their own money to fund the trip. We spent two nights in the homeless shelter and served meals to the residents. That shelter had some very strict rules. One of the rules was that the residents could not stay more than a month unless there were extenuating circumstances. They were required to go out every day and search for a job. There were families with young children living in this shelter.

During our stay, we learned a lot about the circumstances of many of these residents. Some were families who had experienced bad luck with car breakdowns on their way across the country. Others lost jobs because of layoffs or because of their own addictions to drugs or alcohol. All of them expressed the wish to find meaningful jobs and get their lives back on track. This was a real growth experience for my students, most of who were from middle to upper-middle-class families. They learned that not all homeless people are in that situation because of their own shortcomings.

Other activities involved doing charitable work. We did yard work for elderly people and collected food items for the food bank. We painted houses and did cleanup projects around the school.

The most ambitious of our service activities was a mission trip to Costa Rica. Our group raised money to cover expenses, and three students and I joined a local priest who conducted these mission trips annually. My son Matthew was one of the students.

Our mission was to join the priest and twenty other American adult volunteers and help a community of Costa Ricans build a church. We spent two weeks digging foundations and pouring concrete to help these people begin the process of erecting a church. We slept on concrete floors and worked hard in the heat all day, but the camaraderie that developed among our group and with the Costa Ricans was inspiring.

One interesting incident impressed upon me the sense of poverty among some of these Costa Ricans. One mother brought her 14 year-old daughter around to meet Matthew, who was only 16 at the time. Another native told me the mother was hoping to marry off her daughter to the rich American to assure a better life.

The support of the Costa Ricans was overwhelming, and the whole experience was incredibly uplifting. We returned with a new appreciation of the material comforts we lived with, but with a new understanding of the meaning and importance of community.

Because of the success of these activities, I implemented a service requirement for the class. Students had to perform a minimum number of hours of service on their own to receive the full credit for the class. When my service requirement became widely known in the community, I was nominated to be on the first Governor's Advisory Commission on Community Service. This Commission was formed as a result of President George H. W. Bush's Points of Light Campaign.

This commission had the authority to provide grant funding for various service activities throughout the state. It seemed a bit counter-intuitive to me that we were given funding for service projects that were supposed to be done voluntarily. We were used to working to raise our own funds. However, I was not above applying for some of these small grants for our class activities which did involve some expenses on our part.

The other religion class I taught was Christian Morality. This was one of the more interesting subjects. The class came with a textbook, but much of what we discussed was from outside sources. This class provided an opportunity to incorporate current events.

One timely event was the Gulf War which began in 1990. The war enabled us to discuss St. Thomas Aquinas and his theory of the "Just War." We looked at the elements of a Just War as outlined by Aquinas and applied it to the Gulf War. There were no solid conclusions, but we used critical thinking skills to analyze each of the seven principles of a Just War and determine if those requirements were met.

As you would expect, a lot of our topics involved teenage issues. Sexual activity and sexually transmitted diseases were a big issue for this age group. It was tricky to discuss these subjects because Catholic doctrine had to be followed and some parents and the parish priests could be very sensitive about these topics.

As a final project, students were assigned to research and make a presentation to the class on a relevant topic. The topics had to be approved by me, and sometimes I had to recommend changing topics. Some topics were too vague, some were too broadly worded, and some were going to be difficult to research.

Students were allowed to pair up for their presentations. In one case, two girls cooperated on a topic but had not gotten their presentation approved in advance. On the day they were to present, I found out that their topic was AIDS. What I did not know was that they had invited the head of the local Planned Parenthood to address the class about the topic. I knew this woman well, and she had a highly visible reputation as being an outspoken advocate of abortion rights. As such, her views were in opposition to Catholic teaching and thus much maligned by the local priests and Catholic parishes.

When she showed up at the door of my classroom, I was surprised and shocked. I knew this was going to get me into trouble even though the topic was AIDS, not abortion. She was kind enough to speak with me about the situation outside the classroom and offered to go away if I did not want her to speak to the class. I analyzed the situation and decided it would cause more of a disruption if I banned her from speaking than if I allowed her to present. I pointed out to her that she was in a Catholic School and asked her not to propose anything that might be contrary to Catholic doctrine. She graciously agreed and gave a fairly enlightening talk about what we knew about AIDS in the early 1990s.

As I expected, word got back to the principal and local pastors. One pastor called me in to explain why I had the Director of the Planned Parenthood Chapter speak in a Catholic religion class. I gave him the details of what had happened and told him she spoke about AIDS and did not contradict Catholic doctrine. He pointed out to me that this whole situation was very embarrassing for the school and the parish and that there were some who were calling for my dismissal. This priest knew me well and said he would not recommend my dismissal, but such a thing should never happen again. Once again my stubbornness had put my job in jeopardy.

The topic of AIDS also provided one of the most dynamic class periods I ever conducted. Before one of the Christian Morality classes, I planned for a student to come to my door with a note that I was wanted by the principal in the front office. I left the class for a few minutes and then returned with a worried look on my face. I told the students that we were canceling our topic for the day because the principal had asked me to have a discussion about something that was happening in our school right now. This announcement gave me the class's undivided attention.

I explained that the principal had called me to the office to inform me that we had a student who had tested positive for the AIDS virus. She asked me to have a discussion with students about how we should handle this. Keep in mind this was in the early 1990s when there was a lot of misunderstanding about how AIDS is contracted, and there was a lot of fear. At that time, most people believed AIDS was only contracted through homosexual activity.

The question was whether this student should be dismissed from school or whether we should work with the student and take appropriate precautions for others. Most of the students were sympathetic and said it would go against our Christian principles to throw the student out.

To stimulate discussion, I played devil's advocate and suggested that we had to protect the school's reputation and we should quietly remove the student. Several of the students became angry at me and our Parish Pastor, Victoria, became livid. She said that I was a complete hypocrite and went against every principle of loving others that I had taught them in the class. The discussion was beginning to get out of control when I finally explained to them that our discussion had been a test., The situation I had described really hadn't happened. There was a visible sigh of relief, but Victoria was so incensed by my statements that it took her several weeks to warm up to me again. Never have I had students continuing a classroom discussion as vociferously after class as they did in this instance. This was one of those magical moments that happen in teaching. I've seldom seen a class so totally engaged in the topic.

Getting students emotionally involved with a topic is one of the best ways to get them engaged. I learned later that when you engage the part of the brain that controls emotion, the amygdala, students learn and retain much better. I didn't know as much about brain function in learning at the time, but exercises like this one on AIDS confirmed my instinct that emotional involvement was an effective technique. My teaching technique in this second stint was much more effective than my first two years. I was learning how to motivate the students to care about the subject matter.

After two years teaching part-time, I was moved to a full-time position and appointed Religion Department Chairman. During this time, I continued to take classes sponsored by a nearby Catholic College to get a certification in Religious Studies. I enrolled in a class on the Old Testament taught by a local priest. Before we began the class, I insensitively mentioned to him that I had been teaching this stuff for several years. He was visibly offended by my referring to the Old Testament as "stuff." When I turned in what in my mind was a very good paper at the end of that class, I was disappointed to receive a B for grade. In his notes on the paper, he indicated that this "stuff" was not as simple as he felt I had made it sound in my paper. Touché!

During this time, I began teaching a sociology class which was more in my area of expertise. I was able to select a textbook and found a book that engaged students. I loved teaching this class.

Our favorite topic was the section on aging. While studying the changes that take place in the aging process, we took field trips to the local Assisted Living Residence. Some of my students had grandparents in that facility, and I knew some of the residents personally. We had group discussions with elderly people and developed strong bonds. There were some tears as some of the residents told emotional stories. The students talked about this activity extensively. We learned that one of the ways to engage the elderly people was to ask about their experiences in the "old days." They sometimes couldn't remember what they had for breakfast that day, but they could recall minute details about something that happened 50 years ago. Aging has helped me to understand these memory issues even better!

During this time, the school implemented a program called Natural Helpers. It was a program that trained students and faculty to whom others were naturally drawn. I was selected for this training and had the opportunity to work with students who felt comfortable telling me about their problems. The Natural Helpers, both students, and faculty worked together and developed presentations to help students with issues they might confront. This experience helped me gain further confidence in my ability to connect with students.

Parent-teacher conferences were always a challenge. Some of these parents had been my classmates in school. I was sensitive to parents' concerns while also straight forward when assessing their child's abilities and performance. Most of the time, this worked well, and the parents appreciated my approach. However, sometimes my bluntness got me in trouble.

One set of parents came to discuss a conversation I had with their daughter. I was concerned about Kristen's behavior and had told her that if she didn't change her ways I feared she may end up pregnant and without an education. That outcome would restrict her opportunities for a successful life. Her parents wanted to know why I told her this. It was an uncomfortable discussion, but they listened and took my concerns into consideration. I have often thought about whether that warning was out of line and still don't know whether that was the right thing to do. What I do know is that four years later Kristen was pregnant and unmarried. However, her parents helped her as she raised the child and continued her college education.

After being discouraged with teaching after my first two years, I had thought I wasn't cut out to be a teacher. In my second stint as a teacher, though, I learned a valuable lesson. Students are interested if you find ways to engage them. That was a truth that I was not mature enough to understand during my first teaching assignment. During my second teaching experience, I found that I had a talent for getting students involved by connecting with them on their level. I made the topics more relevant and got their emotions involved in the learning. My relationships with students helped me to inspire them to learn because they knew I cared about them.

While writing this chapter, I went back to some old files from those years of teaching. There were some final essays that I had assigned in my last year. Students were asked to describe the most important thing they learned from the class that year. The responses were full of comments about learning more about themselves and gaining confidence in their opinions. Many indicated they liked the discussion days we had on Fridays. This allowed them to talk about the topics they cared about.

Understanding relationships was a common theme. It was gratifying to see that many remarked that the class had been a time of growth for them and they hated to see me leave. Once again, the best reward for teaching is realizing that you had a positive effect on students.

During this teaching stint, several students were expelled from school for a variety of infractions. One such student, James, was a likable kid, but he just kept getting in trouble. He was also an athlete who I coached. We had a good relationship. Finally, after several disciplinary issues and confirmation that he had been abusing drugs, he was expelled.

I played a role in the expulsion because I had brought his drug use to the attention of the principal. James was very bitter and felt I had betrayed him. I felt bad for him but could see no other choice. It was somewhat comforting several years later when James told me that the expulsion had been deserved. He indicated that it woke him up and led to him becoming more responsible. As I moved into administration, I would learn that "tough love" can be hard to administer, but it was frequently the best thing for the recipient.

My second experience in teaching was more satisfying than my first. I was more mature and had a better understanding of how to engage the students. However, after eight years of teaching the same subjects, I became restless. I felt I needed a change and was ready to get into administration.

My restlessness also came at a point at which I needed to make more money. My oldest son was in college, and the other two would soon follow. We were not going to be able to support them with two teaching salaries. Melly and I knew that getting into administration would be a huge change in our lives since we would have to move. It was time to strike out for something different for me. I had no idea what a wild, incredible ride it would be.

4

COACHING

I started coaching again when I began my second teaching career in 1987. My first assignment was as an assistant football coach. The head coach, Gene, was a man I admired greatly. Gene was also the school counselor. He had been very successful in his coaching career. He was universally admired, an effective and empathetic counselor, and a driven, enthusiastic coach. He and his wife had ten children. I was looking forward to coaching with him. He knew I had experience in football and asked me to help scout our opponents.

I had previously scouted with one of Gene's assistants, Leroy, who was also an incredible math teacher. Leroy and I would compile the tendencies of our next opponent by watching their game the week before we played them. I learned a lot from Leroy about how to scout since he was meticulous with his mathematical calculations of a team's tendencies. Leroy was so thorough that we joked about his creating mathematical formulas to defeat our opponent.

A week before that first season when I was going to assist Gene, he was in the fieldhouse checking out football gear to his players when he suddenly collapsed in front of coaches and players. I was at a faculty picnic outside. Someone came running asking for help. I ran to the fieldhouse and saw Gene lying on the floor. I spoke to him and thought I saw a faint response in his eyes. Someone performed CPR while we waited for the ambulance, but Gene showed no further response. A couple of his sons were on the team, and I was asked to accompany them to the hospital. While the rest of his family gathered, doctors worked feverishly in the next room trying to revive him. I was about to excuse myself but was honored when his wife and children asked me to stay with them.

Eventually, the doctor came out to tell us that Gene had passed away. They believed his aorta had ruptured and he was probably dead before he hit the floor. We were all in a state of shock, and I returned to the faculty picnic to give my colleagues the bad news. What a way to begin the school year. We had suffered a tremendous loss and were devastated. The faculty and students loved Gene, and many had become very attached to him because of his caring nature. It was a painful time for all involved.

The administration then had to find a new head coach and counselor in a very short time. I had been a former football player at the school and had some coaching experience. They asked me to take the job as head coach. Having been out of coaching for a long time, I just didn't feel ready to do this. Eventually, the administration named two longtime assistants as co-coaches, one in charge of offense and the other in charge of defense. I agreed to serve as an assistant.

The season went OK considering the terrible start we had. After the season, the offensive co-head coach was named a head coach for the following year. Gene had also been head track coach and had been very successful in that endeavor as well. With that position open, I decided to apply for the job. I had some experience and felt more confident in that role. So began my first head coaching experience.

The first year as head track coach was quite an adjustment for the athletes and for me. They idolized Coach Gene, and there were some things I did differently, which some of the athletes saw as an insult to Gene. The practices were organized differently, and their loyalty to Gene had them nostalgic for the same routine. I sympathized with their emotions and felt a great loss myself. However, we were able to have a successful season after making some adjustments. Some of the girls were particularly resentful of me for taking his place. I realized it was not as much about me as it was about them missing their former coach. They were heartsick about losing Gene and that first year was more about recovering, than coaching, for all of us.

One of the outstanding runners, Shelly, was particularly obstinate toward me from the beginning. She had a troubled home life and had been very close to Coach Gene. I think she saw him as a father figure. We had several talks, and she was considering quitting track. She had been a great 100-meter sprinter as a freshman and sophomore but wanted to run the 200, and 400 meter runs as a junior and senior.

It was not unusual for girls to lose some of their short sprint speed as they matured, so I let her run the longer sprints. She did well, but we also kept her in the anchor position of the 400-meter relay. She was not our fastest runner, but she was very competitive and would not let anyone pass her on the last leg. By her senior year, that relay set a new school and state record with Shelly as the anchor, and we were state champions. By the time she graduated, Shelly and I had a great relationship, but it took some adjustments to understand her emotions. She was an example of how much of an influence Gene had on kids. I had to prove my respect for him before I could get her cooperation. We had many talks about what a good man he was and how we both missed him. It helped her to know that I also held him in high regard.

Shelly had a brother named Kent. He was an even better sprinter than Shelly but was a real challenge to motivate. He was very laid back and easy going. He eventually finished high in the 100-meter finals at state. Kent was also the anchor runner on our outstanding 400-meter relay.

We knew we had a chance to place high in this relay at the state meet in Kent's senior year. As a new coach, I was anxious for the race to start. At the state meet, coaches could not be on the field. Imagine my shock when I heard the announcer call for our team to report to the starting line immediately or we would be disqualified. I quickly ran behind the stands to find out where they were. Sure enough, Kent had fallen asleep in the shade. His teammates dragged him to the starting line just in time to avoid disqualification. I was shaken by almost losing our best chance for a medal.

Our main competition in the relay was a team with an outstanding sprinter, Lance, who ran their second leg. We had competed against this team several times, and we could stay with all their runners except Lance. Our second runner, Dean, was accustomed to having Lance pass him up while they ran their leg. As the baton came to the second runner, Dean found himself in the lead, and he held the lead. He was surprised that Lance did not pass him during his leg. What he didn't know is that Lance's teammate dropped the baton at their handoff and Lance's foot accidentally kicked it into the stands, disqualifying their team. We came in second and set a new school record. As Dean told the story afterward,

"I kept waiting for Lance to pass me and he never came!" Dean thought he was just faster that day. I had always told them to believe in themselves and never think you are beaten.

When we went to state meets we were allowed to bring some alternates for our relay teams. It was the job of the alternates to film our events. I always told the person filming not to talk too much, because we would show the film to the team and parents after the state meet. Curtis was filming for us that year and got wrapped up in the race. As Kent got the baton for the anchor leg, you could hear Curtis say,

"Holy shit, look at that bastard run!"

Later, I had to apologize and explain to parents that Curtis just couldn't contain his excitement. We all had a good laugh about that video.

After Kent graduated, he went to the local college. He came back to the high school occasionally to see me and some of his friends. He talked about how much he missed the fun of high school track. The last time he came back he seemed in a particularly carefree mood. To my shock, Kent took his life one month later. This was devastating and reminded me to be more aware of the moods of my athletes. You never know what is going on in their minds.

Track and field was my most enjoyable sport to coach. There were so many different events for kids with a variety of skills. Anyone could participate no matter how talented or untalented. At the beginning of each track season, I gave a similar speech to the athletes. My emphasis was on improving themselves. It didn't matter if you wanted to be a state champion, lose weight, build athletic skills for another sport or just hang out with other kids. We would find a place for them, and all I asked is that they worked to improve.

On the first rainy day of the season, we took the team inside and passed out note cards. On those cards, everyone was asked to state the reason they were out for track and field. Then they were to set some short term goals and some long term goals. We collected these cards and kept them in a file and reviewed them occasionally on rainy days. This turned out to be a great motivator for the kids as they were inspired by the goals they had previously set.

One of the most strenuous workouts that we developed was called "running the hill." We would occasionally go to a nearby pasture and run up and down a steep hill to build leg strength and endurance. This was a difficult workout, and sometimes, after several trips up and down, kids would vomit at the top of the hill.

This workout was done every week for the runners. However, it became such a rite of passage that the field events kids wanted to participate also. We designed a T-shirt that stated

"I survived the hill" and anyone who could run up and down the hill ten times in an hour earned the right to wear that T-shirt. After a few years, it became a challenge that every track athlete wanted to confront and achieve.

This workout did a lot to strengthen our middle distance and long distance runners and build their endurance. We became known on the track circuit for having runners who finished strong at the end of the race. After a few years of seeing these results, my older runners would encourage the younger runners when running the hill. When they heard the freshmen and sophomores complain they would tell them to quit griping and just do it.

"It works and will make a big difference when you get on the track," they asserted.

It was nice to know that the older kids had bought into the idea so much that they sold it for me.

To inspire the kids to do the hill runs, I would engage parents by asking them to bring watermelon or some other treats to celebrate completing the hill. One time parents grilled some hot dogs for the runners. That didn't work out so well because after that workout some of them got sick on the hotdogs and puked them up. We also had parents bring treats to track meets and sometimes had cookouts after the meet. We had to be careful that those who still had races to run didn't eat before they completed their last race.

Our track team became a real powerhouse, and our numbers kept growing because kids were having success and fun. We won numerous league championships in both boys' and girls' track and were always near the top at the state meet. Sometimes it took two buses to get our team to track meets. Despite our success, personal stories were the best part of the experience.

Jill was a young girl who had no talent as a runner and was very shy and withdrawn. She was also mentally and emotionally challenged. She came out for cross country and track every year just to be part of something. She was a distance runner. We tried to help her improve her times, but she finished last in every race. At one meet, she was running the 3200-meter run when the weather turned bad, and it started to sleet. She was a full lap behind the second last runner and had a lap to go. I told the meet organizer to tell her she was finished so we could get the race completed and take cover. After she got her time, Jill couldn't contain her excitement.

"Coach, I took a whole minute off my best time ever," she breathlessly told me.

I didn't have the heart to tell her that she had only run seven laps instead of the eight required to finish the race. The important thing was she felt good about her run that day and thought she had improved. I admired her perseverance.

By her junior year, Jill was still competing and coming in last every time. I had a very talented girls' 3200-meter relay team that year. Before one of our meets, the girls from the relay team came to talk to me about Jill.

"Coach, we want to get a medal for Jill," they said.

"That's great but how do you propose to do that," I replied.

"Let's put her in the 3200-meter relay, and we'll see to it that we get in the top three," the girls answered.

"To do that one of you will have to drop out of the relay," I informed them.

"That's OK," said Maleia. "I'll drop out and run another race instead."

This was a meet that was not particularly competitive, so the girls knew that it was probably their only opportunity to get that medal for Jill. We decided to let Jill run the second 800-meter leg. Our lead runner took off and ran her heart out and got us a big lead before she handed it off to Jill. Jill took off at her usual slow pace, almost running in place. By the start of her second lap, she was passed up by all of the other runners. During her second lap, the rest of the field pulled far ahead of Jill in spite of our whole team lining the track and cheering her on. By the time she handed off to our third runner, we were more than half a lap behind the second last team.

Our third runner ran her heart out, and by the time she finished her leg, we were back in fourth place. The anchor runner took the baton and quickly passed two more runners to help us finish in second place. Jill had earned her first medal, and the entire team was more excited about that than they were about any of their own performances. The smile on Jill's face as she received that medal was priceless. I hope that medal is pinned on a wall somewhere in Jill's home.

The next fall Jill was running in our home cross country meet. I knew she had never finished any higher than last in all her cross country meets. I was at football practice and saw her come running across the field after the race. She was so excited to tell me,

"Mr. Schmidt, I didn't get last!"

What a thrill for her and for me. I gave her a hug and went back to football practice.

Not all experiences were that positive. One year I had a very talented boys' team. We had a transfer student who was a great sprinter. Jorge was the fastest kid on our team and was running times that I knew would place him high at state. He also anchored our 400-meter relay team which was setting times that would place high at state. However, Jorge was having trouble getting to practice regularly. During spring break I asked my athletes to make it to at least two practices unless they were out of town. Jorge was in town but never made it to any practices. I suspended him for the next meet, and he still wasn't coming to practice.

We were very talented that year and had a good chance to compete for the state championship. However, I didn't feel it was fair to our other athletes to allow Jorge to compete if he wouldn't come to practice. Finally, I dismissed him from the team. We got second place at state that year by one point. Jorge could have easily gotten us some points individually and with our relay. Later on, I found out that Jorge had a serious drinking problem and he left school. I think I did the right thing, but it makes me wonder if I could have helped him had I known about the problem.

Another challenging case that turned out more positive was the case of Dawn. She was one of my outstanding girl throwers but decided she only wanted to come to practice three days a week for her senior year. When I told her that wouldn't work because it wasn't fair to the rest of the team, she quit. After two weeks she came back and asked to rejoin the team. I informed her she must be at practice every day. She had a great year breaking the school record in the discus and placing high at state.

My athletes often surprised me with their concern for others. The story of Jill was just one example. A neighboring school often competed at the same meets we did. They had a young man on their team who was developmentally disabled. Billy ran distance events and usually came in last. After a couple of meets in which Billy trailed the field badly, many of my athletes, and some from other schools would gather around the track and cheer Billy on as he completed his race. Usually, he was the only one still running on his last lap. It was heartening to see the smile on his face as he heard other athletes cheering "Go Billy" and he would sprint the last stretch and throw his hands up as he crossed the finish line as if he had won the race.

Sometimes coaches displayed poorer sportsmanship than the athletes. Jason was an outstanding pole vaulter and javelin thrower. There was always a conflict because these events took place at the same time. At one of our league meets Jason was doing well in the pole vault and didn't want to break his rhythm. They were calling him to throw the javelin. He kept putting the javelin off until he could finish at the pole vault. When he got over to the javelin, the person in charge told him he was too late.

I knew Jason could place high and maybe even win the javelin and we needed those points to win the league meet. There was a meeting of the rules committee, and I explained the reason why Jason didn't make it to the javelin throw. It would not have been a problem for them to wait and let him make all his throws even after the other throwers were finished. However, a majority of the rules committee voted against Jason being allowed to throw. One of the coaches who cast the deciding vote was our biggest rival for the league championship. After uttering a few unkind words to him, I left, and we continued with the meet. To his surprise and mine, we won the league championship anyway.

When I first started coaching track and field in 1988, personal computers were just coming into use. My records were kept on an old Epson II. After a while, I figured out a way to predict track meet scores. From several area newspapers, I got times and distances of all our competitors. This information was given to my ten-year-old daughter, Sarah, and she would enter the data into the computer. I was then able to screen for those teams in a particular meet and project approximate scores. My teams were stunned when my predictions about the next meet were close.

Eventually, I posted the top performance in each event on the door of our locker room so our athletes could see their competition. I hoped that the data would spur them to try to beat those ahead of them. One year we had three outstanding pole vaulters. They were beginning to get rather cocky because there was little competition in our region. At our regional meets, the top three finishers qualified for state. My vaulters clearly had the three best vaults, and they believed they would all three qualify easily. To bring a little humility to the group, I created a phantom pole vaulter. On my list, Wallace was added with a height of 14 feet. He was listed as being from a school in our regional. My vaulters were stunned when his name suddenly appeared on the list and asked me where he came from. I made up a story that he had been injured early in the season and had finally become healthy. I told them they needed to really work hard if all three were going to qualify for state.

When we got to regionals, they looked all over for Wallace. When no such vaulter showed up in the competition, they asked me where he was. After telling them I had made it up to keep them humble, they were pretty angry with me. However, all three of our vaulters made it to state. We later had a good laugh about that one, but at the time they were upset with me.

Before the league meet one year, my computer projections predicted that we were going to have a hard time winning the boys' division. I found a weakness throughout the league in the high jump. Tracy was a great athlete and my best pole vaulter, but he was only in three events and never had high jumped before. Athletes are allowed to compete in a maximum of four events. Tracy was asked to work on the high jump that week. All he had to do was get 4th place. Tracy was willing, and he ended up getting second place with a very average jump. We won the league championship. I refer to that as the year I "stole" a league championship.

Some of my athletes were so consistent that it was easy to take them for granted. Lisa was an outstanding discus thrower and shot putter for several years. She was almost automatic in winning her events at most track meets. We had a throwing coach who accompanied her and other throwers, so I went to other events and seldom watched her throw. I took her for granted. Eventually, her father felt that I did not appreciate how much she did for the team and he called me out. He was right, and I began to take more time at meets to give her encouragement. Not only was Lisa a multi-event state champion but she was an outstanding student and went on to become a doctor. I learned how much it meant for the head coach to recognize her success.

In 1993 we won the state championship in the boys' division. It was a magical year. However, that didn't mean that everything went as planned. During the year we dominated at all of our meets. I experimented by placing athletes in different events to prepare for the state meet. At one meet I scheduled Seth, a good runner at several distances, to run in three relays. As we prepared to leave for the meet, he was upset with his entries and went to tell his mother, who was also a teacher at our school. She came to me to complain. I told her I had already sent in our entries and he would have to run those races. After discussing it with his mother, he decided to quit the team.

We went on without him at that meet, but a week later he asked to rejoin the team. I asked my other seniors if they wanted him back and they replied in the affirmative, so he was reinstated. However, I told him that he would no longer be used on relays because he had let his teammates down. He agreed to these conditions.

As we were qualifying for state at our regional meet that year, we came down to the last event, the 1600 meter relay. Our second best runner got sick and asked to be relieved. I asked Seth to run for Tom, his close friend. It was clear that Tom would be the one to run in the relay at state if we qualified. Seth agreed to these conditions, and we qualified for state.

The next week, as we prepared for the state meet, I asked Seth to be an alternate on the 1600 meter relay. We knew that Tom would be vaulting about the time we ran the preliminaries in that relay. The plan was to have Seth run in his place in the preliminaries. He asked who would then run in the finals. I told him we would take the person with the slowest split time in the preliminaries off the relay for the finals. My son was on this relay and would probably have had the slowest time. However, Seth wanted me to guarantee that he would be able to run in the finals if he ran in the preliminaries. I would not guarantee this so he said he would not go as an alternate. By this time, it was too late to enter another alternate.

When we got to state, just as we had anticipated, Tom was in the middle of the pole vault when it was time to run the preliminaries in the relay. Since we didn't have an alternate, Tom had to run. When he finished the race the pole vault judge was very understanding and tried to give Tom time to catch his breath. However, after running his 400-meter leg in the relay, Tom could not generate enough energy to clear another height in the pole vault and ended up in second place. The sad part of this is that Tom's best jump of the season was almost two feet higher than his closest competitor, but he ended up in second place because he couldn't get his legs back under him after running that relay.

We did qualify our 1600 meter relay for the finals. We went to the finals knowing we had to be no more than one place behind our closest competitor to tie for the championship. That team won the relay, and we placed second with our best time of the year. Our 72 points tied us for the state championship.

After the award ceremony, we were ecstatic. We decided to take the team for dinner on the way home. We had come in two vans. During the meet, several athletes had come to me to get a key to our van to get equipment numerous times. When we got back to the van, I noticed the key was not in my usual pocket. I asked the team who had taken the key last. They all insisted they had brought it back to me.

I was still on a high from the track meet and insisted I didn't have the key. After having everyone check their bags, we still couldn't find the key for the one van. After about half an hour of checking, we still could not locate the key. Disgustedly, I put my hands in my pockets and noticed there was a key in the other pocket. It was the missing key. I felt pretty foolish but told the team to get in, and we would be on our way.

That was an embarrassing incident, but even that fiasco could not blemish the exuberance of winning the state championship. We celebrated all the way home, and the story of the lost key just added to the excitement of the occasion. Also, I was later named Kansas Boys' Track Coach of the Year.

The next couple of years of track and field coaching were very successful. We won league championships and placed in the top three at state. However, I could tell I was beginning to lose some of the enthusiasm and was looking for a new challenge.

An incident happened that almost ended my coaching at this school prematurely. We were preparing for the league meet and one of my assistant coaches, Jim, usually drove the bus. On one occasion, he told me that he would be driving to the meet with the principal in his own car and might not be able to drive the bus home. This was a problem because on the way back from this meet I had planned to fill out the entry forms for the regional meet the next week. It had to be in on time the next morning, and we wanted updated performance information for all of our athletes. This included their results at the league meet. I usually worked on this in the bus on the way home from the league meet and sent it in early the next morning.

Jim came to the meet in his new vehicle with the new school principal. After the meet, I asked him if he would drive the bus and let the principal drive his car so I could work on the regional entries. He would not do it, and we got into a bit of an argument. The principal was also there and got in on the argument. I told them it was not safe for me to be driving the bus while figuring out regional entries. The argument got a bit contentious, and I uttered a few profanities.

On the way home I had an assistant fill out the forms as we discussed who was in what events and what their best performances were. It was a difficult ride back in the dark with me driving the bus with divided attention.

The next day I called a couple of board members and told them what had happened. I expressed my concern that this incident had put the track athletes in danger. They said they understood and would discuss it at their next meeting. I had a premonition that the principal might bring this up and try to use the incident to get me fired. It turned out he did bring it to the board, but they were supportive of me. My job was spared. Once again, my hot-headed attitude almost got me fired.

During my coaching tenure, I had some talented assistant coaches. All of them had participated in track and field at least at the high school level, and some had even competed successfully at the college level. We had as many as 80 athletes out for track, and the school allowed me to have four paid assistants. They weren't paid very much, but at least they were paid. Also, there were usually some assistants from the local college who wanted to help just for the experience. This might seem like a lot of coaches, but with up to 80 athletes and 18 events, a lot of coaching was required. When they assisted, they could put it on their resume for their next job.

I generally grouped my coaches by sprints and hurdles, throwers, jumpers, long distance and relays. There were so many different aspects of teaching that we had to study the latest techniques and strategies and attend clinics continually. There was one assistant, Renard, who admitted she knew nothing about track and field but wanted to help as my "puke" coach. She had a son on the team and said she would give encouragement when the athletes became discouraged or when they had run so hard they had to puke. We had some good laughs about her role, but she came in handy to direct groups of athletes when I was busy with another group. And yes, she comforted the pukers, especially after running the hill.

I was very fortunate to have many talented coaches in specific areas. They spent endless hours with the athletes breaking down techniques and training them. We often used video to analyze our athletes and then made appropriate adjustments. Often my distance coaches were young men who were able to run with the athletes. This was great for bonding.

I generally coached sprinters and hurdlers and through my forties would occasionally run with them. In my later years of coaching, I would have them run intervals of 200 meters and then after they had run several, I would run with them. If I beat any of them, I would point out that they were beaten by an old man. This irritated them, and they ran harder so the old man couldn't beat them. Of course, I only took them on after they were fatigued from running quite a few sprints.

Since track and field is a spring sport, we would often encounter difficult weather. It was not unusual to have sleet and snow hit us at the early meets. At one meet we had to have the athletes shovel snow off the track before we could begin. And of course in Kansas, there was always the ever-present wind.

Coaching track was one of the great joys of my professional career. In that sport, you could really get to know the kids and work with them individually. We developed pride in the quality of our program both among the athletes and the coaching staff. Many of my assistants went on to become successful head coaches. It was a feeling of great pride to have a coaching tree.

We developed close relationships as coaches and frequently went to a local bar after returning from meets to eat, drink and discuss the day's performances. There may have been a considerable amount of alcohol consumed at times. At these gatherings, we analyzed which athletes to put in which events to maximize individual potential as well as team scores. We had a lot of fun and became a highly functioning organization. As I transitioned into educational administration, it became clear that my management of the coaches and athletes was great training for administration.

I also served as an assistant coach in football. This was the sport I knew the best and had played at the Division I level. As mentioned at the beginning of this chapter, the head coach, Gene, passed away suddenly and I was offered the head coaching job. I had been out of coaching for years and turned that offer down but agreed to serve as an assistant.

The school had had success under the previous coach. Gene had been a strong leader and was very passionate about the game. He had produced numerous winning seasons. His passion came out one time after a devastating loss to a hated rival. Gene was on the bus with his team after the game when the rival coach came by and taunted him. I happened to be standing near the bus when this happened. Gene started to come off the bus to go after the taunting coach. I jumped in between them and pushed Gene back onto the bus and told the driver to get us out of there. Gene was understandably furious but calmed down on the way home and thanked me for stopping him from going after the other coach.

Danny and Joe were appointed co-head coaches for the first year after Gene passed away. They had both been assistants under Gene. After the first year, Danny received the head coaching position. Danny was an offensive coach and Joe a defensive coach. I helped with the offensive backfield, receivers, and linebackers.

In the first couple of years after Gene's death, there were still some pretty good athletes on the football team. We had athletes who were good enough eventually to play college ball, and we won a lot of games. Terry was our star running back who racked up huge yardage and also had great hands as a receiver. Gene had a couple of sons still in high school who were among our best football players.

When Terry was a senior, our quarterback was Matt. Matt and Terry were both good kids and had been close friends at one time.

Unfortunately, the publicity Terry received apparently destroyed their relationship. On the day of a crucial playoff game, these two were feuding openly. Danny asked me to talk to them. I met with each of them after school and tried to counsel them.

I stressed that this wasn't about football, but rather it was about life. Sometimes we have to put our personal feelings aside for the good of the team. This will happen in our marriages, our family, our jobs and just about anything we do in life. They both listened politely, but it didn't seem to make any difference. The feud remained throughout the season. I often wonder if they ever reconciled. Hopefully, life taught them the truth of what I had said.

I was also the junior varsity coach. We never knew who we would have available to play in JV games, especially as our numbers dwindled. However, we developed a reputation as a hard-hitting, vicious defense even if we didn't win a lot of games.

Our most memorable JV game came against Larned. We were trailing with a little over two minutes to go and had the ball. My son, Matthew, was a quarterback and my younger son, Nathan, was a running back. We began moving the ball up the field in chunks of yardage. We ran a pitch right, and a pitch left. The two running backs, Nathan and Ryan were picking up 5-8 yards at a time. The other team knew exactly what we were doing, but they couldn't stop us. We marched the length of the field and scored just as time ran out. It was only a JV game, but you would have thought we just won the Super Bowl. Twenty-five years later my sons and I still refer to it as "The Drive."

After a couple of years, the talent level and numbers began to decline, and we encountered some losing seasons. Pressure began to mount on Danny as head coach. The new school president didn't like Danny, and the feeling was mutual. Sometimes we talked in the coaches' locker room about our dislike of the administration. We didn't realize that the walls were porous and people heard our conversations in the hallway. Among those walking by at the time included the new president.

Danny was passionate about sports, and he loved the kids he coached, although he could be very hard on them. In spite of his frequent rants, he always ended a tirade with a little laugh to let everyone know not to take him too seriously. Most of the athletes liked him personally and knew he was just trying to get the best out of them.

One of Gene's sons, Jason, was our quarterback. He possessed outstanding athletic ability and character. When we struggled because we had a weak offensive line, Danny asked Jason to move to the center position to strengthen our line and let a talented young sophomore take the more visible quarterback position. Jason didn't hesitate to give up the glory position, and it helped the team. These were the kind of sacrifices only Danny could ask of our kids.

In our last game one season, Danny was ejected from the game by an official who mistakenly thought Danny called him pathetic. Actually, Danny was just being his usual excitable self and was chastising one of our players. He had to leave the stadium completely, and I was put in charge of the offense.

Danny left the stadium but took a headphone with him so he could communicate with me. Toward the end of the game, we were behind but driving for the winning touchdown. Danny was trying to call some plays that I didn't think would work. I began asking him to repeat what he said and indicated I was losing contact with him. Finally, I said I could no longer hear him, laid the headphones aside and called the plays I thought would work. We scored and won the game. I could hear him just fine but wanted to call my own plays. Several years later I finally admitted to him what happened. We had a good laugh about that.

Frequently, the principal would drive out to football practice in his vehicle and sit there and watch practice with a friend. Danny was very passionate, and sometimes his language was scorching. He could chew out a kid viciously for a mistake, but he always came back and let the kid know it wasn't personal. We developed a method of using the "good cop, bad cop" routine in which he would rip into a kid and then I would come along later and explain that he was just trying to make him a better player. Sometimes this worked and sometimes it didn't. Since we coached together in track and field also, we used the same technique there. We switched up in that I was the bad cop, and he was the good cop. I'm sure the chewing out was not taken well by Joe and his friend who seemed to be trying to gather evidence against Danny.

After a game in which we had played poorly in the first half, Danny chewed the team out at halftime. I heard the entire conversation and didn't think he said anything out of line. The next week I was called in by the president and told that the opposing Athletic Director reported that Danny was using the "F" word frequently in addressing the team. I hadn't heard any of that, but it was clear by this time that he was planning on replacing Danny as head coach.

The announcement that Danny was fired was made before the end of the season. However, he was allowed to complete the season as coach. This created an uneasy situation since it was hard for him to assert any authority after that. There were some editorials in local newspapers criticizing such a move as disheartening to the athletes. Nevertheless, we soldiered on through the end of the season.

Soon the president announced the hiring of a new coach, Jim, a young man who had coached briefly at the local college and seemed to know a lot about football. After he was hired, he interviewed all of the assistants to see if he wanted to retain us. During my interview, I mentioned that the next year he would need to decide who would be the quarterback. The backup quarterback had been my son, Matthew. Matthew was not as athletic as Russ, the other alternative, but he managed the game well and had good leadership. Russ was more athletic but was erratic in decision making.

I learned later that after our interview he thought I was trying to pressure him into selecting Matthew as the quarterback and he considered not having me back as an assistant. As it turned out, Matthew dislocated his shoulder before the season started, so the decision to start Russ was taken care of without controversy. Eventually, Jim and I got along very well, and we had a couple of good years coaching together. That incident taught me to express myself more clearly to someone who didn't know me well. My comments were easily misunderstood.

As the talent level began to decline, we seemed to be getting a lot of nice kids who just didn't have any mean streak in them that you need on the football field. When Jim took over, he made me a defensive coordinator. I enjoyed the role and tried to develop a hard-hitting, aggressive defense. I had some athletes that I thought could be outstanding. Justin was a 6'3"220-pound linebacker who I thought could be an incredible player. I tried to fire up my linebackers by telling them that they had to be a little "deranged" when they were on the field. Unfortunately for our team, Justin was the kindest, softest spoken linebacker in history. He was more concerned about not hurting someone than he was about being a hard-hitting linebacker. He was another nice guy whom I couldn't turn into a head hunter! Justin is now a renowned college professor.

We had another huge lineman, Brian, who was 6' 7" and weighed 260 pounds. We saw him as a Rock of Gibraltar in the middle of our defensive line that no one would be able to move. He was so large that we affectionately called him "The Creature." Imagine our disappointment when we found out he was an easy going nice guy who just didn't like to use his size. Once again we had a physical specimen who was a soft-hearted, gentle kid who didn't want to hit people. This was not the making of a successful football team. Brian is also a college professor now.

So, our football success declined during the years I assisted. However, we had a series of intelligent, sensitive young men who went on to be very successful in a variety of fields. It didn't help our football team, but it was certainly more important that they succeed in life. I hope their experiences on the football field contributed to their success.

I also coached freshman girls' basketball from 1988 till 1993. The head coach, Rose, had been an outstanding player herself and a successful coach. I didn't know a lot of basketball strategy but agreed to assist if she showed me the techniques and strategies she wanted the girls to learn.

It soon became clear that there were some significant differences in coaching girls than there were in coaching boys. One of the things I found out at that time was that boys often thought they knew all there was to know about a particular sport, so you had to convince them that you knew what you were talking about. Girls were generally more accepting of coaching because they didn't think they already knew it all.

One year my girls were very talented, but we were not playing together as a team. I was frustrated and had a meeting with them to find out what the problem was. After some discussion, I found out that their dads were telling them what to do and they weren't listening to my coaching. These dads had succumbed to the belief that their kids were All-Americans and could not see their athletic abilities objectively. This is not uncommon with many families.

I was friends with a lot of these girls' parents but told them they needed to ignore their dads' advice about basketball and start playing within our team concept. I also had a meeting with the parents and made the same point rather gently. One of the ways I got the point across was to have a parent/daughter practice in which we ran through a lot of our practice drills. After this, we had a parent/daughter scrimmage. This helped to clarify how we wanted to play as a team. The parents got a better understanding of the plays we ran and why we used certain drills in practice. Finally, our team started to play together, and we were more successful.

I really enjoyed coaching the girls. They were open to coaching and eager to have fun. They played with a lot of emotion and were very self-critical. We had many laughs and cries about basketball and life.

One year I had a very athletic young girl named Natalie. However, Natalie had absolutely no aptitude for basketball and no confidence in herself. I worked hard to teach her some techniques that would help her harness her athleticism, but she just didn't get it. When she occasionally made a basket in practice, she would be so surprised that she let out a high pitched shriek. Eventually, we called her "The Screecher." She was fun to have around, but she never did develop into a basketball player. Natalie stayed with the team for that season just for the fun of being around her friends. We always got a kick out of Natalie when she accidentally made a basket in practice and screeched. She even made a basket in a game one time, and I thought the whole bench was going to erupt. The fans must have wondered what was going on when they heard my whole team screeching comically. Natalie was never very successful at basketball, but we all have some fun memories of her effort to try.

The point guard on one of my average teams, Bonnie, was a great distance runner and consequently had great endurance. She was the only girl on the team who could dribble the ball well that year. If she wasn't playing well, our team was in real trouble. The problem was that Bonnie was very temperamental. She frequently had fights with her dad or her boyfriend. When this happened, I could recognize it immediately in a game. She would pout and couldn't seem to handle the ball effectively. When that happened early in the game, I knew it was going to be a long night.

Another of my girls, Nikki, was slow and uncoordinated and only came out for basketball to get some exercise and to be part of a team. I tried to get Nikki in the game whenever we were way ahead or way behind. However, I had to instruct the other girls that if they passed the ball to her, they had to do it gently and then come right back to her and retrieve it. If she tried to dribble the ball, it was a sure turnover.

One team we played regularly was notoriously bad. Their school had no sports until they reached high school, so freshman year was their first opportunity to play the game. We always beat them handily. Our activities association limited the number of games each athlete could play. Some of my better freshman girls would occasionally be called up to the JV or varsity teams. We often saved a higher-level game for them by not playing them against this team.

One year I had several outstanding players who were competing some at the varsity level. The head coach told me to hold them out against this team to save a game for them. I was so shorthanded that I had to start Nikki in this game. I instructed the other girls to pass her the ball occasionally, but come right back to get it. Nikki was as anxious to get the ball out of her hands as they were. Surprisingly we were able to play that way, essentially 4 against 5, and still, win the game. Nikki was very proud to start, and everyone went away happy, except that I was a nervous wreck.

The year I had my best team several of the girls were playing varsity, so we didn't always have our best players available. However, when we played in the freshman league tournament, Rose let me have all the girls except Christina who was starting on the varsity. In the finals of that tournament, we played a team that had beaten us previously when we didn't have all our best players. They had one girl, Angie, who was incredibly fast and would dribble past anyone who tried to guard her. (She later was a two-time state champion in sprints.) Because of this, we had to play a zone defense. I knew if we could get into a man defense we could control the game except for their one girl.

On one play this girl ran over one of our best players, Tara, and no foul was called. Her Dad, Ken, was a good friend of mine and was the counselor at one of our schools. He went ballistic on the referee. Soon the referee ejected him from the game. The game went into overtime, and Angie eventually fouled out. Immediately, I put our girls into a man defense, and we controlled the rest of the game and won the championship.

Later we had a celebration with the families of the girls. We played the song "We Are the Champions" and had a great time. We laughed about Ken getting thrown out of the championship game. This freshman league championship was one of the most memorable occasions in all of my coaching experiences.

While I was coaching freshman girls, my daughter Sarah, served as manager. Sarah was in early grade school but was also showing promise as a basketball prodigy. She enjoyed just being around the team and shooting baskets whenever she got a chance. If we were ever shorthanded for a scrimmage, she would fill in. She could hold her own with these much older girls. As a manager, I gave her specific duties and told her that if she was doing her job well during the games, I shouldn't even notice that she was there. She took great pride in taking care of water, towels and all equipment. It became a standing joke that after games I would ask her, "Were you here tonight? I never saw you." It never got old laughing about that one.

When Sarah was a freshman, I was no longer coaching basketball. By this time she was pretty advanced compared to most of the girls. However, when the head coach asked me about moving her to varsity, I told her she should have to prove herself at the freshman level first.

Rose allowed her to play at freshman level until after the Christmas break. I feared that she would get to the varsity level and be overwhelmed in a pressure situation. That could destroy her confidence. When Sarah found out that I had recommended waiting to move her up to varsity she was mad at me.

Later that year when Sarah was playing regularly with the varsity she performed very well. In the sub-state tournament, our varsity point guard was out sick, and Sarah was called to start. She handled it confidently and toward the end of the game when we had a small lead, the other coach told his girls to foul the freshman. Her mom and I were so nervous as she stepped to the foul line that I couldn't look, and her mom was praying the rosary. What the opposing coach didn't know is that Sarah was the state Knights of Columbus free throw champion. She confidently hit 5 out of 6 free throws, and we won the game.

There are so many coaching stories that I will remember for the rest of my life. The intensity and the relationships that are developed are hard to match in any other endeavor. When there are class reunions, sports stories are generally a main topic of discussion. Yes, we overemphasize sports in American schools, but they also play a tremendous role in the development of young people. It is one of the best ways for teachers to develop meaningful relationships with students.

My coaching ended in 1995 to enter school administration. I knew I was going to miss the teaching and coaching, but it was time for a change. This began a whole new chapter in my educational journey. It was going to be a memorable one.

5

FALSE START

By 1990, my Master's in Educational Administration was complete. I was not able to attend the ceremony because of coaching my track team at the league meet. The classes required for the master's degree were informative, and the adviser was a professor who had supervised my student teaching as an undergraduate at the University of Kansas. Dr. Allan Miller took me under his wing. When he was unavailable to teach the History of American Education class in the next two semesters, he asked me to teach the class. That was a great opportunity, and I met some people who later joined me in the administrative ranks throughout the state. For many years, fellow administrators reminded me how much they enjoyed the class because it gave them a historical perspective on what they were doing.

In the summer of 1990, I received a grant from the National Endowment for the Humanities to study at the University of Notre Dame. Recipients attended a month-long class by a professor in the Philosophy Department called "Faith, Reason and the Meaning of Life." It was a study of the works of Blaise Pascal, a 17th-century scientist and religious philosopher.

The class was comprised of 20 religion teachers from all areas of the United States. It was an enlightening experience with some incredibly intelligent and thoughtful people. The class deepened our understanding of religious faith, and we each wrote a short thesis on how we applied these teachings to our personal lives. My wife and I had recently lost a child at birth and I used this opportunity to work through some of my feelings about mortality and the meaning of our lives.

The summer at Notre Dame allowed me to take my two sons along for the experience. We stayed in a dormitory and worked out together at the historic venues on the Notre Dame campus. Matthew was fourteen and Nathan was twelve. On the trip to Notre Dame, in the course of eating an egg sandwich, I twisted my neck and had back spasms for about two weeks. I needed the boys to give me traction with one pulling on my neck and the other on my ankles. It got so bad during the trip that I had Matthew driving on Interstate 80 at the age of fourteen. Every day I would lie on the floor of our dorm room while they applied traction. We still laugh about Dad throwing out his neck eating an egg sandwich. That summer was a great bonding opportunity for father and sons.

In 1992, the position of President/Principal at Thomas More Prep-Marian came open, and I applied. I hoped that my tenure at the school would be an advantage when it came to getting the job. I applied and was invited to interview. The interview went well, but one of the primary decision makers was not present for it. I contacted him and offered to meet with him at his convenience. He responded that a meeting was not necessary. Eventually, he said it wouldn't make any difference anyway. He made it clear he was not going to support me for the position.

I'm still not sure why I wasn't seriously considered. It may have been that they just didn't see me as the right fit. However, I think the issue of my political involvement was a significant factor. The Trust that had me fired from my earlier position was a major benefactor to the school. I was disappointed and hurt when I realized that I was not going to get a chance to lead the school that had been such a huge part of my life. I was discouraged, but later I realized it was the best thing that could have happened to me. It freed me to pursue other opportunities. As the saying goes, when one door closes, another door opens.

In the ensuing years, I applied for administrative jobs and interviewed for several. One was at a Catholic High School in California. Melly and I flew to California and were impressed with the school and the community. However, that cost of living was more than we could afford. Although I received an offer for the job as principal, I turned it down. It wasn't financially feasible to move our family for a salary that would strain our budget. Finally, in 1993 I was offered the position as principal of a small Catholic High School in Kansas. After talking it over with my family, I accepted the job.

I asked the board to allow me to visit and get to know the staff. I wanted to get to know more about the school before my contract started. The school put me up in a motel for a week to acclimate myself. My two sons were in high school at the time. They came with me and worked out with the football team during summer conditioning while I met with the staff. The staff was very gracious and professional, but something just didn't feel right.

A week into my visit, I realized that I was not ready to move my family from our home town. We were all conflicted about our children not attending TMP-Marian. We had already made an offer on a house, but thankfully it was not accepted. The boys and I returned home. Luckily, my old job was still available. The hardest thing was calling the president of the board and telling him I wanted to pull out of the contract. He was disappointed, and I felt terrible doing it because they had treated me very well. However, it was obvious that it was not the right time to move on. He graciously released me from the contract, and I paid back the expenses from my visit. I returned to TMP-Marian for another round as a teacher and coach.

Accepting a job and then backing out of it was a humbling experience for me because I pride myself on sticking to my word. I did not regret the decision, however, because the move would not have been in my family's best interests. I swallowed my pride and went back to work. Later in my career, I learned that my experience was not that unusual. At the time, though, it was wrenching.

I settled into teaching and coaching for the next year while keeping my ear to the ground for "the right" administrative position. There was a restlessness about my career. I was very critical of the administration at TMP-Marian and was quite vocal about it. In retrospect, my inexperience in administration led me to think making changes would be easy. The president of the school, Joe, knew that

I was dissatisfied. However, he was patient with me, and we had a good working relationship.

On one occasion, the entire staff was scheduled to go to Salina for a Diocesan Professional Development Day. Most of the staff rode on a bus, but Joe asked me to ride with him in his car. I was concerned about why he asked me to ride with him since he knew I had been critical of his administration. However, on the ride, we had a productive talk. I discussed some of the things I thought needed to be changed, and he agreed with a lot of my ideas but explained why some of them weren't possible. He was very gracious with my impatience, and we arrived at a good understanding of each other's position. Joe had previous experience in administration, and he told me he thought I was ready to be a principal. Our discussion gave me a better understanding of what it was going to take to get into administration, which made me feel more prepared for the transition. I had a practical incentive also since Matthew was attending an expensive college in California and we needed to increase our family income.

My inexperience and naiveté about the difficulties of administration had caused me to criticize the administration. I learned a good lesson; that it looks a lot different from the teaching side than it does from the administration side. It's not as easy to make changes as I thought. This was a good growth opportunity for me. Thankfully, Joe handled my frustration with courtesy.

Finally, in 1995 a call came from an old friend at Hayden High in Topeka, which had been my first teaching job. My friend told me there was an opening for an assistant principal. I still knew some of the teachers and staff and applied for the position.

Before the interview, some staff members told me that they needed a strong disciplinarian who could bring order to the school. I was invited to interview and offered the position. This was the opportunity I had been hoping would come my way. So, I accepted the position. I wrote an emotional letter to the faculty at TMP-Marian to tell them I was departing. It was difficult to leave a place that meant so much to me.

As I mentioned, Matthew was in college in California, Nathan was a senior-to-be, and Sarah had just completed her freshman year.

Obviously, Sarah would move with us, but we allowed Nathan to decide if he wanted to finish high school at TMP-Marian. He chose to stay, and we planned for him to live with friends for the year.

Leaving our home town was an emotional experience; it was where our children had lived all their lives. Nonetheless, Melly obtained a teaching job in Topeka, so we were able to afford a house we liked and made a move. There were a lot of tears as we left our lifetime home and began a new life. We knew it would be a difficult transition for Sarah and it would be hard to leave Nathan three hours away. He was involved in sports throughout the year, and we returned most weekends to see him play and were there for his other activities as well.

While writing this book, I reviewed old files I had from my teaching assignment at TMP-Marian. There were many thank you notes from students and parents who shared that I had made a difference in their lives. Such accolades are the best you can hope for as a teacher. There were also a couple of notes from parents who criticized me for one thing or another. In retrospect, they had some validity, and I hope I grew from that criticism. There were so many notes related to the activities in which we were involved. It was amazing to see how many activities my classes took upon themselves.

The most touching note was from an outstanding student who I had taught and coached.

It read:
I just wanted to let you know that I really appreciate all that you did for the school and me. Your faith in me helped me through many hard times. Also, all the time that you spent in numerous activities I was involved in really was worth it! I hope you have many memories to carry with you. I will always remember my experiences with you because they were very special. You will be missed, but I wish you all the best of luck.
Love,

Terra

Another heart-warming note:

Mr. Schmidt,

"I thought I'd share this with only you. Not too long ago I was very depressed. I couldn't handle anything. I was almost literally going off the edge. I had so much anger built up inside me that I never knew what I was doing from day to day. I was constantly crying and lashing out at everybody. One day I was sitting in the corner of my room listening to some good music when I yelled out for God to take me away from all of that. A week later I was in the hospital for two weeks. I've never felt more at peace."

Amy

My response to her was,

"I feel privileged that you let me in on this part of yourself."

These kinds of comments make it all worthwhile. If we can touch lives in a positive, personal way, then we have done our job. I felt I had done that.

Move-related emotion notwithstanding, our family marched forward hoping the change would be a good one. The reality was that getting into administration required a willingness to make moves. Every administrator needs to understand that. When Melly and I were a young couple, we hitchhiked through Ireland. When we couldn't catch a ride, I told her,

"There is an old Irish saying I just made up; Just keep on plodding."

Then, we'd keep on doing just that as we made our way to the next adventure. We got moved to Topeka and we "kept on plodding."

6

ASSISTANT PRINCIPAL

I had a rude awakening in my first year as an assistant principal. It seemed I was always the bad guy because I dealt with the negative disciplinary situations. Being the bad guy was stressful and depressing. Handling most of the disciplinary referrals meant that I was constantly immersed in negativity.

The degree to which I was stressed hit home when I attempted to take a vacation during the first break in the school calendar. On the drive to the airport with my wife, I told her stories of unreasonable parents I had dealt with that day. I became so wound up in storytelling that I ran a red light at a busy intersection. Cars were honking at me, and drivers were giving me the one-fingered wave.

"Stop!" Melly screamed at me. "Pull over and let me drive."

It took a while for me to settle down during that vacation. The job had not started as I had hoped. The pressure of the job was taking a toll on my personal life.

My position as assistant principal required a move to Topeka. Moving our family was traumatic because we'd lived in the same place for the children's entire lives. We were also moving away from both sets of grandparents and lots of family and friends. Nonetheless, we knew the move was necessary to advance my career in education. There were times during the move when I questioned whether we were doing the right thing. The reality is that when one gets into school administration, one must expect to do some moving. It's a difficult, but usually a necessary part of the position.

After moving, I began to acclimate to Hayden High School. This was where I had done my student teaching and where I had spent my first two years of teaching. Some of the staff who were there during my first teaching stint were still around. Having a few familiar faces was nice.

One surprise was that the school had decided to go to uniforms for the first time and it was my job to enforce uniform-related rules. This was a big change, and I was not prepared for how much resistance there would be from the students.

The principal, Rose, had been at the school for several years and was experienced. However, she had recently suffered the loss of a daughter and was still recovering from the shock. She allowed me to make the decisions about a lot of difficult situations, so I received a quick baptism into the role of disciplinarian. On the first day of school, some students painted derogatory comments about the administration and the uniform policy on the sidewalks and the walls of the school. The paint was nearly impossible to remove. That was my first crisis.

After some questioning, we thought we knew which students were responsible. Rose and I decided to take a strong stand. We decided to announce that if the individuals responsible did not voluntarily come forward, we would investigate and expel the students responsible. No one came forward, so we continued our investigation. After questioning many students, we determined that there were three students directly involved. Their parents were contacted, and all three were expelled.

This sent a shock wave through the student body. A couple of the expelled students were popular among the students. There was resentment about their expulsion, which showed up as greater resistance to the uniform rules.

Among the expelled boys was a special education student. His parents came to the administration and pleaded his case. They said that he was talked into participating by the other students and didn't understand the seriousness of his actions. We considered his appeal and allowed him back into school with some service requirements. I quickly learned that rules are meant to be enforced, but sometimes you had to consider special circumstances. Consistency wasn't always the same as fairness.

That was my introduction to educational administration. I didn't expect it to be so hard right off the bat. I was used to having great relationships with students, and I had expected that to continue. In retrospect, I know we had to take a strong stand because the school climate had become undisciplined. Our actions made the point that we were going to enforce the rules. I found out that being a high school assistant principal may be the hardest job in education. You spend most of your time dealing with negative situations, which does not make you very popular.

So, I had to learn how to deal with negative encounters. When someone got in trouble, they were sent to see me. Even though their problems were usually with some other teacher or administrator, they had to come to me for a discussion and the consequences. Being the bad guy is something every assistant principal must wrestle with. It's not easy because everyone wants to be liked, but in this position, you must get used to the negativity that comes with the job.

I resented parents making excuses for their kids' behavior. They were quick to blame someone other than their children or to minimize bad behavior. It was particularly disappointing because it was a Catholic School and therefore, I expected parents to be more responsible and inclined to enforce their children's good behavior.

Some of the students who had misbehaved obscenely criticized me to their peers. My daughter, Sarah, heard such criticisms throughout her school day, which was difficult for her. She was also adjusting to a new school. Fortunately, Sarah quickly established strong friendships with some of her classmates.

Gradually I realized that the students' criticism and anger were not personal. They and their parents were reacting to unpleasant situations. Often, their reactions were extreme because they were dealing with other issues behind the scenes; I was a handy person on whom to take out their frustrations. Keeping this in mind helped me keep a sense of humor.

Early in my tenure as assistant principal, I dealt with a student who was frequently getting into fights. (You might recognize the first part of this story from the Prologue.) Gary was sent to my office and suspended for a few days. His dad was asked to come in and visit with me. He came in loaded for bear. Before I got very far explaining the incident, he threatened me and said,

"I might just come over that desk and kick your ass."

I stayed calm and told him I liked his son, but he had a short temper and needed to learn how to control it. Eventually, dad calmed down and allowed me to explain the incident and its consequences. We talked about how we might help Gary control his temper by having him meet with the counselor. By the time we were done, dad and I agreed about the consequences.

"Not sure if you noticed," he said, "but I can be a kind of hot-tempered too. Maybe that's where my son got it."

After that incident, my confidence increased exponentially. I had learned how to calm someone down who was angry. It became a challenge for me to figure out how to handle irate parents or students and arrive at a mutually acceptable agreement. I looked forward to handling these angry parents. When one of them came into the office and was obviously mad, the secretaries would try to stay out of their way and sent them to me as quickly as possible. I told the secretaries that was fine because I liked to deal with the angry ones. The secretaries were glad to get them out of the office. The most important lesson I learned was not to take things personally.

Around the same time, Chris transferred into our school in his sophomore year. He was African American, and he had been forced to transfer by his dad in his sophomore year. He had been running with a bad crowd, had multiple disciplinary referrals, and had also been involved with drugs. Dad was determined to get him under control and see that he graduated from high school. Chris was not at all anxious to attend private school. The school had approximately 600 students of which only five were African American. There were a few confirmed racists and bigots among the student body.

It didn't take long for Chris' negative attitude about the school to draw attention. Chris resented being there, and he felt out of place in the mostly-white environment. In his defensiveness, he adopted a passive-aggressive "I don't care" attitude. This quickly got the attention of a few bigots. I discussed Chris' attitude with his dad who told me that he had encountered racism in the oil fields of Texas and had learned to deal with it. He was determined that Chris had to learn to live in a society that had racism. He felt the solution was to get a good education and rise above the bigotry.

Shortly after transferring in, Chris was in trouble. His arrogant and defensive attitude landed him in conflicts with teachers and other hotheaded students. He became a regular visitor to my office for disciplinary referrals. The frequent complaint from teachers was disrespect and classroom disturbance. When he was assigned detentions and other penalties for his infractions, Chris attended reluctantly and with a resentful attitude because his dad required him to take care of his responsibilities.

By the third month of school, a serious incident took place that would leave Chris' continued attendance in jeopardy. Chris and another student left class and went to the parking lot to smoke marijuana. When they came back the odor and their behavior gave them away. When questioned they admitted the drug use. Dad was called in, and a serious discussion about Chris' future took place. I expressed to dad that it didn't appear that Chris was going to make it in this school. He was resentful of being here and would prefer to be expelled. Dad insisted that he could make it and said he would work with the school to get Chris' behavior under control. He agreed to get him into counseling for the drug use and the anger. We suspended Chris for five days and put him on probation with a strict contract. At that point, I had little hope that Chris would graduate.

Dad was true to his word as he kept the boy in counseling. When Chris came back from the suspension, he stayed out of trouble for a while. Things settled down and other than a few minor incidents we got through that year with a minimum of problems. He successfully fulfilled his probationary period. Chris and I developed a positive relationship. We frequently talked about how things were going for him. Eventually, getting him to graduation became a goal for me, and though he wouldn't admit it, for Chris also.

When his junior year got underway, Chris became less resentful about attending school. He wouldn't admit it, but he seemed to feel more at home and was committed to graduating. He was making passing grades and staying out of major trouble. Unfortunately, some of our bigots had other plans.

Some students began leaving racist notes on Chris' locker and making remarks that aggravated him. They tried to incite him to do something violent, and he fell into their trap. Chris could not walk away from the taunting and teasing. I visited with him about it many times and tried to nail the culprits but could not catch them in the act.

Finally, it became too much, and there was an explosion of tempers in the commons area. Chris went after the kid who was taunting him and shoved him. A fight was about to break out between Chris and several bigots. Fortunately, I arrived in time to get between them and defuse the situation. Chris had to be disciplined for his role. He and the other students were suspended, and they and their parents were warned that if another incident happened, they would be expelled.

The sudden eruption shook Chris' dad's confidence. He was on the verge of pulling him out of school. He was angry and unsure of what action to take. I explained to him that we were embarrassed by the actions of the bigots and would not allow it to happen again. Dad was concerned that he was asking too much of a 16-year-old boy to endure this hostility. After many discussions, we agreed that he would keep Chris in school and try to get through the year. There were no guarantees about the next year.

During one of these discussions, I told dad that if and when Chris graduates he and I would have quite a hug of celebration at the ceremony. Throughout the rest of the year, there were regular conversations with Chris to defuse his anger and help him deal with the tension. I explained to him that many of the students who did not like him were not racists. They simply disliked his defensive, aggressive attitude. If he changed his attitude, he would find that many of the students would like him and treat him better.

Chris would not admit he had a negative attitude, but our discussions made him think about it. He became a little less defensive and more accepting. He began having conversations with other students. We got through his junior year with no further serious incidents.

As a senior, Chris told me that he wanted to graduate. He made the necessary grades and stayed out of major trouble. He even developed a few friendships with other students. He discussed his desire to join the Marines after he graduated. Finally, graduation day came, and I presented Chris with his diploma. He beamed proudly as he walked across the stage and I fought back the tears. After the ceremony, his dad and I sought each other out and had the hug we had planned. Tears flowed down both our cheeks as we sobbed with joy.

That could have been the end of the story, but the next fall Chris' dad called me. Chris had joined the Marines and would be home on leave. He asked if he could come to the school and do some recruiting. I said we would be glad to see him. When Chris showed up, I could hardly believe my eyes. He was immaculate in his marine uniform and stood straight and tall. The respect he had for others and his pride in himself was evident. When I talked to him, he said,

"Yes sir" and "No sir." I teased him a bit and asked if that was him. He made a statement that floored me.

"Mr. Schmidt," he said, "My drill sergeant pointed out to me that I had an attitude."

I replied, "Chris, I told you that many times."

"Yes," he answered, "but my drill sergeant had a way of convincing me to change."

We had a good laugh about that, but after he left the tears rolled down my cheeks as I realized why an education career had been the right choice for me.

One of my least favorite responsibilities was supervising the lunch room. There had been a series of small food fights, and it was always nerve-racking to keep things under control. Toward the end of one of the school years, we heard rumors of planning for a large food fight.

The atmosphere was tense during lunch that day. I planted myself near the door because I knew I would be one of the targets of the food. Sure enough, food began flying everywhere, and some of it was aimed at me. I stepped outside the door to dodge the flying food and avoided getting hit, but there was an uncontrolled mess in the cafeteria. As one of the leaders of the fight came out of the lunchroom, I grabbed him by the arm and told him they would have to go back and clean up. He looked at me menacingly and said,

"Get your hands off me."

I realized that I had put myself in a risky situation by touching this student and had visions of the end of my career. I immediately apologized for grabbing him. I told him those responsible would need to return and clean up the lunchroom. He walked back in as I held my breath. He joined the others in cleaning up the worst of the mess. I had dodged a bullet.

This incident shook me because of the viciousness in these students. A few ring leaders had stirred everyone up, and it turned into a food riot. I was also concerned because I had let my emotions take over. I lost my composure and had put my career in a precarious situation. The lesson was that no matter how upset you may be about students' actions, always maintain a calm exterior and keep your emotions in check. This lesson served me well in later years. But the tension from all the incidents that school year took a toll on me.

On the last day of school that year I commiserated with the president of the school, Benno, in his office at the end of the day. We discussed all of the unpleasant, funny and confusing things that had happened that year. This was a private school, and Benno had a liquor stash in the closet in his office. We went through quite a bit of bourbon in a couple of hours.

Finally, I decided it was time to go home, but I was in no condition to drive. Both my sons were home, so I called them and asked them to come pick me up. One of them could drive me home in my car. I got into the car and reclined the seat and fell asleep waiting for them. Soon I heard a knock on the door, and they took me home. They had a good laugh at me and still talk about the time Dad got drunk telling stories to Benno. That may not have been the healthiest way to relieve the tension, but it worked.

———

One of the trickier issues I handled was the issue of appropriate dress for dances. There had been some controversy about the lack of modesty in some of the girls' dresses in previous years. Some parents had come to the school to complain about what they saw as inappropriate dress. They wanted it cleaned up. The principal asked me to deal with it.

If there is one thing a male administrator never wants to get involved in, it is determining whether a girl's dress is appropriate. I had heard all the stories about measuring the length of skirts and determining if a top was showing too much. These situations are very uncomfortable for a male administrator. However, it was going to be my responsibility. Of course, I didn't have a choice because it had been assigned to me.

My first move was to form a committee of a group of mothers. They could give input, but the buck stopped with me as far as the dresses were concerned. The mothers suggested posting pictures around the school to give guidelines in the months before prom. We knew that some very expensive purchases are made, so we wanted to give the girls and their mothers plenty of time to decide. Magazine pictures were selected and identified as being appropriate or inappropriate and then posted in the hallways. We noticed that girls were very interested in studying these postings. However, the boys were even more interested in studying the inappropriate pictures. We knew this was distracting but decided to leave them up so there would be no misunderstanding.

We had many questions as we got closer to the prom date. Girls were bringing in dresses or pictures before they made a purchase. My committee and I had to pass judgment. We thought it was going well until it was time to have the queen candidates bring in their dresses. The committee asked them to come in one evening and wear their dresses. They came out of the dressing room one at a time to be approved.

As the only male in attendance, it is difficult to explain how uncomfortable this was. I was a 45-year-old male passing judgment on teenage girls' prom dresses as they paraded in front of me! I tried to avert my eyes when the girls paraded by us, but it was my job to look. To make matters worse, one of the candidates, who was a close friend of my daughter, came out with a dress that was clearly too revealing. It was cut very low in the back. The mothers on the committee immediately pointed this out to me and left me no wiggle room. They showed me pictures that had been posted of the inappropriate dresses, and this one closely resembled those samples.

Of course, the mother of the girl in question was very upset. She informed us how much she had spent on the dress and there was no time to make a change before the prom the next week. There was much crying and pleading. I may have backed down had the mothers on the committee not held my feet to the fire. As uncomfortable as it was, I held firm and said that the dress was not acceptable. I said we would have to approve any substitute that was found before she could be a candidate for prom queen. Thankfully, this mother and daughter found a way to add fabric to the back of the dress, so it wasn't so revealing. We approved it, and the event took place without incident. I was never so happy to be done with a prom as I was in that year.

Unfortunately, that wasn't my only experience with determining appropriate attire. The school had a very talented and popular dance team that performed at halftime during games. The team had gotten new uniforms that fall and performed in them at football games without incident.

At the first basketball game, they performed proudly in front of the home crowd. It was evident immediately that this was going to be trouble. Before they were even finished, I was accosted by several parents who informed me that the dance uniforms were not appropriate for a Catholic School. The uniforms were tight fitting spandex, and we had several girls who were quite well endowed. There was noticeable jiggling during the dance. I told the parents that I would investigate the situation.

When I asked the dance team coach why she got such tight uniforms, she pointed out that nobody had complained during football season. I informed her that when performing on the football field the dancers are a long way from the stands and the lighting is not as bright. She then told me the school president had approved them.

Benno was well into his 60's when he became president of the school. He had much experience as a principal before assuming the role of president at our school. We had become close friends, and he allowed me to handle student affairs without much interference. We worked together well and trusted each other. I went to see him about the dance team uniforms. Sure enough, the coach had brought the new outfits to him for approval before the school year.

"They were on hangers and looked fine to me," he said.

"Benno "I replied, "What the heck were you thinking? Hangers are a lot different than these girls' bodies."

We had a good laugh about the situation. There was no way we could make them spend more money to get new uniforms right away. The coach told us they could get tighter sports bras and wear some t-shirts over the top. That got us through the rest of the year. New dance uniforms were purchased the following year.

Many administrators will tell you that dealing with cheerleaders and their moms can be one of the most difficult situations they face. When our girls' basketball team qualified for the state tournament, we had to decide what time to leave for the first tournament game on a school day. Our state activities association kept a log of how much class time was missed for activities. I was very sensitive about that and determined to minimize class disruptions. Since the team could warm up on the court during halftime of the game before theirs, we allowed the team to depart early. The cheerleader sponsor wanted to leave at the same time. I told her they could not leave until later because they didn't need to be there for halftime of the previous game. When she objected, I told her that the team needs to be there for the game. The cheerleaders did not.

She went back to the cheerleaders and told them what had been said. Soon she came to me and insisted that I needed to face the cheerleaders and apologize. At first, I didn't understand what the apology was for but decided to face the music. At the meeting, they pointed out to me that they were just as important as the team. They practiced hard and were also athletes. If they couldn't be there to cheer, the team would not be able to play as well. Besides, they thought that I was being biased in favor of the players just because my daughter was on the team.

I contemplated telling them that the game could not be played without the team, but it could go on without cheerleaders. That was true, but after considering the situation, I decided that alienating the cheerleaders was not going to help. I listened to their concerns and eventually agreed that they could leave at the same time as the team. It bothered me to give in, but in this case, discretion was the better part of valor.

It had been repeatedly drilled into us at administrative leadership seminars that we needed to pick our fights wisely. The term they used was to 'choose the hill you are willing to die on.' This was not a hill to die on.

This was my first confrontation with cheerleaders, but there were others throughout my career. The next year there was a controversy about the selection process. We had a scoring system that was overseen by the sponsor who used teachers as judges. To satisfy some concerns about bias, we brought in outside judges who didn't know the girls. This helped, but there were still candidates and their moms who disagreed with the selections. Later, as a principal, I dealt with more of these cheerleader controversies. I learned that just because an activity wasn't a priority for me, didn't mean it wasn't important to others.

During my years as an assistant principal, I acquired a remarkable on-the-job education. There were also plenty of professional development opportunities to learn from more experienced professionals. I joined the Kansas Association of Secondary School Principals, KASSP. Led by a master principal, Gene Haydock, this organization helped me a lot as I fumbled through my first years. Gene was the consummate professional and provided excellent opportunities for rookies to learn from experienced administrators.

We learned not to react to everything we saw or heard. Sometimes being deaf and blind were not bad things in this job. We learned how to handle the most difficult scenarios with calm professionalism. We also learned to determine the hills we were willing to die on.

Usually, the assistant principal oversees crowd control at athletic contests. Most of the time such work is enjoyable and involves minimal effort. Occasionally, things get dicey.

At one of our football games against a rival school, things got tense. The rival school was predominantly black, and our student body was mostly white. We had our share of racists, and the rival school had plenty of troublemakers. I was sitting in our stands and noticed some of our opponent's students coming into our bleachers. They went to the top of the bleachers, and I watched them to observe what was happening. They yelled at some of our fans as they walked by. I decided that wasn't something to get involved in. However, a short time later, some fans reported that kids were spitting on them as they walked by below. I approached the students and asked them to leave. They became belligerent and initially refused to go. After telling them that I was getting complaints about them spitting on our students, they still resisted. I told them they needed to stay on their side "with their people" and we would stay on our side "with our people."

This made the rival students angry, and at first, I didn't understand why. As I thought about it later; however, I understood my mistake. I meant to stay on their side with their fans, and we would stay on our side with our fans. However, these students were African American, and ours were all Caucasian. They thought I was referring to color. My inexperience and lack of awareness caused me to use that terminology.

I immediately went to the other side to seek out their principal, Mr. Cushinberry. Dale was African American, and we had become good friends in our years as colleagues. I told him what had happened and assured him I didn't mean it the way it sounded. He laughed and said he would take care of it. He reprimanded his students and ordered them to stay on their side of the field.

That incident was a bit of an awakening for me about the issues of race. For the first time, I was in a city with a diverse population. There was not much diversity at our school, but there was at many of our competing schools. I needed to become more aware of my terminology. It was a good learning experience for me and fostering sensitivity to race became one of my emphases as I advanced in administration. Throughout the rest of my administrative career, equal treatment of diverse populations was a priority for me.

Another sticky situation arose when we hosted a basketball game at our gym. The opposing team had a former student who had been expelled and had made threats to some of that school's students. He was known to have access to a gun. The other school's administration was informed of this and were concerned that the expelled student might carry out his threats at our game.

Our administration was notified, and we requested an enhanced police presence outside our gym. They were on the lookout for the former student who had made the threat. Halfway through the game, a policeman informed me that the suspect had entered through a basement door and was in the hallways. We were concerned, but the police sealed off the hallway and eventually caught the suspect, who was carrying a gun. To our relief, he was wrestled to the ground, arrested, and taken away without anyone being harmed. That was not an enjoyable game, and I can't even remember who won. That was not as important as the safety of our crowd.

A tradition had developed at our school where seniors would pull pranks in the last days of school. Each year the pranks escalated as students tried to outdo those from the previous year. Sometimes the pranks were funny, but sometimes they caused a lot of problems.

One year, someone released mice in the hallways. The mice had been purchased at a pet shop, so they were tame and not that hard to catch. However, one student was bitten by a mouse as he caught it. We made an announcement that we needed to know where the mice came from so we could determine if the student needed to be treated for rabies. That wasn't true, but we thought it might help us catch the culprit. Eventually, someone told us who brought the mice, and he was disciplined.

Another time, someone put glue in all the key locks in the doors. Fortunately, we found one door that had not been touched so we could get inside. That was an expensive fix and, though we had a suspect, we could not prove who had pulled the prank. It cost thousands of dollars to fix all the locks.

Another time we arrived at school one morning to find that one of the main entrances had horse manure piled up against the door. It was the last day of finals for seniors. I announced that no finals would be conducted until the horse manure was removed. We guessed who had been responsible because one of the students had a horse farm. The serious students were angry because they wanted to get their finals over with. They gathered up a group and began pitching the manure into a couple of pickups. While supervising this activity, I gave them a couple of trash bags and asked them to fill them up for my use. I told them this would make good fertilizer for my garden. I thanked them for bringing the fertilizer and produced my best vegetables ever that year.

The funniest prank was one that was thwarted by sheer luck. We traditionally had a Catholic Mass on the last day of school for seniors. During the mass, our activities director, Jerry, patrolled the parking lot and heard chickens. He noticed that someone had put some boxes with chickens in them in the back of a pickup and covered it with a tarp. We figured out that the plan was to release the chickens to run down the hallways. Jerry was instructed to put the chickens in the bus garage, and I would watch the student whose pickup contained the chickens.

As students were processing up to receive communion, I noticed the suspect slip out a side door. I followed him to his pickup. He was standing there with a quizzical look on his face when I walked up.

"What are you doing out here," I asked.

"What happened to my chickens?" he mumbled forlornly.

I pretended not to know what he was talking about and told him to get back into the school. Slumped over and puzzled he shuffled back into the building. Many students knew about the proposed prank and were disappointed when no chickens showed up.

By coincidence, we had fried chicken for lunch the next day. Some of the underclassmen, suspicious of the source of the fried chicken, asked me if these were the chickens we had confiscated. I gave them a vague response that left them wondering. We had taken the chickens to another farmer who already had a flock of chickens, but many of the students thought we had butchered and eaten them for lunch that day. I did not dispel them of that notion.

After several years as an assistant principal, I felt ready for a principal position. My daughter had graduated from high school, and it seemed a good time to move on. A position was advertised at a nearby high school, and I applied. The job was at a rural public school and would be my first foray outside of Catholic Schools. The interview went well although I got lost and arrived late. I accepted the position quickly when I received the offer. It meant a commute of about 30 miles since we weren't going to move. Now it was time to prepare myself for the new assignment.

My tenure as an assistant principal had been a mixed bag. I learned a lot and became much better at not taking things personally. I improved my communication skills and learned how to deal with the most volatile situations. The stream of disciplinary issues became tedious, but by the end of my tenure I was also helping with teacher evaluations and working with student organizations that were doing positive things. Rose had been a great help in improving my teacher evaluations.

In my new position at a much smaller school there was no assistant, so discipline issues would still be my responsibility. However, I could also do teacher evaluations, personnel management and have overall responsibility for the school. I wanted to stay involved with students but also felt ready to manage a staff of adults and lead a team. This new challenge had me excited for another transition in educational administration.

7

PRINCIPAL

My first principal assignment was at Mission Valley, a small rural high school just outside of Topeka. This district had been consolidated in the 1970s from three rural K-12 schools into one high school. The three small K-6 schools located in each of the three small towns remained in place. One of those schools housed a district-wide, seventh and eighth grade. The high school building was in good condition and was in the middle of a pasture exactly 8.2 miles from each of the three small towns.

This location had been necessary to get the votes in the 1970s to pass the consolidation bond. Each town was jealous of the other. Their high schools had previously been bitter rivals in sports competition. To convince them to vote for a consolidated high school in the 1970s each town had to be assured that they would not lose influence. One important factor was the distance the building would be from each town. I checked the distance as I drove from each town to the high school location and it truly was exactly 8.2 miles.

The three elementary buildings were outdated and only had air conditioning in the administrative offices. It was not unusual to release students in the afternoon in early fall because of the heat. It sometimes got as high as 90 degrees on the third floor of some of the buildings in the afternoon. Holding school in those conditions was impossible. The high school building was modern and had central air.

This new assignment was exciting to me and the first thing I did was meet with all the teachers before the school year started. I wanted to establish good relationships right from the beginning. Some outstanding, dedicated teachers had strong ties to the community. There were also a few teachers who ended up there because they needed a job.

My term began with great enthusiasm on my part. The staff seemed happy to have new leadership. Just as in my first assistant principal position, so too here I was told that the discipline in the school needed tightening. The previous principal had not been re-newed because the board and superintendent were not satisfied and felt discipline was out of control.

The culture of the school was definitely rural, although most of the parents commuted to jobs in one of several nearby larger towns. Many of them had inherited a small farm and did some farming, but needed full-time jobs to support their families. One hallmark of the school was a highly developed agricultural program and the associ-ated Future Farmers of America club. (FFA) We also were the only school in the state of Kansas that had a trap shooting range on cam-pus. There was a special legislative bill to exempt our school from the ban on weapons. The trap shoot was frequently used on weekends to host contests.

My first confrontation came with the agriculture teacher when he requested that his students be released from school to pick up trash along a highway. This was one of their service projects. I re-fused the request because it seemed to me that if it was a service project they should do it on their own time, preferably Saturdays.

The agriculture teacher had a small farm in the community and had been there forever. He was highly respected throughout the state and was used to getting his way when he requested something. My suggestion was that if students gave some of their own time to do the service, then I would consider periodic requests to also use some school time. This did not endear me to the Ag teacher, but he com-plied. He was not used to not getting his way.

It soon became clear that the board and superintendent were correct in feeling that the students were running the school. They were used to being in the hallways during class and getting rowdy in the lunchroom. When I confronted some students about making a mess in the lunchroom, they told me it was the janitor's job to clean it up. I told them that was not acceptable, and they were to clean up their own mess before leaving lunch.

Bob, the head custodian really appreciated my efforts, and we worked closely together. He was knowledgeable and cared deeply about the school. He was an alum and had children attending the school.

Parents were mostly supportive. We had a lot of two-parent families, and they cared about their children's education. When we tightened up the discipline some of the students complained to their parents, but the parents were glad to see a little more orderliness in the school. As usual in such rural schools, there were also some families in extreme poverty. There was low cost housing, and this allowed for some low rental rates.

Most of the parents enjoyed the fact that their child was in a small school which offered personalized instruction and attention. When there were disciplinary problems parents were usually willing to come in and talk about them and cooperate with the school. However, that wasn't always the case.

Cindy was a sophomore who was a good student and athlete. She was also a cheerleader during football season. The cheerleading was extremely important to her and her mother who was also a former cheerleader. A score sheet was used to pick cheerleaders each year. A significant part of the score was character, and that was determined by disciplinary referrals.

Cindy had been disciplined twice for cheating on school work. Although she was the most athletic and accomplished candidate, her score disqualified her from the team for the next year. She and her mom were devastated. Mom demanded a meeting with me. Cindy and her mom and dad came to my office.

Mom pointed out that Cindy was clearly the most talented of all the cheerleaders. I acknowledged that she was but said her total score kept her from qualifying. Mom angrily suggested that this would be a devastating blow to Cindy and would affect her ability to qualify for college scholarships. Dad sat nervously in his chair trying not to get involved. He was obviously conflicted about the whole situation.

"This is far from the worst thing that could happen to Cindy," I told the parents. "She will have to sit out one year and then she can be a cheerleader again in her senior year."

"That would be devastating to her and totally unfair," said mom.

"Look at it as a difficult lesson for her that isn't that costly in the long run," I suggested.

"Not being a cheerleader for one year might be difficult for her but in the long term scheme of things, it is not that important. She will learn a good lesson about honesty and consequences."

I watched dad's reaction to this comment. He seemed to agree but said nothing. I sympathized with him because it appeared he had been dragged along unwillingly. I understood but wished he would speak up.

"If she can't cheer she will transfer to another school," said mom.

"I'm sorry you feel that way," I responded. "I hope you don't do that."

Sure enough, Cindy transferred to a rival league school. When we played them in football, she was cheering on the sidelines. When we competed against them in basketball and track, she performed like the star she was. Mom loved it while watching from the stands. Dad seemed embarrassed about the whole situation.

I have often wondered if Cindy learned anything from this incident. I felt that staying in our school and serving one year without cheerleading would have made a strong impression on Cindy. It is now twenty years later, and I doubt that missing one year of cheerleading would have been a significant blow to her life.

Teachers in our school knew every student and took a personal interest. When they noticed a change in a student, they were not afraid to approach the administration or parents about the problem.

Several teachers notified me that Robert was continually falling asleep in class. He was generally cooperative but just couldn't stay awake. I called his mother and asked her to come in to have a discussion. She was a single parent and lived in a ramshackle house with her son. Robert was in the room with us as we asked him why he was falling asleep so frequently.

He said he just couldn't get to sleep at night. I asked him if he had a television in his room.

"Yes, I do," he responded.

"Can't you turn it off when it is time to go to sleep?" I asked.

"I just get wrapped up in the shows and can't shut it off," he replied.

"OK, mom. Can't you just remove the TV from his room?" I asked.

She seemed surprised at the suggestion but promised she would do so. After that Robert began staying awake in class. It seemed such a simple solution to me but sometimes the answer is not always so obvious to another person.

One time I was talking with a student in the hallway. Curtis was constantly in trouble and seemed to find pleasure in irritating his teachers. I tried to reason with him and explained that he would be a lot happier if he didn't constantly do things to make teachers mad. He just looked at me like he didn't care.

While we were talking, two of our veteran teachers walked by in the hall. They smiled as they passed. Later Nancy and Carol pulled me aside.

"You were trying to reason with Curtis," they laughed. We have been trying that for years, and it has never worked."

They were right. I never could make any progress with Curtis. They were impressed with my intentions but knew it was fruitless.

Teachers told me that some of the students had guns in their vehicles in the parking lot when pheasant and deer seasons opened. This was shortly after the Columbine massacre, and there was a heightened awareness of guns on campus. I knew that these kids didn't have any hostile motives. They were just used to carrying weapons to hunt on the way to or from school.

Penalties in our state for having a weapon on school grounds were very severe; long term suspension or expulsion. I didn't want any of these students to get caught up in this so an announcement was made that vehicles in the parking lot would be searched in the next several days. By the time I got around to searching, the weapons had been removed. I will admit that some were spotted. I chose to be temporarily blinded and requested a teacher to privately notify the student to get his gun out of his vehicle.

When one high school student was missing a lot of school I went to his home to find out what the problem was. While stepping onto the front porch, my foot went through a rotten board. Thankfully the porch was not very high, so it did not hurt me. I knocked on the door and then stepped off the porch.

The mother came to the door and was embarrassed about the porch. She invited me around to the back door so we could talk. As I looked into the house, I could see it was in a state of disrepair. Windows were rotted out, some were broken, and there was very little furniture in the kitchen. She said her son didn't want to come to school because he had no nice clothes to wear. She couldn't afford to buy anything that would blend in with the other kids.

I went back to his teachers with this information and soon we had over $100 dollars from individuals and school organizations. The money was given to the mother and James returned to school wearing appropriate attire. This is one of the benefits of a small school and community where everyone knows your name. No questions were asked. Everyone just wanted to help out a parent who didn't have the means to help her family.

Busing was always a big issue because of the large geographical area. Sometimes buses had to drive multiple miles between pickups. Occasionally we had students who were out of our district who wanted to attend our school. That was acceptable but the state had a rule that we could not go out of our district with buses to pick them up.

In one case the parent pleaded with the board to go one-half mile out of the district to pick up their elementary child. Otherwise, they had to take her to the nearest point in our district to be picked up, which was a hardship because of their commutes to their jobs. As wrenching as it was to turn them down, we knew that if we made an exception for one, we would get requests to do the same for others.

The school district had a history of strained relations between teachers and the board. There had been some acrimonious contract negotiations, and it got so bad that the state teachers' union publicly urged teachers not to apply at this district. The pay scale was lower than those at most surrounding schools, and it was in a remote area, which made it difficult to recruit. The statement by the teachers' union added to the difficulty.

What I found were some outstanding teachers, including a math teacher with a master's degree from Stanford, a state renowned agricultural program, an outstanding English teacher and debate coach, and other committed faculty. The mood was not very positive because of strained relations with the board, but the teachers were ready for good leadership and cared about the kids. This was an ideal opportunity to test my leadership skills.

The first order of business was to instill a sense of discipline in the student body. It had become a tradition for seniors to pretty much do whatever they wanted to do. I cracked down on leaving school for non-critical reasons and implemented an attendance policy that had been lacking.

Teachers were ready to work with me on the issue of kids walking the halls during class time and creating disturbances in the halls during passing periods. They were assigned to be out in the halls during class breaks and not allow students to leave the classroom without a pass. I patrolled the halls and assisted teachers in their efforts. We did not allow students to leave the lunchroom without cleaning up their tables and we supervised the parking lot before and after school.

Soon we began to see a difference in order in the building. However, the seniors were not happy about this and expressed their dissatisfaction to the agriculture teacher. He agreed to set up a meeting between the senior leaders and me to discuss the situation. Apparently, they sensed that he was more on their side than I was.

We had the discussion in which I allowed them to express their concerns. It was then explained to them that I had been hired precisely because the board and much of the staff felt that discipline was lacking. A few concessions were given in exchange for their agreement to work with me on creating more order in the school. I explained to them that most schools did not have such haphazard behavior and that we would be a better school if we tightened things up. The previous principal was popular with the older students because they had pretty much gotten their way. They were not enamored with the changes I had put in place.

By the next board meeting, word had gotten back to board members about the meeting with seniors, and I was asked about it.

Fearing opposition, I explained the meeting in positive terms. It surprised me when one of the board members laughed and said she was glad they were unhappy because things had been too loose. She stated that the freshman liked me and thought things were fine because they didn't know any better. They had not witnessed the lax enforcement of rules and were adjusting accordingly. She indicated the seniors would just have to adapt. It was comforting to know that I had the support of the board.

Some teachers felt there had not been sufficient attention paid to academic rigor in previous years. This was an area in which I felt competent and that I was anxious to address. We began having regular faculty meetings focused on academic issues. We discussed how to increase our rigor. There had been a recent educational movement to emphasize the three R's: Relationships, Rigor and Relevance. There was also a strong push in our state to become more proficient at problem-solving. I had developed a strong interest in the latest research into how the brain learns. These concepts of brain-based learning were brought to the teachers, and we began sending teachers to professional development opportunities that they had seldom been encouraged to attend.

Teachers became excited about developing more depth in their instruction and holding students to higher standards. Interdepartmental projects were encouraged to show the interconnectedness of the various subjects. One of the most interesting was when our math teacher used the example of raising cattle for the market to do mathematical calculations and problem-solving. The students, many of whom were from farm backgrounds and were also in agriculture classes, were asked to calculate whether it was more profitable to raise their cattle as grass fed in the pasture or grain fed in a feedlot. The exercise demonstrated the relevance of mathematics in many areas of life.

Connie was an excellent counselor, and she and I worked together to encourage students to take rigorous classes. It had been past practice for many students to take as light a schedule as possible, especially seniors. Connie and I began enforcing pre-requisites for taking advanced classes and eliminated some of the less rigorous courses.

An ongoing issue in a rural school like that one is getting qualified teachers. We were particularly disadvantaged because of the low
pay scale and the remote location. I attended small college teacher fairs where it was more likely to find young teachers from small
towns. They were more inclined to show interest in a small rural
school.

The rest of the administrative staff was an interesting mix. There
was a highly competent, supportive staff in the high school office. As
a beginning principal, I learned that the most important people in
your school are the secretary and the custodian. Dixie and Bob were
indispensable to anything we would accomplish.

The other building administrators were an experienced group
that gave me opportunities to learn. Dale was a retired superintendent and a seasoned veteran who came to our district as an elementary principal. He had a wealth of experience and helped me more
than he imagined. Gene was another elementary principal who de-
fied the stereotype of a principal. His alternative views caused us to
reconsider preconceived notions. And Mark was a talented young
leader who was more than willing to learn as he progressed in his
career.

The administrative meetings with the superintendent, Dick,
were always interesting. There were lively discussions and friendly
banter as we challenged each other on decisions about our various
buildings. This impressed upon me the importance of hearing many
viewpoints before making decisions. After a year of leadership from
Dick, he retired and Bob, another experienced superintendent, took
his place. What I learned from them came in handy when I became
a superintendent.

A major issue in the district was the outdated state of the elementary buildings and the uneven distribution of students in those
buildings. In one building there was a class of six students with a
teacher while some other buildings had as many as twenty-five per
teacher.

Bob and the school board took this issue head-on and proposed
building a new K-8 school to consolidate the elementary buildings.
This was quite controversial as each small town wanted to retain its

school. Meetings were held for public comment and to answer questions. I watched as Bob was attacked by many constituents opposed to this move. The concern was that losing their schools meant losing their towns. These towns consisted of less than 300 people, and there was only one grocery store amongst all three towns.

Bob maintained a professional demeanor and tried to explain that the district could not afford to maintain three elementary schools for such a small number of students. By consolidating we could even out class sizes and reduce the number of teachers. He gave financial statistics and explained that operating one building instead of three could be done more efficiently.

The opposition was not only opposed to losing their local schools but was strongly opposed to the increased property taxes that would be necessary to construct a new elementary building. This issue had been discussed frequently in the previous twenty years since the consolidation of the high school. After considerable rancor, the issue went to a vote and failed by a narrow margin.

Even though I was not directly involved, it was a real learning experience that would serve me well later. Bob showed me how to present a proposal that had strong opposition. He demonstrated how to keep it as non-confrontational as possible. I also learned about the strong passions of residents regarding their local schools and taxes. There is always a group in opposition that will make the following statements:

"It was good enough for me, and it should be good enough for them."

"The building doesn't determine the quality of education."

"There are many people in the community that cannot afford a tax increase."

There is an element of truth in all of these statements, but there are many other things to consider. I filed this in the back of my mind for future reference and was appreciative of the opportunity to observe the process.

One of the more interesting parts of the job as principal was the hiring and firing of teachers. I enjoyed interviewing prospective teachers and soon developed a routine for the process. A committee of a few staff members was formed.

If we had multiple candidates, we screened resumes and invited two or three of the best for an interview. On resumes, I looked for activities that showed an innate interest in kids. Since many of our applicants were beginners, I looked for those who worked camps, 4-H activities, volunteer coaching, church youth activities, etc. Transcripts became one of the least important factors in hiring.

Occasionally there was an applicant who flunked out of college early on, went into a job or the military and came back to finish college. In spite of their poor academic records early on, these people often became some of the best teachers. They had experienced failure because of their own lack of effort but matured and succeeded. This helped them understand the students who were not motivated to learn. There were also valedictorians and salutatorians who applied but were ineffective teachers because they could not relate to the unmotivated students. This is certainly not true in all cases, but I learned not to view transcripts as indicative of the quality of a teacher.

Before inviting candidates for an interview one or two references were checked to see if they were viable. Occasionally that eliminated a candidate who may have looked very good on paper. Several times, when calling about a candidate the response was,

"According to our attorney, I can tell you that this person worked here these dates."

That response assured that the candidate was removed from the interview list. It indicated that the person had been terminated but had a legal agreement with the school that there would be no negative recommendation. Usually this involved a situation in which wrongdoing of some kind was alleged but could not be proven in court. I later had a few of those situations myself.

Those who checked out after a cursory reference check were invited for interviews. The questions that gave me the most information about a potential teacher were those that focused on relationships. After determining that they had enough subject knowledge, I would ask questions about their classroom management style.

"How do you motivate students?"

"Give me an example of how you would teach a certain concept?"

"Describe the best teaching moment of your student teaching or teaching experience?"

"How do you deal with the disruptive student?"

There is no one correct answer to any of these questions but listening to the candidate's description gave me a good feel for their style of teaching. I am a firm believer that a teacher must have a positive relationship with students to be effective. The adage, "They don't care how much you know until they know how much you care" is popular because it is true."

Sometimes a candidate eliminates himself early in the interview. One candidate came for an interview with his wife and asked if she could sit in on the interview.

"What is the purpose of that?" I asked.

"She and I operate as one, and she wants to know what it will be like working here," he replied.

I am totally supportive of the idea that marriage is a partnership. However, that spouse will not be in the classroom with you. You must make it on your own. Needless to say, that candidate did not get the job.

Some candidates came to interviews dressed in sweats and t-shirts. I don't necessarily expect everyone to be in a suit, but how you dress does have an impact on how you appear to students. If you can't even dress up for an interview, you may not be as serious about the job as I would like. I believe that if you dress professionally, you are perceived as a professional.

After identifying our favorite candidate(s), there was a more extensive check of references. Candidates give a list of references on their application, but I rarely called the ones they listed unless I knew them personally. Those are almost all going to be positive and will seldom tell you any of the problems that may have existed.

I had become acquainted with educators all over the state in my career. This came in quite handy on reference checks when I knew someone with first-hand knowledge of the candidate. If I knew the reference well, they were asked to be thorough and honest in their description of both the good and bad qualities of the candidate.

Most references don't want to say anything bad about a candidate. The natural inclination is to put the best spin on your evaluation of someone. Everyone has some faults, and it is helpful to know what they are and then determine if those faults are manageable in your school.

Since most references tend to minimize negative statements about an individual, I learned to take the negatives they mentioned seriously and to assume they are more serious than the reference expresses. Sometimes those negatives will not be a problem if you know about them in advance and can manage that person properly.

Despite every precaution, your hires will not always work out. Sometimes you must admit you were wrong and cut your losses. There were times when I didn't feel good about hiring a teacher, but that person was the best of the applicants. That is a frustrating situation, but it can happen when there are teacher shortages and in a remote location.

When terminating or non-renewing a teacher, I found it best to be straight forward. Respect them as a person and let them know they do not fit your expectations.

Richard was a music teacher who knew his subject well and was liked by the students. However, his classroom management was chaotic at best. When we had public performances those who were not participating at points in the program were disruptive, and his transitions between groups were slow and noisy. The audience was frequently restless while waiting for the next group to get in position to perform.

I had many discussions with Richard about his management skills. He agreed they were lacking and finally I requested the board to non-renew his contract. Students and parents came to the board meeting and pleaded on his behalf. They felt that he cared about them and had helped many with their appreciation of music. They acknowledged the lack of discipline but felt he could develop that skill. The board backed down and granted him another contract year. I agreed to work with him to improve his classroom and performance management.

After another chaotic year, Richard and I decided it was best for him to move on. In our discussions, I suggested that his best option was to get a job as an assistant music instructor in a larger school where someone else could give him direction. He agreed, resigned from our school and was fortunate enough to find just such a position. He did well there and was happy with his decision.

When the long-term agriculture teacher resigned, we faced a critical hiring decision. TD had built the program into a state power in his forty-some years as an instructor. It was one of the major points of pride in this district. To maintain that quality we needed to make a good hire.

A young man who had gone through our program had recently gotten his degree in agricultural education. James was intelligent, knowledgeable about agriculture and although he came off a bit arrogant, he stood out as the most impressive in the interviews. I found out about his arrogance soon after he was hired.

The agriculture program had a strong science component and there was a guideline that students could not take the Ag science course without having completed the prerequisite of biology. The counselor and I noticed that some students were signing up for Ag science without having completed biology. The counselor told students they could not do so. The students claimed that the Ag instructor had told them he would waive the biology requirement.

The counselor notified me, and I met with James to tell him he did not have the authority to change the requirements. He did not take it well and criticized the counselor and me to the students. That was the precursor of the problems we had with him. He adopted the attitude that the agriculture program was the starship of the school and they could do anything they wanted to. After two years of this kind of conflict, I finally convinced the board that he should be terminated. He got word of the pending termination and resigned before it was delivered.

At any rate, he was gone, and we had to find another instructor for the highly visible program. Kelly, a female candidate, looked like our best option after the interviews. She had just graduated from college and came highly recommended. She was not as knowledgeable in the traditional areas of agriculture as our previous instructors but she was very impressive. It was a bit of a shock to some of our constituents to have a female in charge of what had been a mostly male-dominated teaching area.

Within a couple of years, Kelly transformed the program by placing more emphasis on speaking ability and leadership. The program continued to win awards and enrollment grew steadily. She was a hire who worked out well and is still there twenty years later.

As I wrote in the chapter on extracurricular activities, the school had a long losing streak in football: in fact, the second longest in the state. Bill, the longtime coach and a respected member of the staff and community, tried his best but could not turn it around. I felt we needed a change to jumpstart the program.

Bill was very professional throughout the difficult decision to replace him. We brought in a new person to coach and to serve as activities director. I found that confronting the issue directly and honestly with Bill helped our relationship because he continued as an effective special education teacher. Later in his career, Bill became the high school principal and then superintendent in this district.

Terminating or non-renewing with a direct and blunt conversation convinced me that was the only way to do it. However, not all instances went as smoothly as the two I mentioned previously. In some cases, no matter how you do it, the person is not going to react well. You do your best to handle it directly and personally. Cut the ties and move on.

As was mentioned earlier in this chapter, changes were not always well accepted by the students. One such change was in the academic awards event. Every school has these events and they are important to parents and students. However, the tradition at this school was to go through every reward and recognize each student for every single award they received separately. Some came forward as many as ten times. This led to an interminably long process and parents who had to wait till the end were hopelessly bored.

I proposed bringing each student forward to receive all of his/her awards at one time instead of being brought up multiple times. This cut the length of the event in half, and each student was still recognized for all his or her good work. The few major awards were still handled individually at the end of the program.

Some parents of the best students were incensed by this change. They liked the idea of their student being called up multiple times for their many awards. They even went to the board to protest. Fortunately, the board supported me, and the event was held as planned. It was a lot of work for the counselor and me to group all of these awards, but most of the parents were appreciative of the time saved.

Our emphasis on improving academic rigor and behavior in the school was not accepted by all students. One girl pointed out to me that she was proud to be a "hick" from a rural school. She resented the attempt to change that image. She saw me as a "city guy" coming in and telling them how to act.

We had quite a discussion about what it meant to be a "hick." I suggested that meant you were crude and out of touch with current times. I proposed to her that what she really meant was that she was proud to be from an agricultural background. I too was proud to be from an agricultural background and did not feel that meant one was out of touch or backward. Being agricultural did not preclude acting with respect, intelligence, and dignity. I'm not sure I changed her thoughts on the topic, but we were not going to tolerate rude, disrespectful behavior.

Graduation was a case in point. It was the tradition to hoot and holler at the mention of every graduate's name and spray everyone with silly string. In my mind, graduation should be a dignified ceremony conducted seriously. I was offended by the rowdy behavior that had become a tradition, and I attempted to change the culture.

During rehearsals, I implored the students to forgo the silly string and ask their families to contain the hooting and hollering at the mention of every name. On graduation day as we prepared for the ceremony, I saw cans of silly string under the seats where the graduates would sit. I confiscated the cans before the ceremony began. One of the mothers confronted me angrily and demanded to have the cans back or that I reimburse her the cost. I told her I would gladly pay her the $2 after the ceremony if we could just conduct it in dignity. Unfortunately, many parents handed their graduate another can of silly string as they marched into the ceremony and the tradition continued. In future years I asked the graduates to wait with the silly string until we did the recessional and then have their tradition outside the graduation venue. This met with limited success.

Maybe I am just old fashioned, but it upsets me to see such boisterous behavior at what should be a serious, dignified event. I am not opposed to getting wild and crazy at other events such as games or playtime. This was just something I had to learn not to get stressed over.

During those three years as a high school principal, I gained an understanding of the high profile the position holds in a small community. Everybody knew who the principal was and most had an opinion on every decision made.

After serving three years as high school principal, it was announced that our superintendent was taking retirement. I was even more surprised when Bob stated that he had recommended me to take over as superintendent and the board had agreed.

During my time as principal, I had taken classes to obtain district certification. I had no great desire to be a superintendent at that time but thought it might be a possibility in the future. I was conflicted about taking the position in this school district. I knew about some of the problems and realized that we would have to propose a bond issue again to consolidate our elementary schools. Bob convinced me that it was better to know what the problems are in your district than go to a new district where you weren't aware of the existing problems.

After much thought, I accepted the position. I still needed a couple of classes to complete my district certification so, while closing out the year as principal, I commuted 30 miles to class at Emporia State University. There were times when I drove 90 miles per hour to get to class on time after finishing some project or event at the high school. Finally, the certification was completed, and I was promoted to superintendent. So began a whole new phase in my educational career.

8

EXTRACURRICULAR ACTIVITIES

Among the things that I enjoyed immensely as an administrator were extracurricular activities. Yes, they made the days much longer, but I felt more relaxed at these events than during the day. It was enjoyable watching the kids perform on the athletic fields and in the arts. It gave a different feel to relationships with kids to see them display their talents.

As a principal, you are on duty at these events and must watch crowd behavior. Occasionally there are problems with students or even adults. But most of the time you can just watch and visit with the crowd.

The kids appreciate the fact that their administrators are taking an interest in something they are passionate about. It is always a thrill to students when a principal sees them in the hall the next day and compliments them on their performance in a game or a play.

In sports, it is expected that principals will go to the varsity contests because this is where the biggest crowds are. However, I tried to go to freshman and junior varsity games as much as possible. These kids need support just as much as the varsity kids.

As a superintendent, it is important to make an appearance at as many events as possible. This was sometimes very difficult because there could be two or three events going on in an evening. It wasn't unusual to have an elementary music program, a junior high game, and a high school recognition program on the same night. As a superintendent people frequently remarked to me, "you are everywhere," because they saw me at multiple events in an evening. It is impossible to stay for the duration of each event, but I at least made an appearance. That was an important part of my job.

I mastered the art of what my second wife, Mary and I called the "Superintendent Shuffle." I would show up at events and enter conspicuously so everyone would see me. I would usually sit for a while and watch while talking to several parents or patrons. Then I would slip out inconspicuously and go to the next event following the same procedure until appearances had been made at every school event that evening. Frequently Mary would accompany me if it was going to be a long evening of events and we would have dinner at the concession stand. We became experts at the concession stand food. I love popcorn, so that was a treat to me anyway. Sometimes I made the rounds by myself and was able to get home early enough to have dinner with my wife, but still usually grabbed a bag of popcorn for the ride home.

Students notice when their administrators show an interest in their activities. There were a lot of games and music programs that didn't really interest me. But if you care about the students who are participating it is important to attend. If it was important to them, then it was important to me. Being present at their events also makes it much smoother when you see those students for disciplinary issues. If they know you care about them, they might not be happy that they are being disciplined, but they are more likely to trust you.

I once had a fellow teacher who did not care for sports. He was an outstanding teacher, very demanding and cared about his students, but he never attended any games.

"Why don't you ever go to the games?" I asked him.

"I have no interest in sports," he said. "They are a waste of time and resources, and I have more important things to do."

"It's not about the sport," I replied. "It's about the kids. I know you care about the kids."

He looked at me a bit startled and walked away. It had not occurred to him that he could show his concern for students outside the classroom as well. To his credit, he began attending some sporting events after that. The students noticed his attendance. They knew he wasn't into football or other sports, but they were impressed that he came anyway.

As an assistant principal, I oversaw crowd control at games. We began a tradition of doing pushups whenever our team scored in football. The cheerleaders and I would line up in the end zone and do as many pushups as we had points on the board. We had some pretty good teams, and it wasn't easy to do 40 or more pushups. Of course, I was young then and could still do it. The cheerleaders loved it, and so did the student body. Some of them even joined in. Decades later I have run into former students who still speak about the pushup tradition.

At varsity football games there was always a contingent of younger kids playing football somewhere nearby. They come with their parents and get excited about the game, so they start their own little game of touch football. Sometimes they got in the way of fans, but they were just dreaming about the day when they would be able to play on the real field like the big kids. As a principal, I often joined them in throwing and catching passes. They loved it that an adult was participating with them in their fun. They couldn't wait until it was their chance to get on the big field.

One year I received a call from a principal from a school we had just played in a freshman football game. We had beaten the team 74-0. The other team's principal was angry because he felt we had run up the score. I had a talk with my head coach about what happened. He admitted they were having fun and it was just so easy to score. After the fact, he realized it was wrong to run up the score like that. I told him that it was unsportsmanlike. I knew enough about football to know he could have played his lower end kids more or run plays that were less likely to score quickly. I told him we were creating adversarial relationships with other schools. There was no point in beating someone that bad. It didn't help our kids, and it hurt the other team. There may be a time when they are good, and we are bad, and they might want to do the same to us. The coach reluctantly agreed he wouldn't do that again and I had him send an apology letter to the beaten down opponent. Later in my career, I would be on the other end of that kind of beating.

In my early years as a principal, I sometimes attended football practices. Our team was terrible and had the longest losing streak in the state. I felt bad for the kids and wanted to support them, but they just didn't have much talent. Because of our poor record, many of the better athletes did not even go out for football. The reputation of our football team was so bad that one kid who had some talent told the coach that he liked football and would like to play in the games, but he didn't like to go to practice. He never came out for the team.

I watched practices and tossed a football around with anyone who was free. When no one was available to play catch, I would set the ball on a tee and kick field goals. The kids knew I was there and watching them and they appreciated that.

Something that bothered me more than anything was when poor sportsmanship was displayed. I could understand the passion, and as a young coach, I sometimes lost my composure. It was not unusual for someone to get out of control and as principal, it was my job to deal with it. The hardest cases were when it was one of our own parents.

Adam was a parent who had been frustrated with our losing football team during my tenure as principal. He was a big guy who had played football at this high school. Listening to him I thought he must have been a great player. But those who knew him said he was terrible. However, in his memory, he was a great player on a great team.

He wasn't satisfied just sitting in the stands. Instead, he roamed the sidelines and criticized players and coaches. I reluctantly went to the sidelines and asked him to be more positive, especially with our kids. I told him they were doing their best and they are just kids. He angrily blamed the coaches for not teaching them the fundamentals. I had been at practices and saw coaches teaching fundamentals. Our kids just weren't very talented. He criticized every unsuccessful play.

"That was a stupid play call," he would say after the play was stuffed for a loss. "They should have run it outside."

"They should have run it inside," he said after an outside play lost yardage. "They keep running the same stupid play over and over."

I finally told him he was the best person at calling plays after the play was over than anyone I had ever seen. It's too bad he couldn't tell the coach what play to run before the play.

After several of these encounters with Adam, he was told he couldn't be on the sidelines anymore. He uttered a few profanities and told me I didn't know anything about football and neither did the coach. In frustration, I asked him for his phone number. I said I would be calling him this weekend to get him signed up as an assistant coach. Since he knew so much about the game, we were going to tap into his ability to turn our football fortunes around.

I called him that weekend and asked him to come in on Monday and sign a contract as assistant coach. I figured he was all talk and no action and wouldn't show up, but I wasn't sure of that. It had me worried all weekend, but when he didn't show up Monday, I knew I had him. The next game he was told he would be removed from the game if he continued to yell insults at our players and coaches. Like most bullies, he whimpered away without a fight. I made it a habit to sit near him at games to try to keep him under control.

Our coach at that time was a wonderful teacher and knew enough about football to be successful, but he just couldn't turn the program around. After several years of no-win seasons, I finally asked him to resign. Bill was a class guy and said he always taught his kids never to quit so he would not resign. I would have to fire him. It was painful to do, but Bill was fired as coach, and we began a search for a new head coach. Bill held no grudge and continued to teach and still coached wrestling.

Our search for a new coach was difficult. We had lost 39 consecutive games, and no one wanted to come into that situation. Finally, another assistant in our league who seemed to have the right credentials applied and was hired.

Rod was a young man who was full of enthusiasm. He immediately began recruiting students to come out for football. He meticulously organized practices and had his assistants teaching the fundamentals. Nonetheless, we lost every game in his first year. There was a little bit of hope because we played some teams close. I again received complaints from parents and patrons who wanted the coach fired. I tried to tell them it was going to take time to turn this around.

In one game that year we were beaten 72-0 by a league team that was a perennial powerhouse. We were obviously outmatched, and at halftime of that game, I appealed to the superintendent of the Eagles.

"We are just not up to your level of ability," I said. "Our kids could get hurt."

He laughed and said, "Well, you just need to get better."

This made me angry, and I responded, "You can play your younger kids in the second half to keep the score reasonable. No one is benefitting from this beating. Your team is not getting any better, and our players may get hurt."

He was noncommittal and walked off to the concession stand.

When the Eagles still had their starting quarterback in the game in the fourth quarter, I was livid and approached him after the game.

He repeated, "Your team just needs to get better."

I said, "You have us overpowered. We can't do anything about this, but you can. Blaming us is like blaming the rape victim for not fighting back. We just aren't strong enough."

He laughed and walked away.

Years later I ran into this same superintendent when we were both at different schools. We had put the incident behind us and got along OK.

But when he sees me, he frequently remarks, "Didn't you call me a rapist or something?"

That 72-0 beating motivated several other schools in our league to join us in looking at other options. Eventually, three of our league schools who had been beaten similarly joined with three other schools and formed a new league. It was a great move for all of us. The new league was much more competitive, and we alternated championships in a more even fashion.

The following year we finally broke the losing streak. We were closing in on the all-time state record for losing streaks when we finally won a game. The celebration was electric. We were so tired of losing and finally felt the taste of victory. You would have thought we had just won the Super Bowl. The mood in the school completely changed that week.

We won two games that year and the following year made the playoffs for the first time in our history. Unfortunately, we had to play the Eagles in the playoff game. They beat us again but not as badly. At that game, I rubbed it into several of our patrons who had been berating me for not firing our coach the previous year.

"Are you still wanting to fire the coach?" I asked them. "You know this is the first time we have ever made the playoffs."

They grumbled something like, "Yes, but we're getting pounded by the Eagles again."

You just can't please some people. The football team continued to win and make it to the playoffs under this coach.

One of the funniest stories I witnessed at a football game was when we were playing another league team at their field. The superintendent, Susan, was a good friend of mine. She was a petite woman who was very mild mannered. She had a patron who was walking along the side of the field loudly criticizing the referees. At halftime, the referees told her to remove that man from the premises. There was no security person at the game.

She looked at them and said, "Look at me. He weighs 300 pounds and is crazy angry. What am I going to do?"

They were adamant that he must be removed.

Finally, she went to the other side of the field where he was hanging out. She was trembling because he seemed out of control and she was afraid he might strike her. Susan mustered all her 120 pounds and confronted the man. She told him he had to leave the field, or she would call the police. Like most bullies, he backed down and left. She laughed as she told me the story, but at the time she was terrified. The patron spent the rest of the game in the parking lot complaining.

There were plenty of examples of good sportsmanship, but they aren't as interesting because they are just cases where people cheer for their team and treat everyone with respect. One example worth relating was a touching event on our home field. The team we were playing had experienced a real tragedy the week before. One of their players collapsed and died on the practice field. We were in contact with them the next day to give our condolences and ask if they wanted to cancel the game. After meeting with their parents and athletes, they decided the best thing for them was to go ahead with the game.

When their team arrived, we had people there to welcome them and make them feel at home. Their mood was somber, but they dressed for the game and came out to the field. We had arranged with their coach to bring both teams together at the middle of the field for a moment of silence for their fallen teammate. Tears flowed on both sides as players and coaches knelt together in the middle of the field. We reflected on the fact that the game was just a game. The loss of their teammate was what really mattered. The game proceeded in a sportsmanlike manner amid a feeling of brotherhood. I can't even remember who won that game.

When I left Mission Valley to become superintendent at Independence, I discovered that they also had a long losing streak in football. They had lost 27 consecutive games by the time I arrived there. I wondered what it was that kept luring me to schools with losing football teams. This school held the record for the longest winning streak in the state from way back in the 1950s, but recent years had not been good. I found out that the city had discontinued tackle football for several years in the recreation league and the school only started football in the eighth grade. This meant that kids coming out for football in high school were very inexperienced in the game.

Amidst the losses, I remarked that this level of football may be worse then what I had seen at my previous school. We had good kids, but they didn't have a clue how to play the game, and we were nearing 40 consecutive losses. The coach was new at the high school level but had been very successful at junior high in previous years. The city recreational league had also started up a tackle football program. He was now getting the first of those kids into his high school program.

There were frequent occasions during that first season when patrons urged me to fire the coach.

"Look at these kids," they said, "Nobody teaches them how to block and tackle. You need to get a new coach."

I had watched some practices and knew that they were teaching fundamental techniques. Several times the complainers got the best of me, and I responded,

"Look at what he has to work with. These are good kids, but they are just not very athletic, and they have never played before. We need to give the coach some time."

The suffering continued throughout that season. I grimaced watching our defensive backs stand still and watch the flight of the ball into the hands of receivers and then try to chase them down. It was unclear if they realized that they could go after the ball also. It was excruciating to watch. However, as bad as the football was, the stands were always full, and we had a good contingent of supporters that traveled to away games. I wondered how we would handle the crowds if we ever started winning. I secretly made a vow to myself that if I ever went to another school, it would have to have a winning football team.

The second year started with a loss, and I was prepared to suffer through another dismal season. However, our second opponent was a team we thought we could beat. We knew we were the better team. The anticipation of breaking a 40-game losing streak was in the air. Plans were made to have a celebration back at the high school if we won. There was a ceremonial victory bell at the school that had been in a state of disrepair for years. That didn't matter because it hadn't been needed during the losing streak anyway. The week of our second game it was repaired in anticipation of ringing the bell.

To the delight of every Bulldog fan, we won the game. The team and its supporters were ecstatic. A huge crowd gathered around the victory bell, and the players took turns ringing the bell. It was like an exorcism for the school community.

We won several more games that season and surprisingly made the playoffs for the first time in years. We were soundly trounced in our playoff game, but the jinx was broken. The next year we made the playoffs again with a winning record, and Bulldog football supporters became used to winning seasons. There were still the naysayers who lobbied me to fire the coach whenever something didn't go well, but most supporters were happy.

We had some increase in our fans at home games, and it became a problem to find seating for the bigger rivalries. Supporters started the habit of spreading blankets on the bleachers the night before games to reserve seats for themselves in the best locations. It reached the point where our board had to make a policy of restricting the reserving of seats until the morning of the game. That was a great problem to have.

Early in my career as an assistant principal, high school soccer was a new sport. A culture had developed that led to a lot of fights. It was accepted as part of the game. It must have come from the European culture in soccer where fights and riots at games were not unusual. Our kids seemed to want to embrace that culture. We frequently had to calm players and fans down at every game to avoid an incident.

Eventually, schools and the state activities association began to crack down on such behavior. Our players were warned that any unsportsmanlike behavior would lead to game suspension and removal from the team. After a year or two of strict adherence to the policy, the behavior changed dramatically. It was a good example of changing the culture with a very intentional purpose.

Basketball presents unique challenges because it is indoors, and crowd noise is more noticed. The basketball tradition at Mission Valley was stronger than football. We were competitive in both boys' and girls' hoops and won our share of games. But this didn't mean that sportsmanship was always at its best in Viking Land. Players, students and sometimes parents could get out of hand.

One parent had a son who had been a star basketball player in junior high. However, like happens often, other kids caught up to him. By the time he was in high school he could barely make the junior varsity. Dad thought this was the coach's fault and frequently complained. At games he loudly criticized the coach, players, referees, and everyone else but his son. Several times I had to ask him to stop his criticism or he would have to leave the gym.

This dad was an electrician and we hired him to replace the gym lights. On the day he was up on his ladder putting in lights, I approached him from the gym floor.

"Are you sure that's how that should be wired?" I asked.

"Do you have the correct wattage in those lights?" I pestered.

He finally came down from his ladder and asked me what I was doing. I told him I didn't know anything about electrical work, but felt I was qualified to give advice anyway. I pointed out to him that his feelings about my advice were similar to what the coaches felt when he loudly criticized them. He looked at me and didn't say much. About a week later he approached me and said,

"You know, I get your point. My criticism of the coaches is just as irritating and unwarranted as your criticism of my electrical expertise." Point made!

The worst situation I experienced with players was when we played a basketball game against the rival league school that had previously beaten us in football 72-0. We were at their gym, and their students were intent on rubbing in the drubbing they had given us in football. There were signs with the score 72-0 in the stands and during the junior varsity game some of the fans from both sides began yelling back and forth across the court. The situation was getting tense.

During the boys' varsity game, it became even more contentious. One of our players had a personal grudge against one of their players, and he had been egged on by some friends to create an incident. During a scrap for a loose ball, the Eagle player shoved our player. Our boy took a big swing and cold-cocked the other player. Officials and coaches from both teams immediately jumped in and calmed things down. Our player was ejected and was escorted to the locker room. It was a very tense situation, but after a few minutes everyone cooled down, and we finished the game without incident.

Our player was dismissed from the team, and our Vikings were censored by the State Activities Association. We sent a formal apology to the Eagles administration and team. We received a notice from the Activities Association that any further incidents would bar us from postseason play.

About a month later it was time for the Eagles to play at the Viking gym. We had been warned that any unsportsmanlike incidents would be dealt with severely. I spent the week talking to our students about the good behavior we expected. I told them the best revenge we could exact was to be the perfect hosts with impeccable sportsmanship and beat them on the court. We made it a point of pride that we would be as kind and respectful as we had ever been.

On the day of the game, I was a bit nervous. All it would take was one student or parent to get out of hand, and our whole strategy would be lost. As the Eagle players were introduced our student body cheered for them. This was quite unusual because they were our hated rivals. As the game progressed, our team was playing well and maintained a comfortable lead through the first half.

At halftime, I circulated among the crowd and told them to keep calm and if our boys could maintain their lead, it would be the perfect ending. During the second half, the Eagles seemed to have lost their intensity. It was as if they were disappointed that there wasn't an unsportsmanlike incident. We beat them comfortably.

It was one of the best feelings I ever had in a regular season game. Kids came up to me and said that we did just what we planned. They were ecstatic. We had treated our opponents like royalty but beat them on the court. They were so proud of themselves. Many of our fans hadn't believed it was possible, but they took more pride in the fact that they had displayed perfect sportsmanship than the fact that we had won the game.

Of course, sports are not the only extracurricular activities. Other activities don't get as much attention, but music programs, plays, debate, and forensics contests, science fairs, art shows, and many other extracurricular events also draw large crowds. Schools have a culture of emphasizing one or the other of these activities. It usually has to do with a particularly dynamic coach or sponsor.

I have seen many fabulous music programs consisting of bands, singers, and orchestras. In some of my schools, these events packed the house. It is not only parents and grandparents who show up. If the arts are promoted, the entire community becomes involved. A crowd will show up for even a sixth-grade band with beginning practitioners and many sour notes.

In Independence, the music program was the pride of the community. Dynamic directors drew huge crowds for the concerts, but student groups also performed in the community. If you didn't get to the concerts early enough, you were doomed to squeezing into the few empty seats in the back rows.

One of the most moving activities was the choir's Christmas concert. Mr. Annable invited alumni to return, many of whom were home from college for the holidays. He invited them to come on stage to sing along with the current choir in a moving rendition of seasonal music. It was gratifying to see how excited these young people were to approach the stage and participate one more time. There were few dry eyes in the auditorium on such occasions.

One of my pet peeves about music programs is when they don't move along efficiently. It is distracting at concerts when one group is performing while another group is in the audience creating distractions. Then, when it is time to switch, the transition takes forever, and the audience gets restless. Fortunately, I have had many directors who were extremely disciplined about this. The program lasted exactly an hour, and the transitions were managed in a way that wasted very little time. The students were threatened with severe repercussions if they were not quiet during other performances.

The theater was a strong part of the culture at some of my schools. I have seen many fabulous performances by young high school kids who were almost professional in their skills. One of the best I have ever seen was Fiddler on the Roof when a high school student, Brion, played an almost perfect Tevya with a marvelous voice.

Debate and forensics have their own cultures. These students often enjoy playing the smart nerd role as they research and argue over relevant resolutions or perform speeches or dramatic interpretations. It is amazing how much time these kids and coaches spend on research and practice. Then they give up most of their weekends to go to the meets. I always encouraged our athletes to be involved in this activity if they had the desire. They could be both an athlete and a scholar. My own kids did both and my first wife was a debate and forensics coach, so I saw how much time and dedication went into this activity.

It was my privilege to judge a lot of debate and forensics contests; some of the contests were even at the national level. Coaches frequently had to bring along judges to tournaments, so I was volunteered often. Many times, I drove the bus and then stayed and judged. Some performances convinced me that those kids could eventually be professional actors or would someday be successful attorneys with their arguing skills. The trips are part of the value of debate and forensics. The kids and coaches do some bonding during those weekends, and they produce lots of stories to remember fondly.

One weekend our team went to Kansas City for a big tournament. Melly was the coach, and two of our children were on the team. After the tournament, we began the five-hour trip back home. We knew we would be running into a snowstorm on the way but thought we could make it before the weather got too bad. Unfortunately, the storm hit when we were about halfway home. Visibility was limited from the blowing snow, and the roads began to get icy.

Driving a bus in this weather is treacherous. Several times the back wheels swerved dangerously but I was always able to keep it on the road. By the time we were within thirty miles of home I had questioned if we could continue, but there was no place to stop, and we had twenty kids on the bus. I slowed to about twenty miles per hour and asked the kids to say their prayers that we make it safely. The coach led the students in the rosary while I nursed the bus the last miles. By the time we got home, my fingers had to be pried from the steering wheel. That was a story that will be remembered for a long time.

Debaters were always full of ideas. They tell stories endlessly and make up outlandish arguments on the resolution just for fun. It was hilarious to listen to them while driving. Teams must debate both the positive side and the negative side on that year's resolution. Frequently they would take their arguments to the extreme and end with the statement, "that would end the world as we know it." It was always an adventure to listen to these bright minds come up with logical, but not always practical scenarios.

Science fairs are always interesting. They are becoming more popular as our schools place greater emphasis on science, math, and technology. It is entertaining to see the ideas these kids come up with. And art fairs can be amazing. Sometimes the talent of these young people is awe-inspiring.

One of the strong points of American schools is the culture of extracurricular activities. In my travels to other countries, I found that some do not value these activities like American schools. They have sports, music, and drama but they are usually not school sponsored.

They are often separate clubs coached or sponsored by non-teachers. I know that we sometimes overemphasize the activities, especially sports, but I truly believe they serve a tremendous purpose in the learning that takes place.

When you talk to American students about their school years, they tend to remember the activities outside the classroom. The relationships that develop, the creativity that is fostered and the self-motivation and leadership skills that are shaped can be just as valuable as what is learned in the classroom. In China, I noticed that their administrators were very conscious of how American schools function and were trying to incorporate some of the extracurricular activities into their curriculum. In recent years, they have put greater emphasis on the arts and physical activity.

Extracurricular activities are sometimes the only thing that keeps less motivated students in school and making their grades. Any educator can relate plenty of stories of leveraging a student's participation eligibility in a sport to motivate them to make their grades. At the adolescent level, the value of an education is not always a major concern. But if I must make my grades to play on the basketball team, that may be the factor that keeps me engaged in school.

Yes, American schools overemphasize the activities, especially sports. At the same time, these activities provide an essential part of a child's education. Most of the time such activities are coached or sponsored by teachers, which provides a whole new avenue to reach these kids. It also allows the students to see their teachers in an entirely different light. In my experience, the relationships were much more effective with students whom I also coached than with those I saw only in the classroom. Many teachers would say the same.

9

SUPERINTENDENT

I never had a great desire to be a superintendent. It had always been my assumption that my career would culminate as a principal. When I was teaching sociology, there was a unit on which occupations carried the most prestige. At the time, a high school principal was considered the second most prestigious occupation after doctor. I felt very good about being a principal and would have been satisfied to end my career in that position.

The superintendent position took away the daily contact with kids, and that was my strength. As a superintendent, you dealt more with adults. However, at 51, it was becoming more difficult for the kids to identify with me as a principal, so maybe it was just as well that I moved on.

My previous perception of the job of superintendent was not very positive. I had seen my friend Bob criticized mercilessly and personally over his proposal of a bond issue in our district. I had seen other superintendents figuratively chased out of town because of public displeasure with some aspect of the district. My hesitation in taking the job came from the realization that the best intentions can sometimes create strong opposition and turn a community against you. However, I had good support as a principal and was fairly confident I could keep that support as a superintendent.

A superintendent has to make controversial decisions that affect the public and people can get very nasty over some change they don't like. In some cases, the pressures of the job caused health problems for several superintendents. I knew that Dick, the superintendent who hired me as principal, had some heart problems that he partially blamed on the stress of the job. The position required exceptionally thick skin or the pressure would be overwhelming.

Becoming a superintendent is a much different job than anything else in education. It is more like becoming Chief Executive Officer of a company. You are now responsible for everything that goes on in the school district. You can easily lose contact with students if you allow yourself to get caught up in all the day to day issues that arise. You spend more time with adults than with students unless you make a concerted effort to keep in touch. And you must deal with issues about which you have no expertise. The position brings something different every day. The focus must remain on student learning to be successful. With all the distractions, that is not as easy as it might seem.

I had always looked at superintendents as mysterious, intelligent characters who lived in a different world. The towns that I lived in were usually small enough that there was only one school district, hence only one superintendent. I vividly remember the public school superintendent in the town in which I grew up. I passed him one day on the street when in junior high. He greeted me as we passed and I was stunned that he recognized an insignificant junior high kid. When I was a superintendent, I found some of the same reactions from the students I greeted.

Most people don't understand what the job entails. When trying to explain budgets, developing standards and building curriculum, hiring staff and negotiating contracts I get a lot of blank stares. Even my own family had a hard time imagining the responsibilities of the job. My daughter, Sarah, could only understand the power of calling snow days. In her mind, all the other responsibilities were insignificant in comparison.

After several years in the job, one of my pet peeves was when people asked me what I was going to do with my summer break. They assumed that since the school was dismissed there was nothing to do during that time. Little did they know that summer is one of the busiest times for a superintendent. You are closing out the budget year, setting a new budget, getting facilities in shape for the next year and hiring and preparing new staff. My wife always cringed when she heard someone ask me this question because I had frequently said,

"I'm going to punch the next person in the nose who asks me that."

In the smaller towns in which I operated, you became a public figure, and it was no longer realistic to expect privacy. Everyone knows who you are and they feel emboldened to carry on conversations about school in any setting. My wife, Mary, often became frustrated when we went to the grocery store together because everyone stopped to talk to me. Grocery shopping took twice as long when I accompanied her. It wasn't that they were unpleasant most of the time, but they look at you as a public figure and are anxious to ask questions or hear the latest information.

I am a social person so visiting with people is enjoyable to me. But like everyone else I find it necessary to have some escape from the job. The fact that you are always in the public eye is one of the hardest adjustments to make in the job of superintendent. One colleague told me that is why he buys all his liquor out of town. And anything controversial that you might do in your personal life is fair game for discussion in the community.

I also experienced the political nature of the position. A strain of conservative philosophy had developed in our state that began to demonize public schools. They complained about how much money education costs and criticized the fact that education is the largest part of a state's budget. As a superintendent, it was my job to defend the purpose of our schools. When doing this, it is easy to become embroiled in political arguments.

There was an instance when I was promoting a bond issue to build a new elementary school. A conservative columnist in a local weekly newspaper took exception to the increase in taxes this would entail. I responded to his opposition with the reasons why the board felt it was necessary. At the same time, he was writing columns declaring that the American Civil War was not about slavery.

As a history major, I could not let this pass. I responded to his columns, and this began a series of back and forth letters and phone calls. He insisted that the war was about states' rights. I acknowledged that this was true, but pointed out that the single most glaring disagreement between states was the issue of slavery. Some states allowed it, and others didn't. Those who felt slavery should be legal were the ones who seceded, which began the war. He argued that slavery was only a minor issue in the conflict and that it was more about the federal government controlling what states can do.

We argued back and forth, and I tried to bring in factual references to support my point. He refused to accept the facts that I put forth and came back with references of his own that were opinions that supported his theory. After several months of this discussion, it became clear that he was not going to change his opinion. That was not surprising but what bothered me immensely was that he would not acknowledge certain facts that were easily verified. It was my first experience with this kind of thinking. I realized that my high profile position was a lightning rod for political controversy. That writer was enjoying taking on someone from the "establishment."

I needed to be careful about being so outspoken about my political viewpoints. What I saw as facts were not always acknowledged as such by others. It made me more careful about researching my facts and thinking about how others might perceive things differently. As I found out over time, this refusal to accept facts if they didn't agree with one's political viewpoint became more pervasive over the years. As I became more engaged in promoting educational issues through the political process, this practice of using "alternative" facts became a source of frustration.

At any rate, I decided to take on the job of superintendent and relished the challenge. I knew there was a lot for me to learn, but I was ready and willing. I was about to learn more than I could have imagined about leadership, dealing with the public and communication.

Because there are so many different aspects to the job, this section on the superintendency will be broken down into several chapters.

It was a wild and crazy ride, but it was the most interesting and stimulating job one could ever imagine.

10

THE SUPERINTENDENT
AND STUDENTS

On September 11, 2001, I was attending a workshop in Topeka. Along with other school administrators I had received a grant to receive training in technology that could improve our adoption of technology in the classrooms. We were just getting started with the instruction when people began checking their cell phones. Soon the TV in the convention center where we were gathered was turned on, and we learned about the attack on the World Trade Center and the Pentagon. Shortly after that, our workshop was canceled, and we left to return to our schools.

I was particularly concerned because my son, Matthew, was in Washington, D.C. attending a recruitment fair for the CIA. After attempting to call him for over an hour, I finally got through, and he informed me he was safe. They were just about to begin the fair when the cell phones of all the CIA personnel in the room began ringing. The CIA recruiters immediately left the ballroom where the recruitment fair was being held. The young men and women who had come for the fair began wandering around the city, and there was an eerie silence throughout Washington. Military trucks with armed soldiers were the only vehicles on the streets. The important thing to me was that he was safe.

I was concerned about how our students would react when they heard the news that the United States had been attacked. To assure them that they were safe, I went to each building to visit with kids.

At the schools, the TV's were already on, and teachers were

talking with students about what had happened. The teachers and I explained to the students what we knew about this attack. We discussed how our country would deal with the attack and what inspired someone to perform such a terrible deed. The discussion broadened into an analysis of the worldwide terrorist network and what we could do about it. Students and teachers had many questions and concerns, and we tried to assure students that they were safe in a small town in the Midwest.

I visited all of our schools and talked in almost every classroom. The topic became a learning opportunity and replaced all other instruction that day. At the end of the day, I was exhausted and concerned, but I felt that we had done the right thing for our students.

This situation reinforced the idea that in my role as superintendent I needed to stay connected to students. There are so many other things that could take my time and attention, and unless I made a conscious effort to stay connected to the kids, I would lose contact. In my evaluation, the board of education complimented me on spending that day assuring kids. Several of the board members had heard from other parents and students who appreciated the fact that the superintendent had taken the time to address the concerns the students had about their safety. If the kids don't feel safe, then there is very little learning that can take place, and on that day their sense of security was shaken. I had just begun my first year as a superintendent and learned a valuable lesson that was applicable for the rest of my career. From that point on, regular visits to classrooms were built into my schedule at least several times a week.

This incident also made me more aware of outside influences that can affect the educational process. There are so many factors that help or hinder a suitable learning environment that one must stay attuned to student attitudes to make adjustments. Taking care of the kids is the most important thing we do. Such care comes in many forms that have little to do with traditional instruction. In this chapter, I share numerous stories about some of those factors.

In Mission Valley, the rural consolidated district of my first superintendency, the district was spread out over more than 300 square miles, and there were only 500 students in that huge area. The elementary schools were older buildings that had only window air conditioning in the offices and no air conditioning in most classrooms. This created a real problem when school began in mid-August. Temperatures on the third-floor hallways were regularly checked, and they often reached as high as 100 degrees by early afternoon. This was unbearable, and there was an established procedure to dismiss school in the afternoons on hot days. If the temperature was forecast to reach the mid-90s outside, then parents were notified that school would be dismissed after lunch. This became a frequent occurrence in early fall.

For this reason and because the buildings were so old and lacked the electrical wiring for modern technology, there was an ongoing discussion about consolidating all of the elementary schools into one modern building at a central location. As I mentioned in an earlier chapter, the previous superintendent and board had proposed a bond issue to do just that. For many reasons, that proposal was voted down in a clear rejection by the taxpayers of the district.

Another problem we faced was an uneven distribution of school-aged kids in the three small communities. The towns were small, around 250 people, which meant that we sometimes had over twenty kids in a class in some of the schools and as few as six kids in a class in another school. It was extremely inefficient to have a teacher in every grade in all three buildings. The goal was to keep class sizes around twenty and by consolidating the three schools we could do a much better job of evening out the classroom size with fewer teachers.

There were three teachers per grade level. Through consolidation, we could reduce to two per grade because most grades had fewer than fifty students. And the curriculum could be coordinated more efficiently if all our teachers were in one building. These were factors that led to proposing another bond issue to build one consolidated elementary school for the district. More detail on how this issue was resolved will be given in a later chapter.

Student learning is the most important factor to focus on in any school district, and student comfort and class size are major factors.

There are a lot of other things that contribute to student learning, and we had to consider everything that had an impact. Instructional outcomes were constantly monitored to determine ways to advance student learning more effectively. The No Child Left Behind (NCLB) federal law required schools to evaluate student achievement by ethnic groupings, which was referred to as disaggregation.

There were very few things I liked about NCLB. It was intrusive and treated all schools the same, regardless of their makeup and location. It had unrealistic goals and created a lot of extra work for teachers and administrators. It also contributed to a distrust of educators and provided the public with misleading statistics.

However, the mandate to track the achievement of various groups, not just ethnic groups, was an eye opener for many educators. Students were disaggregated by income level, English as a second language, and by several ethnic groups. We realized that minority students and students who came from disadvantaged backgrounds were achieving at lower rates than others.

In my second district as superintendent, Independence, there was a more diverse student population. There were approximately ten percent Hispanic, ten percent African American, three percent other ethnic groups and the rest of the population was Caucasian. This is far less diversity than in many schools, but in that part of Kansas, it was significant.

Studying the achievement results of these disaggregated groups soon made it clear to me that our African American students were not doing well academically. They were also not doing as well in other measurements of achievement. This became a distinct focus of my leadership in this district. It bothered me immensely that we were not reaching this segment of our population.

Even though Kansas was at the forefront of the Civil War battle to end slavery, this community of 10,000, like many others in Kansas, had an appalling history of racial discrimination. There were stories of discriminatory policing, an active Ku Klux Klan, separate and unequal facilities, and even a lynching. In spite of unequal treatment, there was actually a Kansas Supreme Court case that determined "separate but equal" was not constitutional in 1891.* That case did not get the attention of the later Brown v. Board of Education in the United States Supreme Court in 1954, but it allowed local black children in Independence to attend the schools in their neighborhood.

Even though the schools were integrated, they had an ugly history of discrimination. There were a few pioneers who stood up against the bias. The high school had an indoor swimming pool that was used for a physical education class. Blacks were not allowed to swim in the pool until one PE teacher pleaded with the administration to allow the black kids to swim. She was told they could swim one time on the day before the pool was drained and cleaned. Track was the only sport that was integrated until the 1950s.

One African American friend of mine, Bob, was in school when black students were not allowed to eat in the school cafeteria. His white friends finally persuaded him to come with them to lunch. He reluctantly went along, and when the lunch ladies saw him, they didn't know what to do. Finally, they called the superintendent and asked for his advice. He said to go ahead and serve Bob, and that ended the segregation in the school cafeteria. As an adult, Bob became a member of the school board and a highly respected member of the community with a park named in his honor.

Older people in town still harbored some resentment over these unfair practices from past history, but there was nothing like this going on at the present time. However, even though there was no openly displayed discrimination, there was still a clear separation in town. Blacks and whites lived in separate parts of town, and there was little mixing of the races.

With this as a background, I began to explore why our African American students were doing poorly compared to our white students. After reviewing and discussing this phenomenon with the help of our administrative staff, I decided to gather some of the African American leaders in the community for a discussion. There was a real apprehension on my part because it was unclear how this meeting would be perceived.

Most of the African American people I knew who were known

*1891 Knox v. The Board of Education of Independence

and respected in town were pastors of local churches. At our first meeting, I showed the statistics to the group. There was a stunned silence, and then the discussion began. Some hostility came out because several of them thought I was saying that these students were not as intelligent as the white students. I explained that my only motive was to show them the facts and ask their help as to how we could better reach the African American students. Being fairly new in town, they didn't really know my intentions, so it was understandable that they would be skeptical. We formed a committee and vowed to meet regularly.

After several meetings, the group became more comfortable working with me, and we began to look for solutions. Charles, a local pastor, became a leader of the group and suggested that other areas should be explored besides academic achievement. He said that many of the black students felt that they weren't welcome in extracurricular activities and that they received a disproportionate number of disciplinary referrals.

After hearing this feedback, we made it a point to track participation in extracurricular activities and disciplinary referrals. Sure enough, we found that blacks had a lower participation rate and a higher disciplinary rate. The issue became what to do about it. The committee suggested that although our teaching staff was excellent, they were primarily middle-class whites who knew little about racial diversity. We had one principal and two black teachers among a professional staff of 130. It was suggested that we get some active training and try to develop a more diverse staff.

I found a nearby urban school district that had provided diversity training for its teachers and brought them in to work with our administrative staff. First, administrators went through the training followed by teachers. There was some resentment but most enthusiastically participated. Eventually, some staff members were sent to intensive training with Pacific Education Group which had a program called Courageous Conversations About Race. Voluntary groups of teachers were formed to do more training after hours. Embracing diversity became an important part of our educational agenda.

After a couple of years of this type of training, I learned of a program in another school district in the state that had been started by Willie, a former college teammate of mine. The program was called Can We Talk and involved bringing a diverse group of students together to discuss the issues foremost in their minds. It didn't necessarily have to be about race, but it involved things that were important in their lives, and frequently the conversation turned to race.

To get this program started adult volunteers were needed to give an hour a week to lead small groups of students. Charles was a mainstay as was Eugene, an African American custodian at the school. We gathered enough leaders and began the program at the middle school. Student volunteers were requested, and the program began functioning.

After a short time, we found that the students liked the opportunity to speak openly about the issues that concerned them. Often the discussions were about race relations, but many other topics were discussed that helped students realize that they all dealt with some of the same issues regardless of their race. The program expanded into the high school and then down to the fifth-grade level.

We began tracking progress on academic achievement, participation in extracurricular activities, and disciplinary referrals. To our delight, there was an improvement in all of these areas after several years of this initiative. When a girl of mixed race was crowned Homecoming Queen, and the basketball team consisted of four African American starters the progress was clearly visible.

As this was taking place in the schools, there was also some action in the community. The Chamber of Commerce formed a Diversity Task Force to look into ways to bring more inclusiveness to leadership in the community. A series of Courageous Conversations About Race was sponsored. Some painful stories about discrimination were told, and there was some visible anger expressed, but some healing also took place.

Training was provided to community members interested in improving race relations, and these events were well attended. The community became more conscious of the need to be more inclusive. When a position on the Board of Education came open, Charles, from our original group of African American leaders, was appointed by the Board to fill that spot. Twice in later elections, Charles was among the two top vote-getters on the entire board.

Charles and I became good friends and had many talks about the lack of African American teachers on our staff. Two of them had retired, and the district was down to only one African American principal. I regularly went to college teacher fairs to recruit but found that there were very few minorities represented among the newly licensed teachers.

A historically black college in a neighboring state had a strong teacher education program, so I began attending their teacher fairs and aggressively recruiting teachers. Charles accompanied me once and our black middle school principal, Patty, went a couple of times. We had no success as most of these candidates were from cities and were not interested in coming to a small town in Kansas.

One year, Patty went by herself to this college. She called me later that day and said,

"I have good news and bad news."

"What's the good news," I begged. "Did you get an interested candidate?"

"Yes," she replied. "But the bad news is that he is the only white student in the program."

So much for our efforts to diversify our teaching staff. Gradually, we built a slightly more diverse staff, but it was a long, slow process.

After several years of intensive efforts to improve achievement levels of minorities, particularly the African American minorities, we saw some success. But there was still a long way to go. What had been achieved was an awareness that there were some disparities and some lack of inclusion in both the school district and the community. If that effort is continued, I believe real progress can be made.

––––––––

There are myriad stories about kids during the time I was superintendent. They range from tragic to humorous. In the chapter "Kids Say the Darnedest Things" many of the humorous ones are described. Some of the stories in this chapter illustrate that the most important function of our schools is to keep kids safe and give them an education. Without kids feeling safe and secure and loved, it is difficult to facilitate student learning.

The busing of school children is an activity that never ceases to surprise. Ask any school bus driver for some examples, and he/she will have all kinds of stories to tell. As a superintendent, many of these incidents came to my attention.

At the beginning and the end of every school day, there is a period during which we made sure there was always someone available to answer the phone immediately during the time that buses were running. Frequently, we received a call from a concerned parent because their child was not yet home. These were always taken seriously even though most of the time there was an innocent explanation.

Occasionally, a child got on the wrong bus or got off at the wrong stop. That frequently happened in the first few days of school. However, after a few days, our bus drivers knew the kids well enough to know who should be on their bus and where they should get off. The problems usually arose when a child made a choice to go with a friend.

In one instance, the mother of an eleven-year-old girl was frantic when her daughter had not arrived home as expected. She called the board office, and I was alerted. The driver of her bus said she never got on his bus. The principal and I both went out in our cars to trace the route to her home. We could find no sign of her. We drove throughout the city looking frantically for the girl as it was beginning to get dark. Finally, the police department was notified, and they sent cars out to investigate. Around dusk, panic was about to set in when we finally got a call from a police officer who had spotted the girl in her neighborhood. Apparently, she had decided to go home with a friend, and the police officer happened to see them walking down the street. The girl was surprised there was such a fuss over her, and we all breathed a sigh of relief after that incident. Mom was visibly upset with her daughter, and I suspect things were tense in the house that night.

I don't know how bus drivers do what they do. As a superintendent, I rode the bus occasionally to get a feel for the process. Drivers are confronted with some of the most outrageous behavior while they are driving the bus. The noise level can be deafening. Many drivers find a way to enforce some control early on, but it is a constant battle. The good ones, like Graham, one of our most experienced drivers, find a way to connect with students and win their respect. Students do not have the same respect for the bus driver that they have for their teacher, so some of their worst behavior comes out on the bus.

We have had drivers lose their cool and say things or put their hands on kids because of some bus incident. One driver constantly berated the same kid every day. One day he told the kid,

"Sit your ass down in the assigned seat and don't make a sound."

The mother called our office to complain. We reviewed the video from the camera on the bus and found that the driver had been unfairly picking on this kid. Other kids were causing disruptions, but for some reason, this driver targeted the wrong child. After an apology letter was written and that driver received some education on how to handle kids, he was allowed to resume driving.

One of our smartest decisions was to put cameras on the buses. We regularly received complaints from parents or bus drivers about behavior. It was difficult to get the facts straight because there were always conflicting accounts. After enough of these incidents, our transportation manager suggested that the cost of cameras was well worth being able to determine the facts. Cameras didn't always capture everything, but when we told the parties involved that we would go to the camera, the stories became more consistent.

In one case, a mother had complained to the transportation director that other kids were spitting on her son. The driver had not noticed any such behavior, so the recordings for several days were reviewed. Sure enough, there were incidents of a kid spitting on other kids. However, the camera showed that the complaining student was the one doing the spitting. After informing the mother, we never heard from her again.

Most districts have a special education bus which transports the most severely disabled students. Often these students have behaviors that do not allow them to be transported with other general education students. Sometimes there are physical disabilities that require special equipment. But there are also circumstances in which special education students exhibit behavior that cannot be tolerated on the regular education bus.

Michael, affectionately referred to as Magic Mike, was a special education student who had severe cognitive disabilities. Some of his behaviors were extreme and unpredictable. For this reason, he was transported to and from school on a special education bus.

Mike had an unfortunate habit of stripping naked at any time. One day, to the horror of the driver and his student riders, Mike stripped naked on the bus and peed on the floor. The driver got the bus stopped, got Mike dressed and continued his route. He calmed the other students down and finished dropping all the students off at their respective schools.

Later that morning, the high school principal, Matt, received a call from an irate mother. She informed him that her 15-year-old daughter was on that bus when Mike stripped and peed. She was furious that her daughter had to witness such a disgusting sight. After trying to assure her that it would not happen again, Matt thought he had mom calmed down. However, he was surprised by her last statement.

"This is not how I wanted my daughter to see her first penis," she declared defiantly.

When he told me this story, Matt acknowledged that he understood it was a serious concern. However, he admitted that it took all his restraint to keep from laughing at that remark.

"The only thing going through my head at the time," he remarked, "was what did she have in mind?"

That question raised all sorts of graphic images in both our minds and we quickly dropped that discussion and moved on.

One of the biggest fears of all superintendents is a bus accident. I had heard plenty of horror stories about buses overturning or having wrecks and kids being hurt. I had driven a bus myself and know how easy it is to lose control of such a bulky vehicle in certain conditions.

Shortly after becoming the new superintendent in Independence, I was sitting comfortably at my desk in the morning when the secretary took a call. Visibly shaken, she rushed in to inform me there had been a bus accident. There was very little detail at the time except for the location. I didn't know if anyone was injured or what the situation was. Fred, the Transportation Director, and I quickly jumped in my car and headed to the accident site.

When we arrived, we learned that the bus had been driving on a narrow paved road with no shoulder and steep ditches. The driver got too close to the ditch with one wheel and started to lose control. When the driver tried to bring it back on the road, she overcorrected and jumped across the road, into the other ditch, went through a fence and came to rest next to a telephone pole. Kids were still on the bus, and the driver was shaken but alright.

Fred and I crawled onto the bus and began checking on the children. There were a few bumps and bruises and some hysteria, but no one was seriously injured. We called the office and instructed them to call the parents of the kids on the bus and tell them what happened and that all the children were OK. They were informed of the site of the accident and told they could pick up their child if they wished. Several of them did and took children with them. Another bus was summoned to pick up the rest of the kids and take them to school.

After breathing sighs of relief, Fred and I questioned the driver about what happened. We noticed that the bus just missed hitting a telephone pole by inches. That would have caused some serious injuries, so we felt fortunate.

Back at the office we visited with the driver supervisor and pulled the file on the driver in the accident. It was found that she had been in a similar accident at a previous school district and had been fired from that district. We told the supervisor that he would need to fire this driver. There was some resistance, but we insisted that we would not take the chance of another accident with her. There were no other bus accidents the rest of my career other than a couple of minor fender benders.

In my Mission Valley rural district almost every kid rode the bus because the school was in the middle of a pasture 8.2 miles from each small town. Some of our kids had to ride for an hour and a half each morning and afternoon. There was a practice of trying to reverse the routes before and after school so that the first on in the morning would be the first off in the afternoon. However, that was just not practical in many cases because it meant driving past some kids' homes and they would be on the bus for another hour. There was just no way to even out the rides.

Some roads that had low water bridges could not be passed when there were heavy rains. This lengthened the bus ride even more because then we had to go the long way around to get to some homes. Busing in rural districts can be a complicated and difficult task.

One of the ways I kept in contact with kids was to wait with them at bus stops before school. Sometimes it was still dark when I pulled up and visited with the kids while they waited for the bus. I didn't tell them that I usually visited the stops with a history of the most trouble. There were occasional fights or complaints from neighbors that the students were trespassing on their lawns or even getting into their outbuildings while they waited for the bus. When I showed up to mix with the kids, these complaints mysteriously diminished. It gave me a chance to visit with the kids before school started and showed them that I cared.

I also made it known that I liked to be invited to classrooms for special occasions. When there were student presentations, interesting speakers or programs, I enjoyed participating, and students seemed to enjoy having their superintendent in class. Sometimes it was just to read to the pre-school kids or the lower grades. Sometimes they would snuggle up close while I read. I think many viewed me as a grandfather.

Several presentations I made to students in the classroom were particularly enjoyable. Our high school had a distance learning class in Mandarin Chinese. The instructor was present on a computer monitor and students could interact with her. This was an exciting program that was fairly unique in a school our size. This internationally syndicated program allowed me to make a trip to China to study their schools. When I returned, I gave a video presentation to the students in the Chinese language class. The instructor was also present via computer, and we had a great discussion about what I had seen and experienced. She also added context to the trip.

In another case, I returned from a trip to Amsterdam where my wife, Mary and I visited the Anne Frank Museum with our grand-children. The fifth graders had recently studied a unit on The Dia-ry of Anne Frank. They listened intently as I described the site and showed them handouts from the museum. My visit made the con-nection with the subject of this story much more realistic. They were full of questions and comments about the life of this young girl of their age.

One elementary student was giving the principal, Dale, a partic-ularly hard time. Roger was a third grader with attention deficit dis-order and was hyperactive. (ADHD) He would sometimes crawl un-der desks and make funny noises. When the teacher could no longer tolerate his actions, she called Dale to come and get him. In Dale's office, Roger crawled around the room and under desks and chairs. Dale could not get him to settle down.

Dale and I had been reading about students with hyperactivity, and there was a theory that stimulants such as caffeine would actual-ly help control the hyperactivity. It seemed counter-intuitive, but ac-cording to some studies, it worked. Dale and I decided to give it a try.

I made it a point to get Roger out of class several days in a row. He was taken out in the hallway and given a Mountain Dew. We had a conversation about anything he wanted to talk about. He enjoyed our visits, and when sent back to the classroom he was calmer. I don't know if it was the attention he was given or the Mountain Dew, but the teacher was certainly glad I took him for a while. This worked sometimes but not always. Dale and I considered it an experiment worth trying and Roger always looked forward to seeing me come to his classroom. I don't know if he liked Mountain Dew that much or he liked getting out of class, but it made everyone happier and our short visits were fun.

Conferences and conventions always had vendors with displays. Most of them had promotional items to give away with their logo on it. These gifts ranged from pens and pencils to key chains, note pads, and even calculators. I made it a point to get as many of those trinkets as I could at conventions and brought them back to give out as gifts for students.

I also tried to have lunch with the kids at least once a week. Each time I did this I loaded my pockets with the convention trinkets. The students enjoyed it when I sat with them at their tables and ate with them. I asked them what topics they were studying in their classes, and asked some questions on that subject and gave them a little quiz. I gave students a trinket from my pocket for each correct answer. They got very excited over the smallest little prizes. Sometimes I had to drop the difficulty level of the questions to make sure that every child at the table got something. Once they answered correctly, they could not participate again until everyone had a chance to receive a prize.

After observing this for a while, the kids begged me to sit at their table when they saw me coming to the lunchroom. Sometimes a kid would pull out one of the prizes that I had given him years ago and show me he still had it. I was moved that it meant that much to these kids and realized that some of them had so little that a cheap pen was a magnificent gift. Never underestimate the power of gift giving.

The principals always jokingly scolded me for getting the kids all riled up and then leaving after lunch. I told them that it was a prerogative of the superintendent. I had already paid my principal dues!

Some kids deal with things in their lives that we can't even comprehend. It was not an infrequent occurrence that a teacher or counselor had to call the Department of Children and Family Services because of suspected abuse or neglect. It was often a frustrating exercise because the department always seemed to be short-handed and frequently took a long time to investigate.

Many foster families brought children into our schools with little or no information. We constantly pleaded with the authorities to give us some information on the child so we could be more effective. Our pleas often fell on deaf ears.

In one case, a fifth-grade girl, Stormy, was brought into the school by foster parents in mid-year. The parents and the school had no information on the girl. We placed her in a classroom and in the second week another student told the principal that Stormy had brought a knife to school. She had hidden it on the playground.

After searching the area the principal found the knife and confronted the girl. She admitted bringing the knife to school to settle a score with another student. The principal called the police, and they handcuffed her and put her in the front seat of the patrol car while they got more information from the principal. Suddenly they heard a terrible noise and saw that Stormy had kicked out the windshield of the patrol car with her feet. She was certainly appropriately named.

It was later discovered that Stormy had a long history of violence. We angrily complained to the Department of Children and Families that someone could have been seriously hurt. If we had known about her violent tendencies precautions could have been taken. They apologized but little changed. At that time I would have taken just about any bet that Stormy would never graduate from our school.

Thankfully, I was wrong. Thanks to a combination of good foster parents, school counselors and teachers who worked with her, it was my privilege to hand a diploma to Stormy in my last year as superintendent. That was a special moment for me when I gave a diploma to the girl who brought a knife to school and then kicked out the windshield of a police car six years earlier. It once again confirmed my belief that teachers can work miracles when they establish relationships.

One year there was a third-grade student who witnessed her mother being murdered by her boyfriend. The poor child was traumatized, and we did our best to get her counseling. She was not functioning well in school, and we tried everything we could think of. While trying to help this child one of our teachers referred me to a book called *The Boy Who Was Raised as A Dog.**

The author, Bruce Perry, was a child psychiatrist who has treated many children who experienced terrible trauma in their early years. He argues that their brain chemistry is permanently altered and they will react to certain stimuli inappropriately all their lives unless they have intensive therapy to create different pathways in the brain.

After reading this book and visiting with our counselors, we began recommending the book to teachers and administrators. Childhood trauma is a difficult and complicated phenomenon, and we realized that some of our students' inexplicable behavior could be attributed to that scenario.

Perry, Bruce D., The Boy Who Was Raised as a Dog

The child who witnessed mom's murder continued in school but was withdrawn and non-communicative. In her case, we knew what the trauma was, but it was a struggle to reach out to her and get her engaged in school. Like others with childhood trauma, she could lose control at any moment, and we had no idea what may have set her off. What we learned about this phenomenon is that something completely innocent could happen that reminds the child of an earlier trauma and set off extreme behavior. This may be the child's way to cope with the memory.

Another incident that may have been triggered by childhood trauma happened in the same month as the previously mentioned bus accident. A boy and a girl who were friends sat down to eat breakfast one morning at the high school. As they were chatting the boy made what he thought was an innocent remark. The girl pulled a steak knife out of her purse and stabbed him in the neck.

I don't know why she had a steak knife in her purse, but there must have been some scenario in which she thought she might need it. Something that the boy said set her off in a violent reaction. Thankfully the stab wound missed his jugular vein by a quarter inch, and the boy was quickly rushed to the hospital and saved. After the bus accident and the stabbing happened in the first month of my superintendency, several board members called to reassure me that these were unusual incidents in our district. They were afraid I might freak out and leave.

Another example of childhood trauma occurred when the parents of one of our students were killed in a car accident. The boy was cognitively challenged and had a difficult time understanding what had happened. He seemed to be enjoying all the attention he was getting because the school staff was concerned about his tragedy and they were going out of their way to help him. In his mind, he was getting positive attention, and this affected his understanding of the traumatic event that had just taken place in his life.

We didn't want to add to his trauma, but it just seemed inappropriate that he was enjoying the attention. He didn't know how to process what had happened except that people were going out of their way to be nice to him. He was eventually placed with other family members, and they gradually helped him understand the situation, but he continued to display inappropriate reactions in school. At least they seemed inappropriate to us, but in his mind, it may have been a way to cope with the trauma he had experienced.

Stormy may also have suffered childhood trauma. We don't know what caused her to be so violent, but it may have been a reaction to something that happened earlier in her life. Fortunately, she was able to do well enough to at least graduate from high school.

In recent years, childhood trauma has become more recognized in schools and mental health circles. The trauma can come from physical abuse, sexual abuse, witnessing a horrific event, family separation, or other causes. Fortunately, many books are being written, and much research is taking place that can help us learn how to deal with the negative effects of this trauma. Schools will continue to struggle with these children displaying negative reactions to stimuli until we figure out a way to better understand childhood trauma.

The death of someone close to young people can be exceptionally traumatic because it is a part of life they are not used to. During my time as a superintendent, we had several drowning deaths. Two of the deaths happened in the same incident. During the summer some high school kids were fooling around in a stream outside of town after a heavy rain. They did not realize how strong the current had become. When one boy began to struggle with the current, the other one jumped in to help. The girl with them could only watch helplessly as they both went under and drowned. It was a devastating loss to their friends in that class. When school resumed, counselors were brought in to help kids deal with their feelings.

In another case, we had a young paraprofessional who had recently graduated from our school and was then working with special needs kids. She was killed in a car accident near the school. Originally the family requested to have the funeral in the gymnasium at the high school. After checking with our state school board officials who had some experience with this, I was informed that it was not a good idea to have a funeral in a school. We were told that the site of the funeral becomes a symbol of the tragedy. Psychologists and school counselors advised against using the school.

When we notified the family and explained the rationale for not having the funeral at school, they were understanding. The deceased had a younger sister in school, and they did not want her to think about the death every time she was in the gymnasium. However, some people in the community were not as understanding. I was excoriated by some for not showing sympathy. Even after explaining that the family agreed with our decision they continued to berate the school board and me. The funeral was held at a local church, and we were able to get everyone inside who wanted to attend. The community was able to grieve together and begin the healing process.

A scary incident happened one day as I was driving up to the board office early in the morning. Police cars were all around the area of our middle school. Curious as to what was happening, I approached one of the policemen and asked him what was going on. He informed me that there had been a multiple homicide in a neighboring town and the suspect was reported to be in this area. We were further informed that the suspect had a stepson in our middle school and they feared he might be coming to get him.

The school was locked down, and precautions were taken until the suspect was finally caught only six blocks away that afternoon. Needless to say, not much learning took place at the middle school that day because everyone's mind was on the search for the killer.

When things like that happen, it is vitally important that students feel protected by the teachers and staff at their school. This only happens when relationships with the adults in charge have already been established. Kids want to be assured that you are on their side and will protect them. This has been demonstrated numerous times when all too frequent school shootings have occurred. Many teachers took bullets, and some died as they tried to protect the kids from the shooters.

When the Columbine shooting took place in 1999, the students and staff at Mission Valley were shocked that something like this could happen in a school. A lot of time was spent assuring them it could not happen at our school. In a small school like ours where everyone knows everyone else, it would be difficult to plan such a crime without others finding out. However, as school shootings became more frequent, students' attitudes changed. They recognized that a shooting could happen at any school. They even began to speculate which student might be a potential shooter.

The Columbine shooting had a huge impact on me. It shocked me that students could be so filled with hatred that they would kill their peers. That attitude now seems quaint. It moved me to reflect upon what I had learned in my years in education. Most of it was good, but it also made me confront the negative things I had seen and how students had changed over the years. This inspired me to write a letter to the editor of a national publication, Education Week, regarding the Columbine tragedy. The published letter follows:

As I watched the tragedy at Columbine High School unfold, I found to my dismay that I knew what the outcome would be. I knew that the perpetrators would be outcast students who were filled with anger and hatred. I knew they would blame others- students, teachers, administrators- for their problems. I also knew their parents would not be bad people, only neglectful parents. And I knew that in the aftermath, others would say that these students gave many warnings.

I didn't know this because I'm clairvoyant. I knew it simply because I see it every day in my job as a high school principal. I have had death threats from students and been vandalized. It has become an occupational hazard. No one who has spent much time in schools could have been completely surprised by what happened, only by its terrible magnitude.

Every school has students who blame everyone else for their short-comings. They resent those students who work hard to accomplish something and experience success. They believe these students have "sold out" to the establishment. They don't have the courage or the perseverance to accomplish the same things themselves, so they take out their frustrations on those who do. Occasionally, a teacher will inspire these students to try, and they realize that they, too, can achieve something positive. But all too often, they, like these killers at Columbine, would rather spew hatred and envy at those who achieve. Yes, I see these students every day.

Kids can be cruel to each other. Many schools have bullies who verbally or physically terrorize   weaker students. This has always been the case, but the difference today is that many teachers and administrators are afraid to intervene. They are afraid because a good percentage of the time they intervene, they will become the targets of hatred – from both the kids and their parents. Parents who don't have the courage to discipline and teach their kids respect are often resentful of administrators and teachers who do.

I remain optimistic, however, because I see so many good kids. I see so many of them rise above abusive parents, neglectful parents, or no parents at all. I see some who spend more time raising their parents than their parents spend with them. I see others who are respectful and try their best with limited talent and limited success. They have no idea how inspiring they can be to a tired or frustrated teacher or principal. This is why we do what we do.

Even as our jobs assume potential danger we never envisioned when entering the field, we persevere, trying to teach kids about life in a society that doesn't seem to value it. Often, what we say flies in the face of what our students see and hear every day – in the movies, on TV, in their video games and their music, and even at home. If I have anger in the aftermath of the Columbine shootings, it is for parents who don't take the time to realize that there is no greater occupation than to raise a child well.

I will honor the memory of the victims of this tragedy by continuing to teach respect and honor and love. And I will stand up to the bullies and the thieves and the liars in our midst so that the decent kids can go to school in a safe and comfortable environment. And if this gets me fired or makes me the target of someone's anger, then so be it. What a way to go!

After reading through this letter almost twenty years later, I can see how Columbine had a profound impact on me as it probably did on most educators. If I were writing that letter today it might be a little softer and more understanding, but the gist of what was said still seems relevant.

Schools try to create a climate where no one would think of doing such a violent deed. As shootings became more frequent, there has been increased emphasis on reporting anyone who indicates an interest in shooting up a school. A numbness has developed such that the shock of each new shooting is less pronounced, and we have accepted it as something inevitable.

For me, this tragedy caused me to reconsider my vocation. The thought of changing careers came to mind. It felt like a crossroad at which I needed to decide what to do the rest of my working life. I considered working toward a Ph.D. in administration, getting into business, or continuing as a principal. Eventually, I decided to stay in education and look for other opportunities at larger schools. It was a good choice for me.

After the Parkland shooting in Florida in 2018 the students themselves took the initiative to stem the slaughter of school children. It remains to be seen if their efforts were effective. We also thought that the killing of twenty students and six adults at Sandy Hook Elementary in Connecticut in 2012 would bring about some major changes. That outrage died, the shootings continued, and they continue today

Inevitably, after each shooting, there is the standard debate about whether teachers should be armed. Although there are exceptions, most teachers indicate that not only is it impractical for them to be armed because of the voluminous questions about security, but they don't want to be responsible for shooting a student. It goes against every reason they are in the classroom. If we have to arm our teachers and turn our schools into prisons to protect our children, then we have already lost the battle to provide a safe and secure learning environment. We won't fix a cultural problem by turning our schools into fortresses.

Let me describe one positive situation amid all the tragic instances. Blaine was a sophomore in high school when I was superintendent at Mission Valley. He lived in Topeka just down the street from me and attended a large urban school. His father had died suddenly of a stroke, and his mother was concerned about him.

Blaine was not doing well in school. He had failed several classes and didn't want to go to school. He was depressed because of losing his dad and didn't care about much. His mom found out that I was superintendent at Mission Valley, which was a much smaller rural school. She asked if he could attend school in my district even though he lived in another district. Mom thought that a smaller environment might allow him to enjoy school more and develop his talents. I told her we could certainly try it, but he would have to make an effort. It was a 30-mile drive to school as compared to just a few minutes to the school in his district, but mom was willing to make the sacrifice.

Blaine came to school and slowly made a few friends. He got involved in band, and his grades improved dramatically. He began to enjoy school and eventually graduated. Recently I saw his mom and asked how Blaine was doing. She enthusiastically told me,

"You and that school turned him around. I am so happy with that decision."

After high school, Blaine showed some interest in going to college. She allowed him to enroll, but he had to get a job to pay some of the tuition. He did well in college and became very interested in business and psychology. Eventually, he earned a Ph.D. in business psychology and is now a college professor and business consultant.

Mom couldn't have been prouder as she told me this story. A smaller school environment had helped him, but it was individual teachers and counselors who made the real difference in allowing Blaine to blossom. The satisfaction of hearing a story like this makes all the hard work and disappointments pale in comparison.

Teachers and administrators show their concern for students and develop relationships in many ways. Even when they are applying disciplinary consequences, they can show their concern by how they handle the discipline. Kids are great at reading the signals. They sniff out concern and indifference better than anyone.

As I paraphrased from Socrates in an earlier chapter, "Kids don't care how much you know until they know how much you care."

During the latter part of my career, the emphasis returned to the

"Three R's." However, this time the "Three R's" stood for Relationships, Rigor and Relevance. It is not coincidental that relationships are mentioned first. Without positive relationships, little student learning will take place. There are many ways in which these relationships are fostered both inside and outside the classroom.

Matt, our high school principal, organized a touch football game between the staff and high school students each year. Even this almost-60-year old superintendent decided to participate. It was a way for the adults to put ourselves on the students' level for an hour of fun and let the kids see us as human beings. When our football team was in the middle of a long losing streak and the staff members beat them in a game of touch, I knew it was going to be another long year. If they couldn't even beat a bunch of old guys like us, then they weren't going to beat other high schools.

After a couple of years of beating the kids in this annual game, the staff was going for the winning touchdown. I was just about to catch the touchdown pass when one of the high schoolers jumped in front of me and knocked it down. I knew then that they were getting better and sure enough, the team ended the losing streak that year.

Another way I tried to create relationships with kids was through our mentor program. Our elementary school recruited local adults to spend an hour a week with kids who were struggling readers. These adults would spend that hour reading and conversing with their mentee. We had a large number of community members who enjoyed this activity. Bev, the coordinator, matched community adults with kids who needed academic help or role models. They met once a week for half an hour of reading or talking. I told Bev to sign me up with her orneriest little boy each year. She certainly followed that directive.

One of my first mentees was Landon. He had transferred from the local parochial school, and his mom was concerned about his reading. Landon and I took turns reading together once a week. As he progressed through the grades, I kept in touch with him and watched his success. He did well in school, had a successful high school athletic career, and received a scholarship to the local community college.

Case was another of my mentees. He was very bright and was a great reader. I saw real potential there, but he had some serious emotional problems. He could be just fine one day, but the next day he would go off on anyone in a position of authority. His mother babied him, and most of his teachers felt she was a big part of the problem. She constantly made excuses for him and would never require anything of him. I had no trouble with him during our weekly sessions, but I was constantly hearing about instances when he got out of control. I think Case figured out that if he caused a big enough commotion when he didn't want to do something, people would let him alone.

I followed his progress throughout the rest of his school years, and the same pattern persisted. Eventually, he graduated, but he was still manipulating his mother and anyone else he could. Hopefully, he has grown up and taken some responsibility.

Another student I mentored in this manner was Nicholas. Nicholas was a bright boy who had attention issues. He just could not stay on a topic or a book. He could read with accuracy for about one page, and then his attention would wander. I found myself constantly redirecting him. When Nicholas was in middle school, I gave a talk to a student assembly. The topic was about how they could achieve anything if they just put their mind to it. I explained that sometimes we don't recognize the genius in each other.

I had talked to Nicholas before this assembly and asked if it was alright to use his name. At first he was adamant that he didn't want to be recognized, but eventually, I convinced him to let me talk about him. I told the assembly that Nicholas was an example of someone that most people didn't realize was a great reader. I had him stand up. The students cheered him and the others I recognized at that assembly. Nicholas was happy to be considered the class goofball but was inwardly proud of the fact that he was a good reader. His classmates saw him in a different light after that incident.

Every year at high school graduation it was emotional for me as I watched the graduates walk across the stage to receive their diplomas. As one of them crossed the stage, he flashed a pen at me that I had given him in fifth grade. I remembered when some of the students had survived tragedies at a young age, engaged in serious behavior problems, doubted their ability to succeed, or didn't seem to care. I watched them walk across the stage together with those who always had confidence and had strong support systems in their families. All were successful because someone cared enough to help guide them. In many cases, it was the teachers and principals and support staff who lifted these kids up and helped to give them a future. And then Stormy crossed the stage and the tears began to flow.

And that's why "It's all about the kids."

Benno Schluterman, president; Rose Fry, principal, and Chuck Schmidt, associate principal pose for a last picture together as they prepare to meet new challenges away from Hayden High School.

Clockwise:
The author's high school graduation picture

The administrative team at Hayden High School, Benno Schluterman, Rose Fry

Schmidt with Kansas Deputy Commissioner of Education, Dale Dennis

Top: Independence booth at teacher recruiting fair

Bottom: Lunching with grade schoolers

Counterclockwise:
The author while touring
Chinese schools

Playing the Harlem Ambassadors
in a benefit game

Mary recording vote count for
Independence Bond Vote

Left:
With Leadership Kansas classmate Shaunta Boyd in troop transport plane

Bottom:
6th grade students making goofy faces. *Top left, clockwise:* Rocky, Adrian, author, Mack, Devlin

Top:
Chuck and Mary at a local
Dancing with the Stars
competition

Right:
Author with friend and board
member, Rev. Charles Barker, Sr.

Top: With Kansas Governor Laura Kelly

Bottom: At KU football game with mentees Isaiah and DeShawna

Top: Restored historic Independence Middle School

Bottom: Restored Shulthis Stadium entryway

Chuck & Mary with grandchildren
L to R, Adelyn, Teddy, Anna Gwenyth, Shiloh, Jasper

11

THE SUPERINTENDENT
AND THE PUBLIC

In my first year as superintendent at Independence, the community was evenly divided about two previous bond campaigns that had gone down in defeat by little more than 100 votes. One of the issues expressed by the opposition was that the buildings we had were not maintained properly. If we had taken better care of the buildings, they argued, we would not need renovations.

In this setting, I received a call from a citizen complaining about a hackberry tree growing out of the chimney at the high school. Finean had been a leader of the opposition in the previous bond campaigns. He said it was embarrassing to see how little we cared for our high school building by letting this tree grow on the roof. He felt this was an example of how poorly kept the buildings were. I disagreed with his contention that we did not take care of the buildings, but told him I would look into the situation.

I had seen that small tree growth in that spot before and had asked our custodians about it. It was only about two feet high and had sprung up in a flat area on a chimney where some dirt had accumulated. It was in a very high and remote location that they couldn't get to without special equipment. It was not harming anything and would be very expensive to remove, but it was in a highly visible spot, and it did look bad.

Paula, the district public information director, suggested that we take this criticism seriously even though the tree was not doing any damage. I directed our maintenance staff to find out how much it would cost to remove. They found that the rental for a crane to get someone to that spot would cost $2500.

That seemed a waste of money to me, but after discussing it with Paula, we decided it might be worth it to show the public that we were taking care of our buildings. I called Finean and told him we had listened to his concern and had removed the offending tree at a considerable cost. He expressed his appreciation, and we went our separate ways. That may have been one of the best decisions I made in my ten-year term as superintendent. We didn't want to burn that bridge. More about that later.

When the Hackberry tree was removed, Paula took a small branch from the tree, put it in a box and presented it to me with a message that Hurricane Chuck had removed this tree in 2006. She nicknamed me Hurricane Chuck because I had brought a lot of changes in my first year as superintendent. I kept that reminder in my office throughout my tenure to remind me that the public always has an opinion on what we do and therefore I should never burn bridges.

When you are superintendent everyone has an opinion about the decisions you make. Their information may be wrong, but they form opinions on what they believe to be true. There were a significant number of people in the community who believed we did not take care of school property sufficiently. If we showed evidence to the contrary, we believed it might change some opinions.

One of the reasons I was hired at Independence was because I had ushered a successful bond issue through in my previous super-intendency at Mission Valley. The board felt that experience would be helpful. Allow me to recount that story before I tell about the bond campaign in Independence.

At Mission Valley, the issue was very different but just as con-troversial. It involved closing three outdated elementary schools and building one modern elementary next to the consolidated high school. It was similar in that they had tried several times unsuc-cessfully. Shortly after I became superintendent at Mission Valley, the board decided to try again to build a consolidated elementary school. A committee of local citizens was appointed. I was an ex officio member to provide factual information as they put their plan together.

The committee was a mix of people with varying degrees of expertise. The chairman, Alex, was an experienced businessman who understood how to work with people of different backgrounds. At the first meeting, he asked everyone to give their ideas on what we should do. The ideas included doing nothing, remodeling the old buildings, building a prefabricated metal building, and building a brick and mortar school.

Some of the committee members' main concern was to do it as cheaply as possible. Others were concerned about building something that would last for many decades. I had my own ideas about what it would take to do it right.

As Alex requested everyone's views, he also asked what I thought was needed. I had researched this issue thoroughly and told them it would take about 35,000 square feet and around six million dollars to do it right. The ones who were trying to do this cheaply were shocked. As I listened to the other ideas, I became concerned that we were going to build something that would look cheap and wouldn't last. I kept insisting that doing it properly was going to be close to my numbers.

At the second meeting, I gave enrollment numbers, estimated class sizes, and other facts to the committee. However, I continued to interject that the solution was going to be close to my earlier figures.

Through the grapevine, I heard that Alex had called the third meeting but had not invited me. When I asked him if he wanted me there, he said it really wouldn't be necessary. They had the information they needed. I got the feeling that he didn't want me around. That was hurtful.

At later meetings, the committee began to come closer to the figures I had given them. They finally decided to build a 35,000 square foot building and make some improvements to the high school for a total of $6.8 million. There was a feeling of vindication when they came very close to the figures I had originally provided them.

Later, as I reflected on how this came about, it occurred to me that Alex knew what he was doing. He accepted my figures, but he knew that the committee would not buy into my plan unless they came up with the idea themselves. If this smart aleck superintendent were going to push them into something, they would not get behind the campaign. They had to come to their own conclusions.

My initial hurt feelings that Alex didn't want me in on the decision making gave way to respect for his wisdom in realizing how to get the results we needed. My expertise was not welcomed early in the decision-making process until they came to an agreement on what they were willing to do. This was a lesson that paid huge dividends in the later bond campaign in Independence.

The board adopted the plan of the committee and put a bond issue up for a vote to the constituents of the district. This plan meant that property owners would have to pay an additional fifteen mills in property tax for the next twenty years. This was not going to be an easy task.

As we began the campaign, the committee members explained how they came up with the plan. They felt their plan would help the district to at least maintain its student population. The district had some parents who were taking their children to other school districts on their way to work because of the dilapidated condition of our buildings. The committee suggested that some of these parents would bring their children back when they saw the new modernized elementary school.

A strong opposition put out signs to "Vote No" on the bond issue." The committee put out "Vote Yes" signs, and in many places, they were right next to each other. In one case, a teacher who was supportive of the bond issue had the property that shared a corner post with someone from the opposition. The teacher posted a "Vote Yes" sign on his post and the opponent posted a "Vote No" sign on top of it. The teacher then extended the post and put another "Yes" sign and the opponent extended it even higher to post his sign. By the time they were done, the signs were fifteen feet in the air, but the "Vote Yes" sign ended up at the top. The teacher later told me he would have had to get a crane if the signs had gone any higher.

My role during the campaign was to give the facts. I tried to explain to people that if we didn't consolidate our schools, then we might not have a district in three years. We could not afford to maintain the three dilapidated buildings and have a teacher for every grade at every school. Before long, parts of our district could be merged into three surrounding school districts. We could save about $100,000 per year in operating budget by consolidating. Since school district funding was on a per-pupil basis, the neighboring districts would be glad to take in our students. Unfortunately, that meant our kids would have to endure even longer bus rides.

Even though the campaign got very heated, we were ecstatic that the bond issue passed with a 68% yes vote. It was exciting to plan and observe the construction of this new building which was connected to the high school. The plan also included improvements to the high school.

Although we had spent a good deal of time understanding construction in my school administration classes, this was the first time I was involved in overseeing a real construction project. As an old farm boy, I found it to be an exciting process. The architects were fun to work with as they designed the building. They were able to organize rooms and layouts from years of experience. All staff members were able to give input. It was like watching an art project coming together.

I got to know the construction company owners very well. I questioned the construction foreman about why they did certain things and observed some of the intricacies of construction that most people never see. No doubt it was irritating to them at times because of all my questions. This was a new experience overseeing a multi-million dollar project, and I enjoyed it immensely.

One of the highlights of the construction was a commons area that also served as the cafeteria. It was a beautiful room with high ceilings and one wall with large windows that allowed sunlight to radiate through the room in the morning. I pronounced it the most beautiful room of the entire construction project and the architects and contractors agreed with me.

On a Sunday shortly before the construction was completed, I received a call from one of the custodians. He told me there had been some vandalism at the new school and I needed to come to see it. I rushed out to meet him at the building and was shocked at the sight. There were huge pillars that held up the roof of the cafeteria. Someone had repeatedly backed a large truck into those huge pillars trying to bring the roof down. It made me sick to my stomach to see what had been done to this beautiful project.

Fortunately, the pillars were strong enough to withstand the force. Decorative brick was knocked off the pillars, but the structure itself was not harmed. Other areas had been damaged as well. The final assessment of the damage amounted to over $60,000 worth of repairs. This delayed our grand opening of the building, but eventually, the damage was fixed.

A disgruntled construction worker was suspected of being the culprit, but he had since been deployed to Iraq. We never were able to prove who did the damage, but this experience shook me and many in our community. We had worked so hard to get this bond issue passed.

The vandalism had jolted me, but the grand opening was a moment of joy. Most people in the community were proud of what they had accomplished and took pride in the new building. It was difficult to find anyone in the community who would admit to voting no on this bond issue. That experience paved the way for my next bond issue in Independence.

When I first came to Independence for my interview, they knew about my experience in passing a difficult bond issue at Mission Valley. Their questions focused on this experience and I got a distinct feeling that they felt my experience might help them. It was clear when I was offered the job that they hoped my previous success with a bond issue would be replicated in their district.

One of my first actions in Independence was to initiate a monthly meeting with several people who were leaders in the community. Our group consisted of the city manager, the Chamber of Commerce Director, president of the community college, the CEO of the local hospital and the superintendent of schools. We called it the Community Leader's Breakfast.

During these meetings, we were able to keep each other abreast of new developments and find areas of cooperation. As the other members familiarized me with the community, I was told that there were two major problems that the city faced. They mentioned a lack of housing and the poor physical condition of our schools. Many were frustrated because almost everyone agreed that our schools needed some improvements. They couldn't get a majority to agree on any specific plan. This was a manufacturing community, and when potential workers came to town, they faced problems finding decent, affordable housing. If they had children, they also looked at the condition of our school buildings and often located in neighboring towns.

Because of the cooperation of this group, we were soon able to address the housing issue. The school district owned half a block in the center of town where an old elementary school had been demolished. We just kept it mowed, and nothing had ever been done with the property.

Saul, the city manager, suggested that the city could build some low-income housing if we were to give them that property. After presenting this idea to my school board, they agreed to deed the property over to the city if the city would build low-cost housing. The city built six duplexes of subsidized housing on that block. Several years later, the district gave another small tract of land that allowed the city to build more subsidized housing in another part of town.

The town was very progressive in creating housing. After a few years, because of the cooperation between the city and the school district, the housing situation was vastly improved. Some of this housing was available to new staff and helped us recruit teachers.

Cooperation between the city and the school was crucial when we addressed the substandard school facilities. The previous unsuccessful bond campaigns had been for $24 million and $22 million. Shortly after I arrived, the board and I began working on another bond issue that might appeal to voters. We reduced the total amount to $19 million. Part of the proposal was to implement a one-half cent sales tax to cover a large part of the costs. This proposal went down in defeat by a small margin. The board and I were very frustrated, and we decided to wait a couple of years before trying again.

After waiting two years, we began the process of passing a bond issue for the fourth time in five years. However, this time we decided to let the community develop the plan rather than having the board present a plan to the community.

The first step was holding a series of community listening sessions. The board held these sessions in four locations throughout the district. People were encouraged to address the board about what they thought needed to be done to improve school facilities. To stress to the board that their role was to listen, not to talk, I placed a roll of duct tape on their table. This was a reminder to keep their mouths shut and listen to their constituents.

There were a lot of nasty comments, and some felt emboldened to make personal attacks since the board was not responding. There were also many constructive comments. We recorded the remarks, and I made notes of who spoke at each of the community listening meetings.

When this process was completed, we recognized that most people believed we needed to improve our facilities. There was a wide range of views on how to do it. Some wanted to build a new high school and renovate the other buildings. Some wanted to keep all the buildings we had and make improvements. Some were concerned about historic preservation.

To show that this was an entirely new process, the board hired a different architectural firm than the one they had previously used. This firm had a process to build consensus. Kevin, the lead architect, advised us to gather a representative committee of constituents and the architect would lead us through this process. We invited everyone who spoke up at the community listening meetings, and 45 people accepted the invitation. Finean, mentioned at the beginning of this chapter, was one of those who joined the committee. Two board members, Fred, the Business Manager, and I served in an ex officio capacity to provide information.

The first action of the committee was to tour our school facilities and evaluate their condition. As we did this, I noticed that Finean began to see that our facilities were outdated, and it was not just because of neglect. Kevin led the committee through several questions, and the committee members responded by anonymously voting with the use of clickers that recorded the votes on a screen. At the first meeting, we found out that thirty percent of our committee had voted no on the previous bond issues.

Members were then allowed to give their preferences for facility improvements, and the architects put dollar figures to the cost of those improvements. When they saw the costs of some of their ideas, they began to look for compromises. Those who wanted to build a new high school realized that the cost would be prohibitive. One of the proponents of a new high school, Galen, suggested we look at a neighboring school that had renovated their high school and their middle school. Both buildings were similar to our buildings.

When we toured the neighboring buildings, committee members were impressed. Some began to see renovation as a viable alternative. We still had a lot of variation in the committee members' preferences, and I was getting nervous about what direction the committee might go. The board and I had no control over their recommendations, although the board would eventually have to approve a final plan. However, my previous experience at Mission Valley taught me to allow the process to run its course and trust that the committee would come up with a viable plan. I kept my mouth shut and only talked when they asked questions.

As we studied various proposals, Finean suggested that whatever else we do, we should take care of all the facilities at one time, so we don't have to come back to the voters in a few years to finish the job. It was a surprise to hear him support a proposal to raise taxes to fix our facilities.

Finally, the committee proposed a $45-million-dollar project to renovate the high school and middle school and to build a new elementary school to replace two aging elementary buildings. When the committee voted on whether to support this proposal only one member voted no.

I was stunned. We had not been able to pass a $19-million-dollar proposal, and now the committee was proposing $45 million. How could we possibly get this approved by the voters? Finean suggested that people would back this plan because it meant our facilities would be good for decades and we would not have to come back to the voters for more improvements to finish the job. I wasn't so confident.

One of the attractions of the plan was that much of the funding would come from a city sales tax. I had proposed to the city that they allow us to adopt a full one percent sales tax for educational facilities and they had agreed to this proposition. The city had passed a one percent sales tax for the quality of life improvements ten years previously, and that tax was about to expire. By working with the city, we were able to continue the one percent tax and apply the revenue to pay off the bonds for the school improvements. This would make no change in the sales tax people were already paying, and it would pick up 48% of the cost of the bonds. This was only available because our board and city officials maintained a supportive relationship. There was a common commitment that what was good for one was good for the other. The monthly Community Leader's meetings contributed to this attitude.

The state also had a cost-sharing agreement with poorer school districts which gave us 42% from state funds to pay for the bonds. This meant that we only needed to raise property taxes to fund ten percent of the bond payments. This amounted to 3.5 mills on real property. The average homeowner would see an increase of about $35 per year in their property taxes.

In previous bond issues, there had always been an organized opposition. However, by the fourth election, two of the major organizers had passed away. Some people teased me indicating I may have had something to do with their demise. This time there were individuals against our campaign, but there was no organized opposition.

In order to convince voters that this was a whole new campaign, we had changed architects from our previous bonds. We also changed the chairperson of our campaign. The previous chairperson had done a wonderful job, but the board felt we needed to change everything, so they went with multiple chairpersons. It was painful to make some of these changes, but it was necessary to convince people that we were taking a whole new approach.

I will never forget that election night when our supporters were gathered in the boardroom and tallying up the votes as they came in. My wife was writing the numbers on the board as I read them to her. When it became obvious that it would pass there was absolute joy among the supporters. After many failures, we had finally gained consensus on how to improve our aging facilities.

After going through this process, I reflected on how our goal was accomplished. There were many people involved in different roles. Many who had previously opposed bond issues worked to pass this one. Fincan was a key contributor because he was respected by many in the community and had been a vocal opponent in the past. He was involved in the process, and this time he convinced a lot of the opposition to support the proposal. Many others who had been involved in developing the proposal became outspoken advocates. This was the best example of democracy in action that I have ever experienced.

Never burn bridges; build them.

The community expressed great pride in the appearance of their schools after the project was completed. After the grand opening of our new and renovated buildings, few in town admitted to having voted no.

One of the things that helped win support for the bond issue was the decision to remodel the 1922 middle school building rather than build a new facility. The cost of either option was about the same, but there was a sentimental factor with the middle school. It had also served as a high school and a junior college during its lifetime. Many local citizens wanted it kept in use. The building was structurally sound, it was just outdated.

The decision was made to remodel it and restore its original appearance. That qualified us to receive Historic Renovation Tax Credits. It cost more money to restore to its historic character, but we were able to receive $2.6 million in tax credits that could be used in any way.

The board and I felt that part of that money could be used to renovate our football stadium. The stadium was used by our middle school, high school and the Community College for football, track, and some other events. The stadium also had a historic value as the site of the first professional, organized baseball night game. Mickey Mantle had played there for the minor league team.

However, the original grandstand for the baseball seating was deteriorating badly and was fenced off from seating. Dark and disgusting restrooms were located under that structure. Newer seating had been constructed alongside the old seating when the stadium was converted to football.

When word got out that we were considering remodeling or demolishing the old grandstand, the local Historical Preservation Committee vehemently protested. They wanted it restored to its original look without alterations.

Several architects and engineers had examined the structure and indicated it may be possible to renovate, but it would be very expensive; almost double the cost of demolishing and rebuilding. The preservationists were virulently opposed to demolition and launched a media campaign to save the structure. The board and I decided to renovate the stadium in two phases. The first phase would not touch the original grandstand but would update everything else. Money from the sale of our Historic Tax Credits helped fund that project. The city also contributed because the restrooms could be used for the surrounding park.

We then launched a fundraising campaign to do a public/private renovation of the original grandstand. Again the preservationists launched a campaign to prevent the district from demolishing the structure, and this negatively affected our fundraising. After about a year of fundraising, we raised almost $1 million but that wasn't enough to complete the project. By the time I retired as superintendent, a decision had still not been made to demolish the old structure.

Finally, the new superintendent and board became frustrated with the crumbling grandstand amid a beautifully remodeled stadium. They decided to demolish the structure and build a new structure that housed bathrooms, concession stands, and locker rooms. They would use the private donations and some of the Historical Tax Credit Funds. The face of the structure would be built to resemble the façade of the original stadium.

On the day that the demolition began, there was a gathering of citizens, some very emotional about the structure coming down. It was sad to see it go, but it was a real eyesore amid the beautifully remodeled stadium.

An attractive new, functional structure was built. It included a gathering area that led into the spectator seating area which had text and pictures that commemorated its history. After a year of use, most citizens were pleased with the appearance of the new stadium, including the façade that resembled the original historic façade. But it was a long and bitter battle to get the stadium to that point. Like with the remodeling of the school buildings, few citizens now admit to opposing the renovation of the stadium.

A superintendent is very much in the public eye. Your private life is no longer private. Everything you do eventually becomes public knowledge. Every decision is publicly scrutinized.

When I was hired by Independence, my wife came along for the interview. However, we were separated at the time, and she made it clear to me that she was not going to move. My story to the board was that she was going to finish her teaching contract and would not be coming with me the first year. In the fall of that year, I finally told the board that we were going through a divorce. One of the board members was not present, and at the next meeting she blurted out,

"When is your wife going to move here?"

I noticed the other board members squirming nervously, and they quickly told her what had been disclosed at the previous meeting. She blushed and changed the subject.

When I was single, I often woke up early in the morning with lots of school issues on my mind. I decided to use this time productively. Often at 5 a.m., I went to the weight room at school and began a lifting and jogging routine, or I went to an indoor pool at the recreation center. A lady was cleaning at that time and would let me in to do my pool workout with no one else around. Occasionally others would show up at the weight room, and we would work out together.

After working out, I would go to the locker room for a shower and dress for the day. One morning, I walked into the boys' dressing room and the sight I saw shocked me. A high school wrestler was trying to make weight for a match that day. He had worked out vigorously and then went to weigh himself. He was stark naked and doing a handstand on the scale. I was staring right into his crotch. Startled, I asked him what he was doing. He remarked that he weighed less upside down because the blood in his feet was weightless. I didn't question his statement, averted my eyes, and quickly moved on to the shower. According to the coach, he made weight.

At the pool, there was a group of elderly women who came in early for an exercise class. We had fun teasing each other, and they invited me to join their class. I tried my best to stay out of their way and joked that they should stay out of my lane.

Shortly after my divorce, I began to date occasionally. I met Mary through a mutual friend, but she was 100 miles away in Wichita. We began a long-distance relationship. I was apprehensive about being seen dating but decided it was my life and there was no need to hide. When Mary came to my town, there was a lot of interest in who this woman was. We went to school events and to restaurants and bars around town. Friends told me that people were wondering when we would get married.

Many people in town had gotten to know Mary, and they were hoping our relationship would become permanent. Mary quickly learned that she was in the public eye just as much as me. People knew she was the girlfriend of the superintendent and were curious about her. After three years of dating this way we finally decided to tie the knot. My board and many in the community were very supportive and attended a huge wedding. We actually had two celebrations: one in Wichita and another in Independence. We felt a lot of support and those who liked the job I was doing were happy because they figured this would keep me here longer.

The summer we got married our air conditioner went out. We had to wait nine days for repairs, and after the eighth day without air conditioning, we could stand it no longer and checked into a motel. The owners knew who I was and were aware that I had been single since moving to the community. I didn't know if they realized I had since gotten married, so when we checked in, I made it a point to tell them,

"My WIFE and I couldn't stand the heat in our house anymore, and that's why we are checking into the motel. It was just too hot for my WIFE."

I may have repeated that several times, emphasized the WIFE part of it, and told them all about the air conditioner. They looked at me a bit skeptically as if they didn't believe we were married. It would be quite a scandal if the new superintendent were shacking up with someone in town. Maybe it was just my imagination, but there seemed to be a smirk in their eyes as we checked in. Anyway, it was all legitimate! As I said, you are very much in the public eye.

Mary learned that when we went anywhere, there would always be people who wanted to talk. It didn't matter if we were at the grocery store, a restaurant, or a school event. There was always someone who wanted to ask about some decision or get the latest information. Sometimes she would have to warn me when we went to the grocery store that I needed to make it quick so we could get home. But there was always extra time built into these excursions so I could visit with constituents.

Not all of these conversations were friendly. Frequently someone would approach me about some issue such as firing coaches or teachers. That frequently happened when we had our losing streaks in football. They always wanted to blame the coach. It was enjoyable when our teams broke the losing streaks and began having success. More than once, I pointedly asked the same constituents if they still wanted to fire the coach.

Some of the conversations with constituents in my office or on the phone were much nastier. One of the issues that always brought out complaints was the calling or not calling of snow days.

When the weather forecast looked like snow, Fred (the Business Manager) and I would go out driving at about 4:00 a.m. He would go to one side of town, and I would go to the other. I used my old pick-up with worn down tires and rear drive that didn't do well on snow or slick streets. If I could get around in that vehicle others could get around better in their cars. We had to make the call by at least 6:00

a.m. because that was when the first buses went out. We also had to post on social media and notify local radio and television stations.

After deciding, Fred and I were usually eager to get some breakfast. In our small town, the restaurants weren't open till 6:00 a.m. so it became a tradition for him to come to my house where I made egg sandwiches with all the fixings. After such an early morning adventure we really looked forward to a good breakfast. Snow days weren't so bad when you could look forward to egg sandwiches.

We always received irate calls from parents who disagreed with whatever decision was made about a snow day. If we did not call a snow day when they thought we should have, there was always someone threatening to sue if their child were hurt in an accident. After hearing enough of those threats I just told them to get in line.

Snow days weren't the only reason people threatened to sue. I have often remarked that if I had a dollar for every time someone was going to sue me, I would be a rich man. Sometimes the lawsuit threat came from parents who were upset about some disciplinary action involving their child. They would start with the principal, and if they didn't get satisfaction, then they would call me and threaten to sue.

I always called the principals to tell them about these calls and explained the parent's description of the incident. It took a while for some of my principals to understand that I wasn't criticizing them. I was just telling them what the parent said to me. Then I would ask them to tell me what actually happened. The story from the principal was usually quite different.

Most of the time the principal had a valid explanation for the action. Only on rare occasions, after investigating an incident, did I disagree with the action of the principal. In those cases, we would talk about it and try to find a fair way to resolve the issue without putting the principal in an embarrassing position.

One recurring problem was when there was a fight between students. If both students struck blows, it would be automatic suspensions. It was always difficult to get the full story on these incidents because everyone had a different version. After an incident in which one parent thought his son only defended himself, the parent came to me with an appeal.

We discussed the situation, but there was not enough evidence to reduce the consequences for his son. However, he suggested we form a committee and try to come up with some guidelines that might make the consequences more fair in these fight situations. We added a few parents and called it the Fight Committee. That got some chuckles when I told my secretary there was a Fight Committee meeting today.

The committee took its commission seriously. They were to come up with a way to more fairly determine fault in a fight between students. One of the problems we discovered was that investigating a fight took an enormous amount of time. Many people had to be interviewed, and it could tie up a principal or assistant principal for an entire day. It was easier just to suspend both students and get it over with.

The committee decided that it wasn't fair and with the use of our security cameras, we could often get a clear picture of what had happened. The committee suggested that if one of the students tried to defend himself and remove himself from the situation, that student shouldn't receive disciplinary action. If that could be determined, then different consequences were justified. Sometimes there was verbal antagonism that initiated the fight, but verbal and physical altercations should have different consequences.

After going over this policy with the principals, we decided to put it into action. Even though it was sometimes difficult to determine fault, this gave principals some backing for assessing different consequences. The policy also helped encourage students who were physically attacked to remove themselves from the situation rather than fight back. It wasn't a perfect solution, but it was a good example of allowing parents to help the school come up with a fair policy that affected their children.

One parent who was particularly difficult to deal with was Mr. Strauss. He had several kids in our schools, and they were all in special education; some of them had severe disabilities. I met Mr. Strauss in my first year when he complained about his children not qualifying for free lunch. The state had a formula which determined qualification for free or reduced lunch based on family income. His income was low enough to qualify for reduced-price lunch but not free lunch. This angered him, and he verbally attacked the food service director, Mrs. Speer. He sent her a nasty letter addressed: "Dear Speer." After she felt threatened, she requested that I deal with Mr. Strauss from now on.

My first meeting with him involved showing him the formula and apologizing that he didn't qualify. He was not satisfied, but there was nothing he could do. He became a regular in my office always complaining about something. He felt that the teachers were always doing something wrong with his kids. I would try to calm him down and explain their reasoning, but he always found fault. His wife would come along, but she was very timid and let him do all the talking.

They had a son who was severely disabled and would frequently soil himself in the classroom. This happened so frequently that the teacher, Mrs. Striker, kept clean underwear for him and changed him when this happened. Mr. Strauss came in to complain about this to me.

"She is getting her jollies changing his underwear, and she has no right to do that," he announced angrily.

"Do you really think she enjoys changing his dirty underwear?" I remarked angrily.

"Do we ever do anything right for your kids," I asked? "I'm tired of your complaints."

By that time, I had had enough of Mr. Strauss and let him have it. I informed him that if he didn't want Mrs. Striker changing his son's pants, then we would call him every time and he could leave work and come change his son's pants himself. He didn't like that idea.

"The teachers are just trying to help your kids, and all you ever do is complain. You should be thanking them," I fired back at him.

Mr. Strauss looked at me in surprise. For once he was silent. He was used to people handling him with kid gloves, but I had confronted him aggressively. He suddenly became subdued and listened to me. He left my office promising to try to appreciate the teachers' efforts.

The next time I saw Mr. Strauss was at a parents' night. He was telling other parents what a great school district this was. He told the other parents that teachers were going out of their way to help his kids. He said he was going to encourage his other family members to move here and have their kids attend our schools. This was a shocking reversal of attitude.

Sure enough, one of his sisters moved into town and enrolled her son in middle school. The boy had some severe asthma problems and had been sickly for some time. However, he got along well and was making friends and enjoying his time here.

After attending for less than a year, a tragic incident occurred. The boy died in his sleep one night. The students and staff were devastated and came to the support of the family. They had a memorial for him, and we provided counselors for the kids who struggled with the death of their classmate. Many staff and students attended the funeral and were visibly moved by the loss of their fellow student.

After this incident, Mr. Strauss told everyone that this was the best school district in the state. That was quite a dramatic turnaround from the father who complained about everything. He finally realized how much our teachers cared about all of our students. His sons eventually graduated and were doing as well as could be expected with their disabilities.

Occasionally the public was asked to participate in some decisions for the school district that would affect their children. When the Great Recession hit in 2008, the district was confronted with a serious shortage of funds. There had been a considerable increase in funding that was to be phased in over three years as a result of a court case. But when the recession hit that increase was no longer feasible, and state funding was cut. A reduction of $800,000 from an operating budget of about $12 million was required. This was going to involve cuts in staffing. One of the board members suggested that we have a public meeting to get suggestions from the parents on how we should make these cuts.

A large crowd showed up for the public meeting. The staff and I gave an overview of the financial situation. We explained the reduction in state funding and informed them that it would cause a significant reduction in our budget requiring some cuts to programs. There were some small items that could be done away with, but the only realistic way to cut that amount of money was to eliminate some salaries. Figures were provided to show the cost of various programs and salary positions.

After giving this overview and taking some questions, we broke into small groups with a staff member to provide information to each group. Some of the groups became angry and confrontational. Some had strong feelings about what should be cut and what should be spared. After about an hour of small group discussion, everyone came together.

Each small group gave a report and then discussion began with me moderating. It was clear that these parents did not want any teachers cut. They also did not want classroom aides cut. Before long the discussion settled on the salaries of administrators and their benefits package. The discussion became heated when parents realized that teachers received a single health insurance package while administrators received full family coverage. They also bristled at the salaries of administrators which were in the $90,000 range for most principals and well over $100,000 for the superintendent. Explaining the number of responsibilities that administrators had and the number of employees they supervised did little to temper the anger.

As the moderator of the meeting, I became the target of several of the parents. Even a board member attacked administrator pay and benefits. I tried to explain that we could not get good administrators to come to our district if we didn't offer competitive pay and benefits. Some of the parents even suggested that we had too many administrators. It was encouraging to hear the teachers come to the defense of administrators on that idea. A spokesperson for the teachers said that they didn't want fewer administrators because they wanted to teach, not spend their time disciplining. They appreciated the role of the administrators in taking care of disciplinary issues and other administrative functions.

By the time the meeting ended, all ten administrators, including myself, felt under attack. I spent the next several weeks trying to rebuild their morale. Several of them said they felt unwanted and maybe they would move on to another district or leave education altogether. Even though I had become the primary target at the meeting, I had to maintain a positive attitude. The anger and hostility had shaken me, but I managed to hide my anger and hurt feelings. It wasn't the first time nor would it be the last time that I had to suppress my personal feelings to take leadership and keep staff morale from plunging.

In the end, we made numerous adjustments to address the funding shortfall. No teachers were terminated, but plans to add a couple of teachers were canceled. This resulted in larger class sizes. We also terminated a few aide positions, reduced coaching staff by one assistant per sport, and reduced the athletic travel budget. These moves made some difference but did not get us anywhere near the $800,000 reduction that was needed. Most of the reduction came by canceling scheduled transfers of general fund money to other funds and reducing our reserves significantly. This was a feasible short term strategy but would cause serious problems if it continued.

It took a long time for administrators to heal from the beating we took in this community budget meeting. The attacks were a precursor to attacks that would come against administrators from the politicians as outlined in the next chapter. However, none of our administrators left, and we did not change pay or benefits. When negotiations for teacher salaries took place, some adjustments were made. Normally, administrators were given the same percentage increase that teachers received. That year we gave a smaller increase to administrators, and as superintendent, I declined any increase in pay.

After that contentious meeting, the board discussed the wisdom of bringing the public in to help make decisions about cuts. We understood that it did seem unfair that administrators had better benefits than teachers. This had been a long-standing practice, and it was not financially feasible to give 130 teachers full family health insurance. It would also have been quite a financial hit to the ten administrators who were accustomed to full family coverage to have it taken away. There was no easy solution, but the board realized that allowing the public to attack our administrators was not good for staff morale. They indicated we wouldn't be doing it again anytime soon.

We weathered the storm of a budget reduction, and our district continued to grow. Eventually, we were able to restore some of the cuts because of the increased funding that came with increased enrollment. We assumed that after the economy began to recover from the recession, our funding would be restored, and the promise of increased funding by the legislature would be realized. We did not know that the political landscape was about to change and the hopes of desperately needed increases in funding would not materialize.

The attacks from community members were difficult to deal with. Later we were to experience even more vicious attacks from the politicians.

12

THE SUPERINTENDENT
AND THE POLITICAL LANDSCAPE

One thing every superintendent quickly learns is that the job is political. I don't mean that in a bad sense. The definition of political is "relating to the government, public affairs." Education is definitely a function of the government. However, it also means relating to public affairs, and you are clearly in the public eye.

The superintendent is hired, supervised, and fired by the board of education. In Kansas, board members are elected in non-partisan elections. They meet once or twice a month, make policy, and give direction to the superintendent whom they hire to run the business of the district.

Board members are the unsung heroes of public education. They rarely hear from their constituents unless there is a complaint. They put in many hours studying difficult issues and receive no compensation. Most of them do it because of a strong belief in the value of education and a commitment to help their community.

Since board members are elected officials, they hear from the public about their perceptions of what is happening. So does the superintendent. One way to keep the public informed is by getting involved in community affairs. This was an aspect of the job that I enjoyed.

I made it a point to be engaged in community activities, whether it was a charity function, a social event, church activities, or participation on boards and committees. While serving on the Diversity Task Force, I became friends with Jack, the local United Methodist minister. Despite my being Catholic, we agreed on almost all religious issues. He had a regular informational program in which he invited guests to present on various subjects. Because of my prior experience teaching religion, he invited me in as a regular presenter. Jack and I chuckled about the novelty of having a Catholic presenting to the Methodist congregation. More in line with my religious background, I also taught a class in church history at the local Catholic Church.

When there was a large social event in the community, it was important to attend. It was beneficial to meet people in a social setting. It sometimes became tiring to go to so many events, but people noticed if the superintendent didn't attend. This is especially true in smaller communities, but I believe it holds true for superintendents in any district.

Superintendents have to keep board members informed and satisfied. It is the responsibility of the board to give direction to the superintendent and to evaluate the superintendent annually. In superintendent circles there is an old saying:

"The only thing you need to know as superintendent is how to count to four."

The point of this statement is that there are seven members of the board and as long as you have support from a majority you will retain your job. Of course, it's not that simple, but it does contain an element of truth.

I have heard many stories about board members who wield unethical power. There are cases where board members go after coaches or teachers if their child does not get to play or get the grades they want. I've heard stories about board members who have an agenda when they are elected and carry out that agenda regardless of its impact on the welfare of the district.

Fortunately, very little of that attitude was displayed in my fourteen years as a superintendent. Most board members had the welfare of the entire district as their primary purpose and showed wisdom and discretion in their job. That said, there have been a few instances in which I felt a board member might have stepped out of line.

One instance that comes to mind happened in my term at Mission Valley. When I went to the district, there was open hostility between the teachers' union and the board members. Teacher pay was among the lowest in the state. There were people on the board who made less income than teachers, and they resented that fact.

When we went into negotiations for teacher salaries, the meetings became contentious. It was my role as superintendent to provide budget facts and to give a recommendation on salaries, but the board had to approve the salary scale. Teachers always wanted more than the board was willing to give. That was standard procedure. The idea was to negotiate in good faith and give teachers a fair salary within the budget constraints of the district.

I had experienced how difficult it was to recruit good teachers because of our remote location and low salary scale. It was my recommendation that the board provide a sizeable raise and gradually try to bring our pay scale in line with other schools. During negotiations, the teachers make a proposal, and the board makes a counter-proposal. After some discussion, the two sides separate and discuss how much they are willing to give to reach an agreement. During one of these meetings with the board one member complained that,

"Teachers are making more money than most of us."

He was not interested in trying to compromise and made the remark, "F**k them."

I was shocked and let him know that this was not negotiating in good faith. Fortunately, other board members had cooler heads and eventually came to an agreement. During the four years at this district we were able to improve salaries but never could get near the state average.

Because of our tight finances, I was always looking for grants. Finally, I was able to secure a sizeable grant for Continuous School Improvement. This involved spending time evaluating and upgrading our curriculum and teaching practices. Some of the funds were used for professional development activities while a good percentage was used to pay the teachers and administrators for their extra time in meetings to develop an improvement plan. Board members questioned me about this, and some of them thought we were just using it to supplement salaries.

They were particularly concerned that administrators, including the superintendent, were receiving extra pay for meeting time. This was completely within the terms of the grant, but a couple of board members resented the extra pay for the committee members. This contributed to my loss of some board support. I was beginning to count to four to see if support was still there.

In retrospect, I shouldn't have taken the extra pay for the committee meetings. We spent hours of time in after-school meetings, but the extra pay irritated some board members. However, the committee was able to upgrade our curriculum and teaching practices as a result of that grant. One distinct improvement we made was to implement the first Advanced Placement classes in high school. These courses incorporate college-level academics, and students can receive college credit if they pass an exit exam with a high enough score.

Another problem I experienced with board members was the practice of confidentiality. Most board business must be conducted in public. However, there are a few instances where board members can meet in executive session and what is discussed in those sessions is to remain confidential. Personnel matters and the discussion of negotiations of salaries are some of the more common issues for executive sessions.

Several times during my terms as a superintendent we had former teachers who were elected to the board. They certainly knew the business of the school better than most, but sometimes they forgot that they were no longer part of the teaching staff. Their loyalties were to be with the board. Occasionally, those board members were too close to teachers, and they passed on information about personnel or negotiations that should not have been disclosed outside of an executive session. This can create problems and hard feelings when difficult decisions must be made. Sometimes board members just enjoy the privilege of knowing confidential information. It becomes a temptation to show others how much they know.

Generally, I agreed with my boards on the issues. However, in one instance near the end of my term in Independence, I had to carry out a decision that I disagreed with. There had been some tension between the principal and assistant principal in one of our elementary buildings. I had counseled both and insisted they work out their differences and present a united front. They both agreed to do so, but there was some obvious disagreement about how to lead the school.

After extensive discussion with the two administrators, the principal decided to resign. The assistant principal, Tammy, was happy to stay on as assistant to the new principal who came from another building. She and the new principal already had a good relationship. However, the board insisted that Tammy move to the other building and take the assistant-principal position vacated by the new principal. I argued against that move but was just months away from my retirement. I believe the board disregarded my advice, seeing me as a lame duck. Tammy had a long attachment to this building and its teachers and did not want to leave.

Because it was my job to carry out the board's wishes, I had to announce the administrative change to the staff at that building. It was the most uncomfortable action I had ever taken as a superintendent because I believed it was the wrong move and knew the staff would not take it well. The staff was gathered in the library after school, and I made the announcement to gasps of dismay from most of the staff. I tried to put a happy face on the decision, but many on the staff were angry and shocked. Several of them confronted me afterward and expressed their disappointment. They were upset with me personally. I wanted to tell them that I didn't like the move any more than they did, but I presented a unified front with the board and insisted it would be a good move for everyone.

That was one of the most painful announcements I ever had to make. My heart was not in it, but it was my job to carry out the board's wishes. If I had not already announced my retirement, that incident might have caused me to consider resigning and move to another district.

Tammy made the move to the other building and was a good soldier. After two years she took a principal position at a neighboring district. The new principal then returned to his original position that had been vacated by Tammy and a new administrative team took over. This whole incident was a painful experience that still bothers me to this day.

Kansas has an elected State Board of Education which sets policy for schools and makes recommendations to the legislature on funding and other issues. Early in my career as a superintendent, we had a supportive State Board and an excellent Commissioner of Education. But in 2005 an ultra-conservative majority was elected to the Board. When the Commissioner of Education resigned, the first order of business was to hire an ultra-conservative as Commissioner. He had no school experience except for his role in a think tank in which he advocated cuts to education funding. He promoted charter schools and school choice. Combined with a Board of Education whose majority had the same sentiments, it was clear we were in for a contentious time.

Bob, the new Commissioner, quickly confirmed our worst fears as he became the spokesperson for the anti-education lobby. I realize this sounds extreme, but there were significant numbers in the legislature and on the State Board that did not value public education. They preferred education to be provided by private funding. They despised taxes and education is by far the biggest expense in the state budget.

Bob began touring the state and expressing his ideas that public education was inefficient. He declared that many schools were failing and that there were too many administrators. His solution was to implement charter schools and provide vouchers to parents for private school tuition. He joined the majority on the State Board who did not believe in evolution and adjusted the science standards accordingly. Evolution was de-emphasized, and Creationism was given equal billing.

To be open-minded, my local board invited Bob to speak at a legislative forum. We invited all of our local elected legislators and our district member of the State Board.

The meeting proceeded with presentations by some educators, and then Bob gave his speech. He tried to soft-sell his policies, but it was obvious he was both uninformed about public education and out of step with most of the people in the room. The meeting confirmed my fears that he would not be an advocate for public education but would work mostly as an opponent. It was a strange position for someone who was supposed to be our leader

Iris was one of the most conservative members of that Board, and she attended that meeting. She had gotten into a public controversy about banning certain books in one school district. The contested books were The Catcher in the Rye and some of the works of Toni Morrison. These were some of the usual books attacked by fundamentalists. The superintendent in that district followed policy by forming a committee to review the controversial books, and the committee came up with a solution. They did not ban any of the contested books but made some of them available only upon request. Iris disagreed with this decision and had publicly stated that:

"Some superintendents are promoting pornography."

I strongly resented her comment and confronted her at the meeting. I told her I was offended by her statement about superintendents.

"Do you really think that superintendents promote pornography?" I asked.

She replied, "Yes, I do believe that some of them promote pornography."

"I would like you to retract that statement," I responded.

"No, I believe some of them do promote pornography," she repeated.

"Well, then we will just have to defeat you in the next election," I responded.

To my pleasure, she declined to run at the next election cycle. However, her son-in-law ran for the position with the same ultra-conservative opinions. Fortunately, he was defeated by a pro-education candidate who had previously been a teacher and a curriculum director. When the next election cycle brought a more moderate board, the anti-public education commissioner moved on as well.

Thankfully, there was a knowledgeable and dedicated public servant in the Department of Education throughout this difficult time. Dale Dennis had been Deputy Commissioner for Fiscal and Administrative Services for 33 years. He knew more about education in Kansas and about the budget for the state than most people could ever imagine. During the tumultuous time when we had an anti-education commissioner, Dale was our primary source for accurate information.

As a new superintendent, I was fortunate enough to attend the annual budget briefings with Dale and his sidekick, Veryl. Those workshops were held every summer to help us put together our district budgets based on whatever changes the legislature had made that year. Dale and Veryl (Veryl eventually retired and was replaced by Craig) did their presentations in a tag-team form that was informative and entertaining. They knew each other so well that they finished each other's sentences. In the field, we referred to them as a married couple.

There was so much confidence in Dale that when each school district finished setting its budget, they sent it to Dale to review before they sent it to the board for approval. He could look at the budget of any of the 300 districts in the state and immediately tell if anything was out of order, or if you could adjust some numbers to make it better for the district.

The legislature depended on Dale to give them budget figures. He was a fixture at legislative committee meetings to guide them in their deliberations. No one knew the budget better than Dale. Those of us in the field relied on him for information on almost anything having to do with education. During the times of hostile boards or a hostile commissioner, he was even more crucial.

Ultra-conservatives in the legislature did not particularly like Dale because he was supportive of education funding and defended our expenditures. They wanted to see less money put into education. It was difficult for them to discredit Dale because he was so much more knowledgeable than they were on fiscal issues. Finally, in 2018 they thought they found a budget violation on his part and began attacking him. Some called for a suspension or termination, and they tried to discredit him publicly.

Educators throughout the state immediately came to his defense. They characterized him as one of the greatest public servants in the state and defended him. Most legislators supported him, and the Board of Education confirmed his continuation in the position on a

9-1 vote. It was one of the most impressive shows of support for an embattled public servant I have ever seen. This incident was an example of the tension that existed between ultra-conservative factions and the education community.

Our special education cooperative held legislative forums every year. It was our opportunity to meet with our legislators about education issues and establish relationships. Depending on the makeup of our legislators these forums were sometimes effective and sometimes a waste of time. At one forum, we were told by one of the most extreme conservatives that they were in charge now and we needed to get used to it. He made a big issue about guns and suggested that we should have guns in schools. That conversation got a bit testy.

The hardest part of the political environment is dealing with the state legislature on education issues. Education is the primary function of state government, and the funding of education is always a contentious issue. The more conservative legislators resent that education takes up almost half of the state budget. However, past legislators put the wording "suitable funding for education" in the constitution.

Several times while I was a superintendent the conservatives tried to claim that education was so expensive because there were too many administrators. They attacked administrators for having unreasonably high salaries and taking money away from the classroom. The code word for this movement was "more money in the classroom." Some developed an arbitrary rule that 65% of school funding should go directly to the classroom. This sounded like a reasonable goal, but there was no research to show this had any direct effect on student learning. It was simply a number pulled out of the air. It was also misleading because the rules for coding how money was spent are not very clear.

Counselors, social workers, and librarians are not coded as classroom spending. Coaching salaries are coded as classroom spending. Most teachers will tell you that counselors and social workers are critical to student achievement. Without these support services, many kids would not succeed. Some of the items not considered classroom spending are very necessary for schools to function. Items such as busing, utilities, construction, and textbooks were coded as non-classroom spending.

Some of the schools with the lowest percentage of "classroom spending" actually had the highest achievement rates. It was interesting that the Teacher's Union was generally supportive of the number of administrators. They felt this freed them from having to do administrative tasks and allowed them to concentrate on their teaching. The argument in the education community was that local school boards knew best what was needed to provide the best educational outcomes for their district and they support that by budgeting accordingly.

Our Kansas Association of School Boards produced a flyer comparing the number of school administrators per worker to other industries. Education was by far the least top heavy in administration compared to any other industry. Even when statistics from the Department of Education showed that the number of administrators had been declining while the number of teachers was increasing, conservative legislators continued the attack. Facts didn't seem to make any difference.

When the attack on the number of administrators didn't catch on, they began attacking administrator salaries, trying to drive a wedge between teachers and administrators. My base salary was approximately $130,000 by the end of my career. I oversaw 300 employees, 2,000 students and was responsible for a budget of over $20 million. Any CEO of a business this size would receive much higher compensation. The lobbyists and legislators opposed to education funding levels pulled out a few salaries of the larger districts in the state in which some superintendents were making $250,000 to $350,000. Again, these were huge districts with large numbers of employees, students, and a huge budget.

The attacks continued, and some of those people even began attacking teachers insinuating that they were overpaid. They criticized their pay for what they believed was only nine months of work. Most teachers are attending professional development or attending college classes throughout a good part of their summer vacation time. Some coach without compensation during that time and others use the time to update their lesson plans. The reality is that most teachers have only a short vacation during the summer and work much longer hours than most people realize. Their evenings are taken up with grading and planning.

Political climate changes in the legislature have a dramatic effect on schools. In the early years of my superintendency, we had a supportive legislature and governor. But even with a supportive administration, the recession of 2008 hit school funding hard. It was understood by school leaders that this was a time of belt-tightening for everyone. However, as the economy began to recover we anticipated that funding levels would be restored. Unfortunately for schools, the election of Sam Brownback as governor and an ultra-conservative legislative majority had no intention of restoring funding. In fact, they passed a massive tax cut that reduced individual income taxes and eliminated taxes altogether for many businesses. This action caused a state budget shortfall that eliminated any possibility of restoring funding to pre-recession levels. It also caused the legislature to renege on the promise of increased funding that the previous legislature had proposed as a result of a court case.

At one of our KASB conventions, Governor Brownback was a speaker. He told us how important education was and that he supported strong public schools. This was after he had gotten his tax cuts passed which eliminated any possibility of restoring the funding that had been cut as a result of the recession. He was proposing a block grant to schools that would lock us in at pre-recession levels. This was opposed by virtually every school district in the state.

After his speech, he stood near the back of the room while another speaker addressed the crowd. I was sitting with several superintendent friends and noticed the governor was standing by himself. To their surprise, I walked over to where the governor stood and told him the block grants were not a good alternative.

"You're killing us with the cuts in state funding," I said.

"But you're not giving me credit for the increase in capital outlay," he replied.

"We only got that because the courts ruled in our favor," I answered. "You forgot about the previous court ruling that required a significant increase in the general fund."

He just turned away and shook his head. I walked back to my group of friends, and they were stunned that I had approached the governor.

"Somebody has to tell him directly what he is doing to us," I said. "I'm not afraid to talk to him."

Finally, in 2018 I actively campaigned for a pro-education governor, Laura Kelly. She was successful, and it was like a breath of fresh air when she took office. By that time, I was retired, but it was such a change to have a governor who would listen to the needs of schools.

While still a superintendent and trying to negotiate with key legislators to increase funding, I was part of a small group of educators who met with legislative leadership in 2014. We told them that if they continued to refuse to adequately fund education the State Supreme Court would rule against them. They argued that the state had no money available and we argued that they had no money because they had given a massive tax cut. Our efforts were to no avail, and the Supreme Court eventually ruled against them as we had predicted.

The legislature continued to refuse to make significant changes to funding until the election of 2016 finally gave a Democratic and moderate Republican majority in the legislature. With power in numbers, this group finally reversed the tax cut and overrode Governor Brownback's veto. This action dramatically improved the revenue available. They then passed a modest increase in funding for schools, which the Court still ruled inadequate. After the election of Governor Kelly in 2018, they finally passed a significant school funding increase. As of this writing the Supreme Court has yet to rule if this funding meets constitutional demands.

Fighting these battles became a regular part of the job of superintendent. I testified numerous times before legislative committees with very limited success. My testimony never seemed to have much impact. Those who were opposed stayed opposed and those in favor stayed in favor. It was more of a battle of ideology than an exercise in finding facts.

Once when I testified to a Senate committee about how they could find additional funding, I was interrupted in the middle of my testimony by the committee chair.

"Have you read the rules for testimony? She asked.

"No," I replied. "But I think I understand the procedure. I have done this before."

She said, "The rules state that testimony should never attack individuals on the committee."

"Have I said anything offensive about anyone?" I asked.

"No you haven't," she replied. "Continue."

I was puzzled why she had interrupted me, and it temporarily threw me off my point. Afterward, I asked some people in the gallery if I had said anything offensive. They saw nothing of the sort and felt she was just being vindictive. She just didn't like what I had to say. Maybe her purpose was just to disrupt my presentation.

Participating in the political process was a tricky maneuver for a superintendent. You could not be too partisan in public because your constituency involves all parties and every political persuasion. However, it was important that we inform voters about the stands of the candidates on education issues.

When I first came to Independence, we had a state representative who was ultra-conservative. He was not inclined to do anything to help with school finance. After two years of getting nowhere with him, several of our board members and I decided to support his opponent in the next primary election. Jeff, the opponent, was a young lawyer who had attended our schools and seemed to be supportive of education funding. Since my board was open about their support, I publicly supported Jeff and even contributed to his campaign. Jeff won the seat, and we thought we had a strong advocate for schools.

Unfortunately, after a few years, Jeff moved up in leadership and came under the influence of the most conservative wing of his party. When the Great Recession hit and education funding was cut drastically, there was a bipartisan movement to impose a one percent sales tax for three years to get schools through the next several years until the economy could recover from the recession. Despite our pleading with Jeff in a private meeting, he refused to support the sales tax.

Fortunately, the coalition was successful in getting the sales tax passed despite Jeff's opposition, and it helped schools weather the storm for a few years. Surprisingly, when three years had passed, and there was an effort to terminate the sales tax increase, Jeff voted against eliminating the increase. At that point, I knew we could no longer depend on him to support our schools.

After retirement, I decided to run against Jeff for the Senate seat. He had lost some support by that time, and there was some chance to win even though I was a Democrat in a heavily Republican district. However, he dropped out of the race shortly after I entered. My run was unsuccessful, but the district did elect a Senator who was far more supportive of education issues.

Another incident that soured me on politics was when our district was in the process of passing a bond issue to do some major renovations on our aging buildings. Our then-state senator was also the majority leader of the Senate. He carried a lot of influence in our community, and he didn't want us to run a bond issue for the improvements. He had another idea about how he thought we should go about it.

Several board members, Fred, our business manager, and I met with him. We made our case for running a bond issue. Fred pointed out that the Senator's proposal would not work both legally and practically. Suddenly, the senator got loud and went into a passionate speech about how we were always asking for money. He attacked me personally and referred to my salary and how I made much more money than he did as a state senator. That had nothing to do with the issue we were there to discuss. We were all stunned at his tirade. After the meeting, we just shook our heads and moved on. It was clear we weren't going to get his support.

We never did figure out what that blowup was about. We assumed there was some other issue that had him stressed, and he had taken it out on me. Those present in the room just laughed it off as inappropriate and said it had nothing to do with our purpose.

One of the best ways to get away from the pressure of being superintendent was collaborating with other superintendents. Such opportunities were available at conferences with some of our professional organizations.

Kansas Association of School Boards (KASB) was a great organization in which superintendents and board members could receive professional advice and even legal advice when needed. Their legal department was on speed dial in my office. Donna was the person I generally consulted at KASB when there was a legal question. She had been doing her job for a long time and had seen every possible situation. When there was a unique circumstance, I called Donna to find out how it had been handled in other districts. She usually had an example for me.

One of my most difficult cases was when we non-renewed a tenured teacher. The principal had some technical violations in the process, and the teacher brought a lawsuit to retain her job. Donna guided us through the courts and back and forth with the teacher's lawyers for almost five years until it was resolved. In the end, we paid the teacher a settlement in the amount that we had originally proposed five years earlier.

KASB had an annual convention which was a highlight of the year. Attendance was strong. We had a chance to meet board members and superintendents from all parts of the state. It was a huge social event as well as an educational experience. There were breakout sessions on just about every topic you might face. There was always a huge display of vendors who gave away trinkets with their logos. This is where I gathered the most loot that I took back to students as prizes. There was always a large drawing for some really valuable goods that vendors donated. I still have briefcases, backpacks, and calculators from those events. Spouses were also welcomed at these events, and we got to know each other on a personal basis.

Kansas School Superintendents' Association (KSSA) was another helpful organization. Superintendents could get together to share experiences and develop policies. By listening to each other's stories, we learned how others dealt with the myriad dilemmas we faced. It was helpful to know we weren't the only ones who faced strange predicaments.

Both organizations were active in lobbying the legislature on education issues. They helped us prepare testimony and gave us a support group as we tried to influence legislation that would be helpful to schools. Some legislators resented these organizations and vilified us for using state funds to lobby. It's true that we used state funds, although the amount was minimal. We argued that we were the practitioners in the field and we knew what worked and what didn't work. Still, there was always a group of legislators who saw our organizations as the enemy and paid no attention to our testimonies. Some legislators really listened to what we had to say and believed we were trying to do what was best for schools and students.

One of our biggest fights was when the legislature tried to take away state aid for capital building projects. Districts that had high property values could easily raise the tax dollars needed to build and maintain good school facilities. Poorer districts did not have this ability. The law had a formula that provided state aid at various percentage levels based on the relative wealth of the district. Some legislators introduced a bill to eliminate that formula at the same time we were proposing a bond issue in Independence.

When testifying against that bill, I showed them that one wealthy district could raise one million dollars per year for a project with only a 1.5 mill tax increase. A neighboring poor district needed a 40 mill increase for the same amount. It was not possible to do it in the poor district without state aid. It would create a tremendous disparity in the quality of facilities based on zip codes. The discouraging part of the effort was that a maverick state school board member testified in favor of eliminating the state aid. Fortunately, the bill was killed, and the aid was maintained.

For me, the greatest value of our professional organizations was the camaraderie that developed among our colleagues. Being a superintendent was a very stressful position, and the ability to get away and relax was a major relief. We could talk about things that we were not able to discuss in our local communities, and our colleagues understood. There were always great speakers at our conferences that provided needed insight into relevant issues. The ability to commiserate with fellow superintendents was a necessary diversion.

We shared foxhole stories. The stories we heard from other superintendents were helpful in some of the situations we had to deal with later. Some of the stories were funny and provided relief from the constant pressure.

One of my superintendent friends, Jim, told a story about a bus driver who transported the debate team to a tournament in Wichita. During the day, Jim received a call from someone in Wichita complaining that his school bus was seen parked at a stripper bar. When the driver returned home, Jim told him about the complaint he had received. The driver assured him that he had gone to a pharmacy to pick up some medications while the students were debating. The pharmacy didn't have enough space in the parking lot for a bus, so he had parked it in a lot across the street.

Jim filed this story in the back of his mind until he had to be in Wichita. He went to the location to check out the veracity of the bus driver's story. There was no pharmacy anywhere near the previously mentioned stripper bar. The bus driver was terminated.

Another humorous story from a superintendent friend was about the coach of his basketball team. The coach had told the boys that if they won the upcoming tournament, he would take them out to eat at a restaurant of their choice. When they won the tournament, these typical teenage boys selected Hooters. The coach took them, but a patron happened to see the school vehicles in the parking lot and complained to the superintendent. The superintendent admonished the coach for his choice, but admitted that he later chuckled about the pickle the coach had gotten himself into. Some constituents were offended at seeing their taxpayer-funded vehicle parked at Hooters.

Usually, our conferences involved some golf. This seemed like a luxury, and it was certainly an enjoyable break. It was also an opportunity to develop professional networking that came in very handy in our jobs. I may have gained more insight into difficult issues while golfing with other superintendents than from all the presentations I attended. My golf game didn't improve, but I gained a lot of insight into decision making.

As I said, politics is a necessary part of the job of superintendent. It does not have to be a negative thing if you have politicians who appreciate the importance of good schools in their state. Unfortunately, some politicians are more interested in making political points and getting re-elected than improving education. There is always going to be some disagreement, but if we can agree that public education is a vital function of the state, most differences of opinion can be worked out.

13

THE SUPERINTENDENT
AND STAFF

The first issue I had to confront as a new superintendent was finding my own replacement as high school principal. In a remote location like Mission Valley, that was not going to be easy. We advertised in several statewide publications and websites and soon received a few applications. After interviewing and checking references, Bruce was offered the job. He was experienced and had an impressive interview. I was very pleased with my first major decision as superintendent.

That feeling of satisfaction quickly turned to concern. I had been pressuring Bruce to sign a contract as soon as we hired him in May to get him locked in. It seemed suspicious that he kept putting me off even though he verbally agreed to take the job. He was continuing to hunt for a better job and found one. Since he had not signed the contract, he was able to back out of the job.

June is not a good time to be looking for a principal. Most of the good ones have already been hired and if you are still available there is probably a reason. But there was no choice, and we advertised extensively once more. We received many applications, but most of them had some glaring deficiencies which explained why they were still available.

However, one candidate looked good on paper, and he was called in for an interview. James had been a principal before but had to give up the job because of a medical condition. He was currently teaching and felt he could now handle a principal's job since his health was better. All his references were good, and I felt comfortable hiring him. This time I made sure the contract was signed immediately.

James was good with kids and soon established himself as an effective principal. He was doing a good job, but soon he started calling in sick frequently. He was starting to have the same health problems he had experienced previously. Finally, by February he asked to meet with me to tell me he could no longer do the job because of his health. The stress of the job had caused his health problems to recur. That was very disappointing, but there was nothing I could do about it, so we let him out of his contract.

We needed someone to handle the job, so I found a retired principal who agreed to take the job on an interim basis. He got us through the rest of the year until we could find a permanent replacement.

After reviewing the original applications, I found a physics teacher who had no administrative experience but seemed to have the potential. He accepted the offer, so this gave us our fifth high school principal in one year. Wow! Was my job always going to be this difficult?

Kenneth was an extremely intelligent young man, but his personal skills needed a lot of work. I received some complaints from parents that he did not communicate with them and seemed to lack empathy. I knew he cared about kids, but he was not very good at expressing it and came across as cold and uncaring.

We had numerous talks about this, and I tried to guide him. He made some good decisions for the school and was very good with technology which was a rapidly developing method of instruction at that time. But his interpersonal skills were going to ruin his career if he did not improve them.

During his evaluation, he was directed to make concerted efforts to improve communication. I suggested that when he attended games, he makes it a point to sit with at least two parents and visit. All he needed to do was make small talk and ask them about their children. Every parent wants to talk about their child.

Kenneth followed my instructions even though he was stiff and uncomfortable about it at first. But the more he did it, the better he got, and I received fewer complaints. He did an acceptable job as principal. He learned enough to continue his career and eventually he became a superintendent. Kenneth lasted the rest of my term as superintendent, so there was no need to fill that position again.

It is widely accepted in education circles that the most important job of a school board is their selection of a superintendent. I believed the most important job of a superintendent is the selection of principals. The leader of a school can make a huge difference in how that school operates. Even if you have good teachers, if the leadership is weak the school has a difficult time being successful.

Throughout my career, I have been blessed with many good principals. I have learned more from those effective principals than they ever learned from me. Just as a great principal can make your job easier so too, a weak one can really add to your workload.

Shortly after becoming superintendent at Mission Valley my junior high principal accepted a promotion to principal at a much larger school. Mark had been an effective leader, so we were anxious to get another good one to replace him.

After an exhaustive search, we found Don who seemed to be just what we needed. His references had spoken of him in glowing terms. He was intelligent and experienced. There was some mention of his being independent-minded, but it didn't seem to be a big problem. Unfortunately, I found out later that Don's insubordination would have gotten him terminated in his previous position had he not found this job first. The reference I had talked to was anxious to get rid of him, so he only told me about his good qualities. He made only a passing reference that Don sometimes didn't take direction well.

I soon found out that Don's arrogance convinced him that he was always right, and it didn't matter what the superintendent or administrative team wanted to do. He was going to do it his way. In administrative meetings, the team was encouraged to express their opinions. Then we hashed out an issue and made a decision for all to follow. Several times I was astounded when Don acted directly contrary to something we had decided. When I asked him why he wasn't doing what we had decided he said he thought that was what we decided.

In my frustration with him, I said, "How could you come out

of the meeting with exactly the opposite interpretation of everyone else? The other principals understood what we decided."

"I thought that was what we had decided on," he replied.

But then he let it slip that he thought his way was the best solution. As you can imagine, there were many conflicts.

I tried to convince him to leave after the first year, but we had given him a two-year contract, and he would not resign. Finally, he was moved out of the position and was assigned to teach a class in which the regular teacher was on sick leave. However, he still received the principal salary because that was what was on his contract. My first two experiences in hiring principals had not gone smoothly.

Despite my initial difficulty in finding principals, I was blessed with an outstanding and talented group of principals throughout my career as a superintendent. They also provided me with some of the most entertaining stories.

Brad was an elementary principal. He was a large man who had been a lineman in college football. It was funny to see him with the tiniest students in his school which covered kindergarten through second grade. At our first meeting, I assumed he must be intimidating to the students, but I soon realized that while he was an excellent leader; he was also a large teddy bear.

Brad was the only male educator in the building most of the time. All the teachers were women except for a young, male kindergarten teacher. The women in the building called Brad "The Man" and Brett, the kindergarten teacher "The Boy." Later he was lucky enough to add a male music teacher. There was always the concern that the women teachers might resent the lone male administrator, but that was not a problem. They had the greatest respect for him and teased him relentlessly.

Students looked up to him and feared him at the same time. It was hilarious to watch him walk down the hallways and see tiny first graders run up and hug him around his knees. Despite their admiration, they often trembled in fear when they were sent to his office because of bad behavior. Brad seemed to know every child and knew their tendencies and interests.

Brad was always good for some funny stories about what his students did or said. One first grader had constant behavior problems and was sent to the office. Brad set him in the corner and gave him some school work to do while he returned emails. Within a short time, he heard hissing noises coming from the offending child. Brad asked him to stop, but the hissing continued.

Finally, Brad asked, "What are you doing?"

The boy hissed back at him.

Brad repeated, "What are you doing?"

"I'm a snake," said the boy.

"Well, I don't speak snake," said Brad, "so stop it."

"You're a dumb ass," said 'snake boy.'

Eventually 'snake boy' and his parents left the district, so we didn't have to deal with them anymore.

On another occasion, I went to Brad's building to visit with him about a district issue. The secretary informed me that he was on the phone. After a long wait, he came out with a second-grade boy. When I asked what he was doing, he said they had skyped the boy's parents in prison. Both parents were incarcerated, so once a month the boy came down to the principal's office and skyped first mom and then dad. What a sad situation for such a little guy.

Every year there were the stories of the new kindergartners who couldn't adjust to a full day in school. It seemed like every year there was one who ran away to go back home. The concern was that they didn't know their way home and would get lost wandering the streets. Sometimes moms were as bad. They often had a difficult time dropping off their kindergartener and stood in the hallways crying.

On snow days, Brad would find a few kids sitting at the entrance waiting to go to breakfast. They didn't know there was no school because their parents didn't get them up and ready for school. They did it on their own. Brad would take them to breakfast at McDonald's and then drive them home.

Brad also told me about the mother who stood outside the school entrance at dismissal time in a tube top without a bra. Emblazoned on the shirt was "Armature (sic) Porn Star." That was a difficult conversation.

Then there was the father who was involved in a domestic dispute. He didn't want the mother to drive away with the child, so he laid down in front of her car and forty others behind her in the pick-up lane to keep her from leaving. No one could move, and the police were called. After twenty minutes of Brad and the police trying to reason with the man, he finally walked away. You can imagine how irate the line of parents was in that lane.

Debbie was another elementary principal who was very strong in curriculum and had great relationships with kids. Her meticulous attention to using the most effective teaching techniques was sometimes aggravating to teachers who were not used to such attention to detail. However, it made them better teachers.

She knew every child in her school and talked to them constantly. When I went to visit her school, it was very difficult to have a conversation with her. We were always moving through the halls while talking. She was frequently interrupted by a student with whom she struck up a conversation. She was protective of the kids like they were her own family. I didn't mind the interruptions to our conversation because she was putting first things first.

One time she dealt with a girl in a split family situation. The father had custody, and the mother was not supposed to have any contact. One day the mother got out of jail and came to pick up the girl. The secretary was suspicious and checked the records and found a no-contact order. Debbie instructed the secretary to call the police and the father while she delayed the mother. As mom was walking out the door with the girl, the police finally arrived and took custody of the girl. Mom was irate and screamed at the principal. Debbie responded that she had no choice because she had to follow the court order. She told mom that when she had a legal document that gave her a right to see the girl, she could do so. In the meantime, they would not let her take the daughter.

Dale was mentioned in an earlier chapter. He had retired as a superintendent and came back as an elementary principal. His experience as a superintendent helped me immensely as a beginning superintendent. I frequently quizzed him on how he would handle certain situations. He always had good advice but gave it in a way that was respectful and cognizant of our respective roles. I sought his guidance frequently.

In an earlier chapter, I mentioned the story of the hyperactive kid in Dale's school that was fed Mountain Dew. Dale's only advice was,

"Don't make him worse."

One of Dale's frustrations was parents who always found fault with the school when their kid got in trouble. One time, two foster kids who were brother and sister were fighting on the bus. The bus driver came in to get Dale. When he got there, the boy had the girl down and was on top hitting her. Dale told him to stop and get off. When the boy didn't respond Dale picked him up and kept him away from the girl. The next day the stepmother came in and accused Dale of physically abusing the boy.

"What did you expect me to do? Let him keep hitting her?" he asked.

When it was put in those terms, the stepmother finally understood and stopped complaining.

Mark was a middle school principal. I always teased him that you had to have something wrong with you to want to be a principal at that level. Middle school kids are full of hormones and crazy behavior, and it takes a special person to be able to handle hundreds of kids like that. Mark had the right demeanor to deal with that age group. He had kids of his own and understood the incomprehensibility of some of their behavior.

In an earlier chapter, I recounted the story of the troubled student who baked Mark a cake and his skepticism about what might be in it. On another occasion, Mark had a gifted student whose parents thought she should be taking advanced algebra in the 7th grade. The girl was adopted from Russia and was very bright, but her dad was very hard to deal with. If he didn't like something the school did, he would immediately attack everyone via email. In that case, we needed to work out details before she could take the advanced math course. We scheduled a meeting for the following week.

Immediately, dad sent out emails attacking everyone for denying the girl the opportunity to take advanced math. He wanted it done immediately. He said the principal didn't care about the needs of the kids, and the superintendent was too busy hiding under his desk.

On the day of the meeting, I notified Mark that I would not stay in the meeting but would come to greet dad and his family. When I entered the room, the dad was shocked and tried to avoid eye contact. I went right up to him, shook his hand, introduced myself and said,

"I just crawled out from under my desk to tell you that we are going to do what is best for your daughter." He grudgingly nodded.

We did work it out for the girl to be transported to the high school to take the advanced math course. A few years later at the high school academic awards program I purposely sat at this family's table. I wanted to show dad again that I wasn't hiding under the desk. By that time, the girl had done great in high school and received some nice college scholarships. This time dad was very congenial.

Patty was an African American middle school principal who had served as a teacher, counselor, and administrator in our district for many years. She told me the story of an African American student who was constantly in trouble. Mom was in the office with her son and told Patty:

"You're just prejudiced against him because he is black."

Patty looked at her in amazement and said, "Take a good look at me. Do you still think I'm prejudiced against blacks?"

After a guilty pause, mom replied, "No I guess not."

Matt was a young high school principal who was brought in to establish tighter discipline at the high school. One of his students was habitually early for school. Students were not normally allowed to come into the building until a prescribed time, but this student said he was dropped off early by mom. Matt let him come into the building anyway. Eventually, the boy began hanging out in the wrestling room because he wanted to sleep on the wrestling mats. That went on for a while until one day Matt checked in on him. He found him under the mats masturbating. That was the end of his entering school before the prescribed time.

Matt had another student whose father had committed suicide some years ago. Darwin was a bright kid and a good athlete, but he was regularly in and out of trouble. He was suffering from depression and seeing a counselor regularly. At one point, he was very unstable and began talking about killing himself. He even discussed doing it at school. This was at a time of frequent school shootings, and we became very concerned. Darwin had gotten suspended from school for disciplinary issues. This meant he was not allowed on school grounds or at any school functions. His counselor expressed concern that he was suicidal.

Darwin's sister was among the cheerleaders to be honored at the last football game while he was on suspension. He and his mother asked permission for him to attend. They said he would come for the ceremony and then leave immediately afterward. We consulted with counselors and were advised not to let him attend. The counselor was concerned that he might try to make a violent statement in front of the crowd. We denied his request to the dismay of Darwin and his mom. It was hard to turn him down, but we discussed our responsibility for the safety of our students and came to the same conclusion.

Darwin eventually left town. He received intensive counseling and gradually got his life back together. A couple of years later he came back to town. He had worked through his crisis and was doing well. He eventually started up a business, got married, and had a child. Matt and I felt we had handled that situation correctly. Darwin was very unstable at the time, and it could have resulted in a tragedy.

There was another incident involving Matt and me which was funny after the fact, but it wasn't very funny at the time. A bomb threat had been called into the high school, and Matt notified my office. I rushed over to the scene of students being evacuated. Matt and I talked with the law enforcement people and asked what we should do.

They told us to go through the building and tell them if anything looked out of place. We were both a bit wary but figured that made sense. The only thing we saw that seemed out of place were some boxes stacked on top of a trash can near the auditorium. We told the police and asked if they were going to check it out. They responded that they would not do a check. It was our responsibility to examine it.

"But what if it blows up?" I asked.

"You will just have to decide if you want to take that risk," they responded.

Matt and I looked at each other, and we both asked, "Which one of us should do this?"

I told Matt, "My kids are grown, and you have young kids, so I'll do it."

Matt replied, "No, it's my building so I'll take responsibility."

Finally, Matt walked up and gingerly started going through the boxes. I stood back but was close enough that if anything blew up, I would still be in the line of fire. I'm not sure what I was thinking, but maybe it was just a bit of guilt.

Matt went through the pile, and everything was clear. We breathed a sigh of relief and walked away. By this time, word had reached Matt that some kids knew who was involved in the bomb threat. That student was brought to the office, and he confessed that there was no bomb. He had asked his mother to call in the threat. We directed students back into the building, and the police went to question the student and the mother. Sure enough, she admitted that she had called in the threat at her son's request. He just wanted to get out of school early that day.

Afterward, Matt and I laughed about the incident. We didn't really think the threat was legitimate, but you never know for sure. I commended him for his courage but noted that I was close enough that I would have been blown up also. That didn't really make either of us feel any better. We were just glad that it turned out all right.

Sometimes the teachers can cause more problems than the students. At one school there was a young English teacher who also coached track and cross country. Steve was an enthusiastic young man who seemed to have great relationships with students, particularly the ones he coached. He seemed to be one of our best teachers, and his enthusiasm was contagious.

However, I began to become a little uneasy with his closeness to some of the girls he coached. Steve was previously divorced and lived alone in the country. I began receiving some complaints from parents about topics he discussed in the classroom. He was uttering veiled sexual references that were making some of the girls uncomfortable. I observed him more closely and had a talk with him about boundaries with his students. He denied any impropriety but admitted he might have said things in class that were of a sexual nature and may have been offensive. A written warning was placed in his file and observation continued.

Soon I heard that he had a party at his farmhouse with alcohol and some of his students were present. This was the last straw, so he was called in to verify the rumor. He confessed that there were students at the party but said they had not been invited. They just showed up. I advised him that he should have immediately asked them to leave. Since this was a continuing pattern, he was asked to resign.

He submitted a resignation the next week, and we ended the school year without further incident. Two years later I received a call from an administrator at another school district where Steve had been employed. He asked if we had had any trouble with him regarding student relationships. I explained the incidents to this person. I reminded the caller that I had made this clear when I was called for a recommendation two years earlier. He acknowledged that he remembered but thought he could help Steve establish boundaries. Steve had developed a relationship with a senior girl at that high school, and they were planning to marry that summer. He was terminated from that job also.

This made me curious because Steve had already been in place for two years when I came to be his principal and superintendent. I looked through his files and called his previous employer who confirmed that there were some questions about improper relationships at that school also. None of that information was in his record. Since researching Steve's work history, I have concluded that a leopard doesn't change his spots, even if he changes location. Probing questions became a staple of my research on references from that time on. I was also determined to give full disclosure to anyone checking references on one of my employees.

Several years later after moving on to another school, I was informed by the high school principal that we had a problem with a long-time teacher and coach. Some of the girls were complaining that he was a bit handsy with the girls in the hallways. He was prone to slap the girls on the butt and tell them they were doing a good job. The girls liked him and didn't want him to get in trouble, but they were offended by the physical contact. That had also happened to some of the girls who were managers for the football team.

The principal and I met with Randy and told him what we had heard. He didn't deny anything but said he was just friendly, and he would stop the touching. We explained that the girls didn't see it that way. We also had some parents complaining as well. They wanted him terminated. There were no other charges other than the slapping on the butt, so we didn't have a lot to go on.

After visiting with the board of education, we decided that Randy needed to move on. There was not enough to bring any charges, but we were not going to tolerate his behavior. We reached an agreement that he would be suspended for the rest of the year with pay and would then resign.

That summer I received a call from a neighboring district that was checking references on Randy. I told them about the situation and said he had been asked to resign. They were not too concerned about his behavior because they ended up hiring him. Later, he became an administrator at the district, and nothing was heard about him for several years. About five years later word came back that he had been removed as an administrator for similar activities. Some people never learn.

I was determined to give all relevant information to anyone checking references. After discussing this with school attorneys, I was told you could tell them anything factual. However, if you can't prove it, you could be liable for damages if that person doesn't get the job. I worried about this, but when someone calls me about a reference, I ask them to keep our conversation confidential. I tell them anything that might be relevant to that person's employment. Most incidents of inappropriate contact do not rise to the level of criminal acts. Nevertheless, they are of great concern. I did not want someone accusing me of withholding information that might result in a student getting hurt. This is why I disclose all relevant information.

But those were the rare cases of teachers violating boundaries with students. Most of the time the relationships are perfectly innocent. Despite the sensational cases we hear about, most teachers care deeply about their students and will go out of their way to help them. Sometimes this invites criticism, but if a teacher can help a kid, they will generally risk that judgment.

The occasional termination was always a difficult task. Sometimes it had nothing to do with improper behavior. It could simply be a performance issue. John was an orchestra instructor who taught at elementary through high school level. He had been a good instructor at one time, but as he got older, he began to lose the interest of students. The program was shrinking, and he was not always showing up on time.

This was a program that was highly valued in the community and parents were becoming restless. I approached John in the middle of the year and asked him when he planned to retire. He said he thought he might go in a few years. I told him there were some complaints and that it was time to retire now. He said he would think about it but didn't believe he was ready. We began tracking his tendency to come late to the buildings, and when this was pointed out to him, he decided he was ready to retire. I needed to apply pressure, but it was clear it was time for him to go. Fortunately, we were able to find a quality replacement, and the program soon flourished again.

Jean was a district administrator who had been in the district before I became superintendent. In the early years, I depended on her to familiarize me with the curriculum and the staff. We had a good relationship, and she was doing her job. She had been in the district for a considerable amount of time and seemed to know everyone in town. I relied on her judgment for many issues including information about staff.

After several years, some negativity began to creep into her demeanor. She criticized people whom I perceived as doing a good job. As I became more familiar with the community and staff, I was figuring out for myself who were the most valuable employees.

At board meetings, she regularly gave a report on her area of expertise. While giving these reports, she began contradicting some things that I had told the board. Board members noticed this and asked me about it. I told them I was aware of the problem and would address the issue with her. We had what I call a "come to Jesus" meeting. She was told that the negativity needed to end, and it was noted in her evaluation.

Over time she reverted to the same negative behavior. The board unanimously recommended that I terminate her. However, we were in the middle of a huge construction project. I informed the board that I didn't have time for the drama that would ensue. I wanted to wait until the next year. They agreed, and we postponed that conversation.

Finally, at a board meeting, I was giving a report on the number of non-English speaking students in our district. I explained to the board how many we had and said that the number had remained steady in the past few years. When Jean gave her report, she directly contradicted me indicating that our numbers had increased dramatically. I knew this was not accurate because I handled that aspect of our curriculum. Board members were startled and noticed the contradiction in our reports. In the next board report, I provided the exact numbers for the past several years. As I had indicated, the numbers had remained steady.

That was the last straw for me. The board was notified that I would be advising her that her contract would not be renewed. She was angry and tried to generate support among the staff for her position. Most staff wanted nothing to do with the controversy. She then requested a meeting with the board to propose a contract buyout. The board refused, and she was terminated at the end of that year. That was an unpleasant termination which dragged out much longer than it should have.

Most of my experiences with terminations were handled professionally by both sides. It is never easy, but if you can do it without demeaning the individual, it can be a growth experience. Matt was a principal who had done a good job for several years. He had accomplished what we asked him to do originally. After several years we sensed he was losing support from his staff. There were also a few incidents that I felt were handled poorly. We had a good personal relationship, and I was very blunt with him in his evaluations.

Finally, it was obvious to the board and me that it was time for a change. When he became principal, we asked him to tighten up the discipline. He had made significant improvements in that area. We were pleased with that aspect, but we needed our staff to improve the rigor of their instruction. Matt was not the right fit for that job. He was surprised and disappointed when he was told his contract would not be renewed.

Matt still had another year on his contract, and a settlement was negotiated. He was unhappy about the situation. I stressed to him that this would not derail his career. He would have plenty of opportunities for good jobs. He just needed to find the right fit.

At the time, this was of no comfort to him. However, he found another good position and is now doing very well. Sometimes it is not about the talent of the person in the job. In some cases, a very talented person may just not be the right fit. This was the case with Matt. Similar things had happened to me in my career when I did not get jobs I had applied for. It took me a while to understand that it was not necessarily a deficiency on my part. I just didn't fit what was needed.

Another example of not being a good fit involved a young math teacher. Josh had been a salutatorian at his high school and had outstanding grades in college. He was a first-year teacher at our high school. Unfortunately, he was teaching some of the lower level math classes and students could not relate to him. He had always been a motivated student and could not adjust to the unmotivated students he was dealing with. After a rough year, it was a mutual decision for Josh to move on. In the right situation, I was sure he would be a good teacher. The position he was in was not a good fit for him.

Sometimes there are uncomfortable conversations that need to take place. At one time I had an older physical education teacher, Mr. Wilmington, who was great with the kids. He coached most sports at the middle school and was highly respected. I was shocked when the principal came to me with a report from one of his students. The student indicated that the teacher was in the bathroom at the urinal next to the student. He said that after the teacher finished, he stroked his penis several times and it made the student very uncomfortable.

The principal and I couldn't believe that Mr. Wilmington would do anything inappropriate, but he had to discuss the incident with him. When the principal had the discussion, he was told that the teacher had prostate issues and he needed to do this to avoid dribbling in his pants. Later, as I became older and developed prostate problems myself, I understood exactly what he was talking about. This is why we have faculty only bathrooms.

The staff in a board office have a special bond. They deal with a multitude of issues with the board, the public, building staff, and students. Many of the issues are sensitive in nature and must remain confidential, such as personnel issues. However, most of the business that goes on at the board office is part of public record and is available to anyone. It is important to know the difference.

My personal secretary, Carla, was the consummate professional. She had served as secretary to the community college president and to my predecessor as superintendent and then throughout my term until she retired. Her experience helped her understand what was confidential and what was public information. She also took great pride in any written material that came from the board office.

I considered myself a good writer and usually proofread anything that was sent out to the staff or the public. When I gave it to Carla to disseminate, she occasionally suggested some improvement in the presentation. Sometimes this was a bit irritating, but most of the time she was right. It became sort of a game between us to see if I could write things in which she could not find any mistakes.

Because of her experience, Carla was also excellent about providing warnings when some report or project was due. She kept me out of a lot of trouble this way. She also notified teachers when their licenses needed to be renewed. It was surprising how frequently teachers let their licenses lapse.

One teacher had received several notices from Carla that his license was up for renewal in eighteen months. To renew, a teacher had to accumulate continuing education credits or complete graduate level courses. This teacher waited until the last two months before getting serious about renewing. Then he requested that the district allow him to use the school vehicle to get to a college to take summer classes to fulfill the requirement. He was reminded that he had received several notices from Carla starting eighteen months earlier. He complained that he and his wife had only one car and he couldn't afford the rent to live at the college for two months.

It was explained to him that it was his responsibility to take care of this and he could not use a school vehicle. Somehow, he worked it out and had his license renewed just in the nick of time. Carla and I shook our heads in wonder why renewing his license wasn't urgent enough for him to take care of it promptly.

The office staff always dreaded when the inevitable irate parent came into the board office to complain about something. Parents were often loud and clearly angry and said something like,

"I want to talk to that damned superintendent."

The staff was anxious to get such people out of the main office and in to see me. I teased them that I looked forward to seeing these parents because it was a challenge to calm them down. They responded that they were anxious to send them to me. They didn't want anything to do with the angry constituents.

When school shootings became more common, we talked about the safety of our office staff. It would be easy for an angry person to come in with a gun. I jokingly told the rest of the staff that they didn't have to worry because I would be the one they wanted to shoot. However, we did have a back door to get out of my office if something like this happened. Eventually, we locked the outside door with a bell to ring and a camera to identify the individual. We used the same security measures we used in the school buildings. It is a sad state of affairs when you must go to these lengths, but unfortunately, it is necessary.

There were also times when we had to provide information to someone who had a complaint. A teacher named Jane who had been terminated before I came to the district, occasionally showed up to complain about her treatment. She had originally taken sick leave for mental health issues but had eventually been terminated. She came in five years later and told me she wanted her entire personnel file. By law, we had to provide this to her. I told her that we would copy it and have it ready for her the next day. She made it clear that she wanted the file to bring a lawsuit against the district for wrongful termination.

When I reviewed the file, there was nothing that indicated her termination had been done on unlawful grounds. When she came in the next day, she complained that there must be more information in her file. She alleged that there had been several instances of mistreatment. I told her this is all we had. There was no more information about her case, and what was in it took place before I was in the district. She was angry and let me know that we would hear from her lawyer. We never heard from her again. As stated earlier, if I had a dollar for every time I have been threatened with a lawsuit, I would be a rich man.

Sometimes there are confidential issues in the board office that are not to be shared outside of that office. There were a few instances where things got out that created controversies among staff outside of the office. On those occasions, reminders had to be issued to board office staff that it was not their prerogative to take things outside the walls.

A board office staff develops close bonds because they deal with important issues and are the face of the school district. The staff I dealt with always took their responsibilities seriously. We were in the foxhole together. When one of them retired, it was a sad occasion and difficult to break in a new person. When Carla retired a year before me, I was really concerned. Fortunately, we were able to find a very capable replacement, although she lacked the institutional knowledge that Carla had.

One of the highlights of working with the staff was awarding the Teacher of the Month. A local car dealership wanted to do something to recognize quality teachers and get some advertising for the business. They came up with the idea of donating the use of a brand-new car for one month for the Teacher of the Month. Other local businesses joined in on the presentation, and they provided flowers, coupons, free dinners, and other rewards.

After developing some criteria, we had students nominate a teacher from each building every month. We then had a random drawing to pick a monthly winner from a jar with the names of all the nominees. When the winner was chosen, the principal of the building was notified and set up a time to surprise the teacher while she was with students. The teacher was always stunned when I walked into the classroom and announced to the students that their teacher was Teacher of the Month. It was touching to see how proud the students were of their teacher. Teacher and students then went outside to take a picture in front of the new car. The picture was placed in the local newspaper.

The elementary students were especially fun to watch. They were giddy about the award and often wanted to ride around the parking lot in the new car with the teacher. Seeing the smiles all around was one of the highlights of every month.

One month the winner was a long-time teacher who had announced her retirement at the end of that school year. She was a farm girl who was accustomed to driving old farm vehicles around. We decided to play a trick on her. The dealership came up with a beat up, rusted out truck as her prize. When we took her out to see what she thought was a new vehicle everyone had a good laugh at the sight of the old truck. She said she was fine with that. She was used to driving old farm trucks anyway. Soon the dealer came around the block with a brand-new car, and the old truck was taken back to the used car lot.

———

One of the most successful learning experiences we provided for teachers was the practice of classroom walkthroughs. This was a technique in which a team observed several classrooms for five minutes. The team had a checklist and marked the effective teaching practices that they observed at that time. This was done in at least twenty classrooms per quarter by each team, and the cumulative data was compiled. These walkthroughs were not used to evaluate individual teachers. They were used to analyze how frequently researched effective practices were being used in that building. Most of these practices related to the higher levels of thinking as identified in Bloom's Taxonomy.*

The checklist was developed by teachers and administrators.

*Bloom, Dr. Benjamin, Bloom's Taxonomy of Learning Domains

It identified several research-based best teaching practices. When these practices were witnessed by the team, they were recorded over those five minutes. The walkthroughs gave us a broad look at teaching throughout the district.

The goal behind the technique was for teachers to become more conscious of research-based practices that enhance student learning and incorporate them into their lessons. At professional development meetings, the teachers discussed these practices and shared ways they each applied them in the classroom.

It was difficult for teachers to adjust to walkthroughs at first because they couldn't display many practices in such a short time. They felt the walkthroughs were going to affect their formal evaluation negatively. However, we emphasized that walkthroughs were not evaluations. They provided only a brief snapshot of their teaching, and the snapshots of many throughout a building were grouped. The value of the exercise was the compilation of data to improve classroom effectiveness.

When this practice was first implemented, the visiting team was comprised of administrators. Because of the outstanding teaching that was witnessed we quickly realized that this was a great learning tool for teachers, so they were added to the teams. It was amazing to watch the teachers witness so many outstanding practices in many classrooms. The team members took what they saw back to their classrooms and implemented them. Our teaching was raised to a higher level as a result of this practice. Higher level learning was becoming more frequent. It also gave the other administrators and me an opportunity to get into more classrooms and compile helpful data.

The data that was compiled from walkthrough visits was used to determine our professional development. The areas in which we were deficient were selected for more training. As we continued to compile data the increase in the incidents of effective teaching practices was dramatic.

My chapter titled "Back to School," chronicles the semester in which I returned to the classroom after retirement as superintendent. On several occasions, the walkthrough teams visited my classroom. When they did, I immediately became very conscious of using effective practices and soliciting higher level thinking skills. I chuckled at myself about the impetus the visits gave me to use best practices. It was effective.

Working with the staff was the most rewarding and the most frustrating part of the job of superintendent. The frustrating part of dealing with staff is when there are performance issues. Inspiring, advising, and directing staff members who are only doing their jobs to receive a paycheck is fruitless. Others are simply not competent for the job they are assigned. Sometimes they are just not a good fit. Such situations are difficult to handle, but I always asked myself one question when faced with decisions about fit:

"Is this person contributing to student learning?"

The rewarding part is working with so many talented teachers, paraprofessionals, administrators, and office staff. Being the person in charge is humbling. I learned far more from them than they learned from me. The ability of teachers to manage a classroom of 25 kids of any age and keep them engaged and learning is rare. Many people might think teaching is easy, but few can do it effectively. The ones who do are not paid enough.

14

THE JOB: THE TOUGHEST JOB YOU WILL EVER LOVE

Eskridge was a small town of around 250 people. This was one of three small towns in the Mission Valley District when I first became superintendent. It was an hour drive to the nearest city, and there was very little recreation for kids outside of school activities.

Maisie Devore was a lady who wanted to provide recreation for the kids in town. Maisie hated the fact that the kids had to go so far to enjoy a pool. She decided that she would get a pool for the kids of Eskridge, so she started a drive to raise money in the 1970s.

Maisie had little money of her own, but she began collecting aluminum cans to raise funds. People began to call her 'Crazy Maisie" because they thought she could never raise enough for a pool. Those who believed in her called her 'Amazing Maisie.' By 2001 she had raised $83,000, and the community got a $100,000 grant from the state and construction began. Maisie received a national Community Service award for this accomplishment. In 2001, at the pool opening, I was asked to address the crowd and give the signal for the kids to jump in.

Noticing the anxious anticipation of the kids I kept my remarks short. Eighty-year-old Maisie was in her swimsuit as she gingerly entered the pool on the steps. The pool was completely lined with kids chomping at the bit to get wet. Finally, when Maisie got down the steps, I gave the signal.

"OK kids. Jump in," I yelled.

Splashes of water hit me, and kids screamed with joy as they flung

themselves into the pool. I have seldom seen such pure, unadulter-
ated joy in my life. It was thirty years in the making, but 'Amazing
Maisie' had come through for these kids. In all my years as a superintendent that may have been my most enjoyable moment.

The reason this chapter is titled "The Toughest Job You Will Ever
Love" is because of the tremendous variety of issues that a superintendent deals with. You are confronted with so many issues, granted
so many opportunities, and meet so many amazing people that every
day is different. That's what I enjoyed so much about the job. I would
never have been picked to be the master of ceremonies for the pool
opening if I weren't in this position!

In my first year at Independence, I was asked to judge the Neewollah chili contest. Neewollah is a huge festival (Halloween spelled
backward) in Independence. It runs for two weeks and includes a
popular chili cook-off. Everyone wanted to meet the new superintendent in that first few months, so they asked me to be a judge. What a
great treat for a true chili aficionado. The only problem is that I ate so
much chili that I got sick that evening. But it was worth it!

Every small town has some festival like this, and the superintendent in a small town is a celebrity. You get asked to join many different organizations and get invited to all the great parties. This is one
of the many benefits of the position.

At the same time, you are in the public eye and can be criticized mercilessly. I always remembered the story from Bob, my first
mentor as superintendent. He got his first superintendent job in a
small town in Nebraska. With the increase in salary, he immediately bought a shiny new Corvette. According to his story, that really
rubbed some people the wrong way, and he was never fully accepted.

The superintendent may be one of the highest paid persons in
a small town. That can cause some envy and resentment. There are
always those people who are critical of anyone in a position of authority, and every superintendent gets some of that. But most people
respect the position and assume you know what you are doing until
you prove otherwise. That's why you get so many fun opportunities
like judging the chili contest, giving the order to jump in the pool, or
having Mary and I invited to participate in a local Dancing with the

Stars contest.

Being an avid University of Kansas sports fan, I was privileged to receive some great seats at the games provided by friends in the community. They had no expectations of any favor in return. They just wanted to be friendly. One good friend, Ray, regularly took a group of people to the games because he wanted to pick their brains all the way up about community issues. I was more than willing to have my brain picked for good seats.

As recounted in some of the other chapters, superintendents are involved in the legislative process as actively as they want to be. This allows you to meet many elected officials. Because of involvement in this process, I was able to be part of critical meetings with other school officials and legislative leaders. Sometimes these meetings could become adversarial, but you were at the highest levels of decision making.

One of the most meaningful organizations I was involved in was the Independence Diversity, Task Force. This group did some significant outreach in our community and made available some community changing diversity training. The members of this committee were able to access some incredibly insightful trainers that helped us understand the issue at a much deeper level. One trip with a group of educators to Chicago was especially helpful. I finally gained insight into what was meant by "white privilege."

All the conventions and conferences had great presenters about educational issues as well as items of personal interest. The author of the book Always Take the Stairs inspired me to be more conscious of exercise in my life. I was able to witness the emotional play Life in a Jar. This is the story of Irena Sendler, a Polish woman who saved thousands of Jews during the Holocaust. The story was developed by high school students at Uniontown, Kansas when they researched her life as a history day project. They eventually went to Europe to meet her.

I had the privilege of singing in a choir of superintendents at the National Association of School Boards convention. And every year we heard a presentation by the Kansas Teacher of the Year and the Superintendent of the Year. One enjoyable presentation was by the

"Cooking Superintendent." He explained how he used cooking to relieve stress. The food samples were incredible, but his obesity made me wonder if he wasn't adding to the stress on his heart. I heard Kent Rader a couple of times with his billing as "The World's Cleanest Comedian." His humor was a great stress reduction tool.

I was privileged to join a group of superintendents who journeyed to Washington, D.C. to lobby our congressional delegation on education issues. We experienced a magnificent view at a rooftop reception overlooking the Capitol. The scene was breathtaking.

One of the most amazing opportunities was touring schools in China. The Confucius Institute is a Chinese educational organization that promotes Chinese language and cultural cooperation between China and the rest of the world. Through that organization we offered Mandarin Chinese language class at Independence High School. To further promote their language efforts they provided a trip to American educators to tour Chinese schools.

We were escorted around the country and visited with school administrators, teachers and students. It was impressive to see that most Chinese students could speak English because they started learning that language in pre-school. The emphasis on education as a way to build the economy and propel that country into a world economic power was impressive. It helped me gain some perspective on the American educational system.

The friendships developed in this job bring smiles to my face. Our colleagues learned, partied, worked and cried together. The most fun times were when one's rank at work did not make a difference. There were a few after-school sessions at the bar. For some reason, the superintendent was always expected to buy a round.

Special memories were the times we had scavenger hunts with staff during Christmas break. Items were hidden at different homes of teachers, administrators, and parents. We carpooled to each site and were treated to refreshments at each house. I hid behind my fence when they came to my house and scared the daylight out of several teachers.

One time, we decided to play a trick on the middle-school principal. With a group of teachers and administrators in the background,

I called Patty, the principal.

"Patty, some of your staff was having a party and a scavenger hunt. They were too loud, and someone called the police," I told her. "Several have been arrested and are down at the police station," I continued.

"Oh my gosh! What should I do?" she asked.

"They need you to come down to the station to bail them out," I said.

"OK, I guess I can go down there," she answered hesitantly.

Before we got any further, we could not contain the laughter. The whole group was cracking up.

"We got you, Patty," they screamed into the phone.

It's possible there may have been some alcohol involved that night.

At every stop in my superintendency, we organized pickup basketball games. I love to play basketball, and it was always easy to get some middle-aged men together to play. At Mission Valley, there was a regular Sunday game. This included high school students and up to adults in their 70s. It was supposed to be for fun, but frequently our competitiveness took over, and the games got contentious. Of course, no one ever admitted to fouling, and if someone missed a shot, it was always because they were fouled. Dick, our organizer, and former teacher is still participating after retirement and well into his 70s.

Many of us looked forward to these games with great anticipation and wouldn't miss them for anything. We older guys were trying to maintain our pride against the younger set. Occasionally, we had a few very athletic young women playing with us. They would often guard the older guys, and we would guard the women. It was a little hard on our egos when they drove around us and scored. My defense was to gross them out. I sweat a lot, and when one of the girls tried to drive on me, I threatened to 'slime' her. This was disgusting to the girls, but it didn't stop them from frequently making me look like an old man.

It was a custom for some of the athletic teams to use a Lift a Thon to raise money for their teams. People pledged a certain amount of money per pound that the competitor lifted in weights. I had been lifting in the mornings so recruited several board members to pledge ten cents a pound on several different lifts. Trying to raise a significant amount of money, I loaded too much on the deadlift bar and threw my back out. As I limped away, the board members said,

"We'll give it anyway."

It cost me more for the chiropractor than I raised in the Lift a Thon.

The beginning of the school year was always a stressful time, but it was exciting to kick off the year. There were several days of staff meetings highlighted by an Opening Convocation. At the Convocation, we had motivational speakers and presented some awards.

It was also a time for the superintendent to address all staff. I was always a bit nervous but excited to do this. There were introductions of new staff members and thanks to those who worked during the summer to get things ready. We especially thanked the maintenance staff and technology for all their summer work. A State of the District report gave information on the budget, legislative activity that affected our school and our latest achievement test scores. The latter was of great interest to the teachers.

I felt it was important to give an inspirational message to the staff. One of my favorites was a quote from Garrison Keillor.

Nothing you do for children is ever wasted. They seem not to notice us, hovering, averting their eyes, and they seldom offer thanks, but what we do for them is never wasted.

Another favorite was a quote from James Michener:

The master in the art of living makes little distinction between his work and his play, his labor, and his leisure, his mind and his body, his information and his recreation, his love and his religion. He hardly knows which is which. He simply pursues his vision of excellence at whatever he does, leaving others to decide whether he is working or playing. To him, he is always doing both.

I also tried to inject humor into situations. I felt it was important to be able to laugh at ourselves. Some of the funniest were samples from student work. One time I used analogies and metaphors that students had developed. Some samples:

"The little boat drifted across the pond, exactly the way a bowling ball wouldn't."

"Long separated by cruel fate, the star-crossed lovers raced across the grassy field toward each other like two freight trains, one having left Cleveland at 6:36 p.m. traveling at 55 mph, the other from Topeka at 4:19 p.m. at 35 mph."

Student essays were another favorite. Some of the more humorous ones include:

"Queen Elizabeth was the Virgin Queen. As a queen, she was a success. When she exposed herself before her troops, they all shouted, 'Hurrah.'"

From a child's understanding of the Bible we had:

"Another important Bible guy was Moses, whose real name was Charlton Hesston. Moses led the Israel Lights out of Egypt and away from the evil Pharaoh after God sent ten plagues on Pharaoh's people. These plagues included frogs, mice, lice, bowels, and no cable."

We always tried to have a good laugh at ourselves by emphasizing something about our subjects. For English teachers, we stressed that commas save lives. For example:

"Let's eat Grandma."
"Let's eat, Grandma."

Early on, I developed a theme for the year. It related to something that was being emphasized district-wide. One year when we were in the middle of a large construction project, teachers had to change classrooms a couple of times throughout the year. The theme was "Flexibility." We were going to experience a lot of change anyway, and we might as well be flexible about it.

One year, after completing a large construction project, I suggested a theme of "Reinvent Yourself." The idea was that we had new facilities and it would be a good time to change the things you don't like about your teaching and your image among students. In this way, you reinvent yourself to the students.

Another year, the theme was "Connections." The idea was to connect with students, parents, the community, and other staff. In this way, we would work as a more cohesive unit.

A theme that I used several times was something I developed on my own. I stressed to the teachers that we needed to adjust to whatever the students needed. It was put in these words:

"Whatever we do in this school district is to advance student learning. If it helps to change the way we do things, or if something must be delayed or eliminated or altered, we will not hesitate to do so at our discomfort, if it advances student learning."

Starting the school year with excitement and enthusiasm was important. There would be plenty of disappointments and dull times throughout the year, so we needed to begin on a high note.

State and federal requirements were always a source of stress. No Child Left Behind made everyone irritable including staff and students. We tailored so much of our professional development to meet the standards of NCLB. But even with the stress and extra work, we all became better educators. Our professional development was more specific and focused. We learned an incredible amount about effective teaching practices over the decade under NCLB.

When it seemed like everyone was just worn out with the requirement, a board member suggested we should have an assembly to demonstrate how much we had improved. That turned out to be a great idea. The curriculum director, Kellie and I, outlined all the things we had done and then picked key teachers and administrators to demonstrate our growth. In a two-hour session at the end of the school year, we were surprised by how far we had come. That may have improved morale more than any other action we took.

Do I have any regrets from my career? Of course, there are things I would like to change and situations that could have been handled better. I wish I had taken the time to get a Doctorate in Education. I also wish I had taken the opportunity to drive a bulldozer on some of the construction projects. It would have been a fun experience to push up some dirt with such a powerful piece of equipment. I regret that someone was so bitter that they felt the need to vandalize our brand new construction at Mission Valley. And I regret that it was a constant battle with the legislature to get adequate funding to do the job right. But many of these things I could not control anyway.

There are just too many highlights in my career to dwell on any regrets. The frequent contacts with former students fill my heart with gladness. I recently connected with one of them who is now a firefighter in New York City. Max was a great kid who I see doing great things in his life.

Several years ago I had a hip replacement. When I went in for the pre-surgery routine, the doctor who was administering anesthesia was a former student. I jokingly asked him if I had ever given him detention.

"No, I was always a pretty good kid in school," he said.

"Well, I hope you learned your trade really well, because it's very important to me right now," I replied.

"Don't worry. I've got you covered," he said reassuringly.

A couple of years later I had a knee replacement, and again as I was going through the pre-surgery routine, I met another former student.

"You don't have any resentment toward me, do you?" I questioned.

"No, I was sent to the office a few times, but I always deserved it," he answered.

"That makes me feel much better to know that," I replied.

In 2015, I had announced my retirement as superintendent. I lost my composure as I announced it to the administrative staff at the beginning of the year. The year went faster than I expected and soon it was time for a retirement reception.

My secretary made the arrangements and people were invited to drop in. When I walked into the room for the reception, I told my wife, "This could be kind of embarrassing if no one shows up."

We went into the room and saw that the food service staff had made an artistic cake that had a replica of a diploma from all the schools I had attended. It was a real work of art. And then people began to trickle in. Soon there was a large, boisterous crowd in the room, and I was enjoying greeting everyone and revisiting old stories. It was such a warm feeling to see so many people, and it made me feel loved. I told my wife that it was more than I could have expected.

Then Brad, one of the principals came up and said, "We're just getting started."

He put me in a wheelchair and blindfolded me. Then he strapped a body cam on my forehead and wheeled me into the auditorium. He took off the blindfold, and to my surprise, there were hundreds of teachers, students, and community members cheering. I was overcome with emotion, and all I could mutter was, "I don't deserve this."

The band began playing, and cheerleaders were dancing and doing cheers. As Brad wheeled me to the front, he told me to relax and take it all in. It was an incredible feeling, and it cemented my belief that I had picked the right vocation. The support and appreciation I felt that day filled me with warmth and gratitude.

When I finally walked out the door on my last day of work my emotions were mixed. I was glad to be rid of the stress of the job, but sad to leave all the great co-workers that I had been privileged to encounter. And I was starting a whole new chapter in my life.

Little did I realize that my educational career was not over yet.

15

KIDS SAY THE DARNEDEST THINGS

When I was a kid, there was a television show hosted by Art Linkletter titled "Kids Say the Darnedest Things." Bill Cosby also did a routine in which he asked kids their opinions on a variety of subjects. The responses were hilarious because kids don't have a filter. They say exactly what they think. This is one of the most enjoyable things about being around kids as a teacher and principal.

As a superintendent, I knew that it would take a special effort to develop relationships with the kids. My office was always away from the schools. There is a good reason for this because it is nice not to be interrupted by the daily crises that happen in each school building. However, the downside is that you must make a special effort to get to the schools to connect with students if that is important to you.

Student relationships were something I valued highly. I thought of myself as a better principal than superintendent because I got along well with students and enjoyed that part of education more than working with adults. However, after a certain age, it becomes more difficult for students to relate to an older principal, so it was best for me to move into the superintendency.

Even knowing that, I vowed to stay connected with students. That helped me remember that every decision should be based on how it affects students. That should be the most important determination. To accomplish that end, principals and teachers were aware that I would visit their schools including the classrooms as much as possible. Of course, there are always formal occasions like assemblies and award ceremonies, but I wanted to have personal contact with the students in the classroom.

One of my favorite things to do was to visit the lower elementary classes and read to kids. It was fun reading children's books and putting voice inflection and facial expressions into the reading. Hearing the kids laugh or respond with various emotions was a real high for me. When I became a grandparent reading out loud became important in my personal life as well. My grandkids taught me what kinds of stories are of interest to various age levels.

Dr. Seuss Day was always a favorite. The teachers would usually get the kids in a circle on the floor, and I would sit in a chair in front of them. Wearing a Dr. Seuss hat, I would read his stories to the lower elementary students. It was fun to play with the words that were such a recognizable component of his stories. The kids loved it.

Teachers sometimes get a little nervous when an administrator is in their class. They want their students to be on their best behavior. They sometimes forget that every administrator was also a teacher at one time and understands occasional chaos.

When I was in pre-school or kindergarten classrooms, the kids were particularly squirmy. I didn't mind that at all, but teachers often wanted them to sit quietly in front of me and pay attention. There was always the kid who raised her hand every minute or so to ask a question. Many times the question was completely unrelated to the story, but to that kid it was important.

"My mom is scared of mice," one kid remarked in the middle of a Dr. Seuss book.

That had nothing to do with the story, but it was important that I heard it. After an appropriate acknowledgment, I continued the story.

"My dad and mom had a fight last night," was another one I heard frequently. Sometimes you hear more than you want to know.

"The police came to our house and arrested Dad last night." I didn't want to hear that.

Poor kid is supposed to concentrate on learning today after that trauma.

"I'm going to Grandma's this weekend and we're going to the

zoo," one child remarked with visible excitement.

Some of the most touching occasions were in a pre-school class when one of the kids wanted to crawl up on my lap while I read. The teacher would try to get the child back in the circle, but I would wave them off. Some of these kids were just very affectionate, or they were really lacking attention at home.

"Do you have a cat?" asked a kindergartner while listening to me read about the Three Bears. "Ours ran away last night," she informed me.

"How old are you?" was frequently asked. When I asked them to guess answers ranged from 25 to 100. Of course by the time I was a superintendent I was like their grandpa.

The funniest remarks always came from the little ones. They are blunter than adults. They are curious and have no filter. They often misunderstand the meaning of words and don't understand nuances.

As a superintendent, I dressed formally, usually with a coat and tie. When the little ones saw me come into their classroom, they were curious about who I was. Because I was dressed up, they assumed I must be somebody important.

"Aren't you the president or something?" they asked frequently.

Another common remark was, "Aren't you the president of this town?"

When I explained to the students that I was the superintendent, they didn't understand what that meant. I told them about budgets, hiring teachers, keeping the buildings functioning, etc. They were not impressed with that. It just didn't mean much to them. Finally, I figured out the best way to explain my job as superintendent.

I asked if they knew what a principal is. Of course, they knew who their principals were and understood their job as best an 8 year-old can understand. I then explained,

"The principal is the boss of your school. I am the boss of all the principals."

Their eyes got as big as saucers. In their little minds, they couldn't imagine anyone more important than their principal. That was as high as it got. If I was the 'boss of the principals', that was quite a lofty position.

Usually, when entering a classroom for the first time, the elementary teachers would tell their students that I was the superintendent. As I said earlier, that didn't mean a lot because they didn't understand the school organization. Many times I was asked,

"Don't you own these schools?"

I chuckled and explained that their parents own the schools. As you can imagine, that brought interesting responses. One of the more common ones was: "I'm going to tell mom to ban homework" or "we want no homework and more free days."

My daughter, Sarah, was in college when I became a superintendent. She had been in Catholic Schools all her life and didn't really understand the role of a superintendent. When she asked what this job involved, I explained about budgets, hiring and firing and overseeing the buildings. Her eyes glazed over a bit, but then she asked,

"Who calls snow days?"

When I informed her that was part of my job she perked up and remarked,

"Wow, that's real power."

I had never thought of it that way. But in the minds of school kids, the power to call a snow day is much bigger than the power to hire teachers or set budgets. This power had an immediate impact on them. I would sometimes toy with the kids when snow was in the forecast.

"Do you think we should have a snow day tomorrow?" I teased.

Of course, the answer was always an emphatic "Yes."

When I didn't call a snow day, and they thought there should be one, they let me know. If I were in the schools on those days, the kids would catch me in the halls and give me reasons why we should be out of school. Usually, it had to do with their concern for safety. They told me I was risking their lives by making their parents drive in this terrible weather. They tried their best to make me feel guilty even when the roads were safe despite a little snow.

Even the parents could get nasty about snow days if my call didn't go their way. If there was any snow at all and we didn't call off school, we always got phone calls at the board office.

"If someone gets killed you're going to have a lawsuit on your hands," was a frequently heard comment.

"Who was the idiot who decided to have school today? I'm going to complain to the school board," was another commonly heard remark.

If I got that call, I would tell them, "I am the idiot who did that."

That stopped them for a beat, but they soon went on about how unsafe it was. Of course, if schools were closed because of road conditions, many of the same parents would be out driving around with their kids.

Those on the other side made sure to let me know what an "idiot" I was. Once when school was called off based on a weather forecast, we ended up just having an inch of snow and roads were not bad at all. I got a call from a parent who had just moved here from Michigan.

"What kind of idiot would call school off for one inch of snow? In Michigan, we have school even when we get over two feet. Do you think we are too stupid to know how to drive in snow?"

There wasn't much I could say in that instance. But I can guarantee that parent that if I hadn't called off school, there would still be phone calls accusing me of being an idiot for not calling it.

Even the older kids sometimes blurted out some funny lines. For a while, I drove an old rusted out, beat-up pickup to work. It was in such bad shape that someone played a trick and had the police put an abandoned vehicle notice on it while parked at the board office. I never found out who pulled that stunt.

I drove the pickup to an awards dinner for middle school students. After the dinner, the students saw me leave in my nice suit and get into an old, rusty pickup. One of the boys remarked to Sharon, the counselor, "That's not right that the president of our schools is driving an old truck like that. We should get him a better vehicle."

The beginning of the school year is always an emotional time for kindergartners. They are excited, but some are also scared. It is not unusual to see the child ready to go to school and a kindergartner's mom crying uncontrollably. There is usually at least one "runner." Occasionally, a kindergartner can't take being away from home, sneak out the door and try to run home. We always kept a close eye on them early in the year, but occasionally one slipped out unnoticed. The scary part was when a child wanders around, because at that age they can't find their way home.

On the first day or two of school in the kindergarten classroom, teachers get to know the students and students bond with the teacher. Elementary kids often mistakenly call their teacher "mom" because they truly become like a mom away from home.

In the excitement of the first days of school, some kids are so distracted that they forget their names. One year, the students came back from recess, and a little girl returned to the wrong kindergarten classroom. The teacher whose classroom she should have been in got worried and alerted the office about a missing student. Concerned that we had lost one, all kindergarten classes were directed to take roll to check if anyone was missing. The missing girl was in the wrong classroom, and when the teacher called the name of an absent girl, this girl responded "Present." Since the students were so new, the teacher wasn't sure of the identity of the girl. Thankfully, before police were called to do a search, a student pointed out to the teacher that the girl who called out "Present" was not who she said she was. She was the missing student.

It is not unusual for a staff member or the principal to address a new student and ask them who they are. They may stutter and because of nervousness be unable to come up with their name. Most teachers or principals are aware enough to calm the child at which point she remembers her name.

Not all the children are so shy. Some have already developed self-sufficient independence.

A new kindergarten teacher, Brett, was just getting the school year started. He had great potential but was very inexperienced. One day as his students were lined up in the hallway waiting to go to lunch one of his kindergartners saw that there were a lot of other kids ahead of them in line. He bluntly turned to Brett and confidently stated,

"Looks like we're going to be here awhile. I'm going to go take a crap."

Later Brett told me he didn't know how to respond. He didn't want his students talking so coarsely, but he was sure this kid heard that talk at home all the time and didn't see anything wrong with it. We laughed about the incident and Brett went on to become a master teacher.

Like most principals, our elementary principal used lunchtime to get to know the kids. Brad was always highly visible at lunchtime and carried on conversations with the little ones. One day Billy, a first grader, came to Brad and said,

"The kid next to me stinks. It's so bad that the smell is following me around even when I move away from him."

Brad checked on the student he was referring to and didn't notice anything out of the ordinary. Finally, when back in class Billy told one of his teachers,

"The smell from that kid is still following me around."

The teacher noticed the smell also and suggested to Billy that he might have had an accident in his pants and that he should go to the bathroom and check.

Sure enough, Billy came back and said,

"Yep, you were right. I pooped on myself." He had cleaned himself up as best he could. Mom had to be called to bring some clean clothes.

I have always enjoyed the slightly ornery kids who are honest when they get caught doing something wrong. The honest kids and I generally developed a pretty good relationship, and when they came to my office there was a mutual understanding. If they told me the truth, I usually went easier on them than the ones who denied everything.

One young man, Cory, was a regular visitor to my office when I was an assistant principal. It was never anything serious, but he just wasn't very good at not getting caught. I developed a good relationship with him as well as his frustrated mother. Whenever she got a call from me her first words were,

"What did he do this time?"

One day I noticed a lot of students walking around the halls with candy, particularly tubes of Smarties. I became suspicious about the sudden appearance of this candy. I didn't understand where so many students would be getting the same candy at the same time?

The concession stand was in one of our classroom buildings. The building sat behind the football stadium, and the stand could be opened on game days to serve spectators. There was a door in the student hallway, but it was always locked. It occurred to me that this might be where the candy was coming from.

I asked a few of the students where they got the Smarties. Several of them mentioned that Cory was selling candy in the hallways. Apparently, he had quite a thriving business. Sure enough, after checking the concession door, I found it had been jimmied.

I took one of the opened tubes of Smarties and called Cory into my office. When he came in, he played it cool as if nothing was wrong. I pulled out my opened tube of Smarties and said,

"Would you like a Smartie, Cory?" as I flipped one to him.

Cory knew he was caught, and he began singing like a bird. He nervously confessed,

"I only took twelve of them, and I was just selling them to other students. The door was open, so I just went in and helped myself."

"Cory," I said, "I didn't even accuse you of anything, but it seems you've confessed anyway."

That was one of my easiest detective jobs. Cory coughed it all up before even being questioned. Of course, mom wasn't very happy with him when I called her about the incident. Cory kept his nose pretty clean for about a year after that incident.

The next year we had about ten students who left school after lunch every day to go to a Vocational-Technical School. Cory was one of those students. They were to go directly to the parking lot from lunch, leave the school grounds, and not return till the school day was over. I usually followed them out the door to observe and make sure no one was speeding out of the parking lot.

One day, I got delayed following them out. Finally, I got out to the parking lot, and as this group of students was walking toward their cars, I noticed someone in the back of a pickup. Suddenly he pulled down his pants and mooned the whole group of boys and girls. I walked toward the pickup staring at Cory's derriere. With his pants still down, he finally turned around and laughed until he saw me right behind him.

"Oh crap," he remarked. "You always catch me every time I do something."

The call to mom met with the usual,

"What the hell did he do now?" She was mortified when I told her about the incident.

The nice thing about kids like Cory was that he always admitted when he did something wrong. We developed a very good relationship, and he eventually graduated in good standing.

You just can't help but be amused by some of the things that kids say. It's refreshing when they blurt out exactly what they mean without applying a filter. I often wonder what things I blurted out to my teachers when I was a kid.

16

DIFFICULT STUDENTS

Throughout my career, I have worked with some very difficult students. In some cases, it didn't turn out well for either of us. In other cases, the outcome was positive. One of the things I tried to keep in mind when dealing with these students was not to let it get personal on my part. There were times I was able to do so and times when I failed in this endeavor.

Often it did become personal for these students since they saw me as the enemy. But I was the adult and had to handle it better than students. However, on occasion, it became personal on my part and most of the time that did not work out well. Most incidents happened early in my administrative career. If there were do-overs, I would certainly have handled some cases differently. Hopefully, my inexperience did not do lasting damage to any student. The learning process caused me to change how I did things after some unsuccessful efforts. Moreover, when the situation turned out well for the student, I learned more about how to deal with difficult students.

Vince became an ongoing challenge. He did everything possible to defy authority, and I'm sure it became personal for him. I tried my best but must admit that it also eventually became personal for me.

Vince was a decent student. He was a rebel and liked by many students. In fact, he was elected Winter Homecoming King by the student body in his senior year. His campaign was based on the fact that this would be a way to stick it to the administration by electing a rebel to this honor. He had a real problem with authority of any kind. He had confrontations with many other teachers and administration in general. However, I became the focal point of his anger.

One of my neighbors had two students attending the school. They were generally pretty good students, and I got along fine with them. However, when their parents were out of town, they frequently had unsupervised parties in their home. In those cases, my home would often be vandalized in some way during and after their parties. The assistant principal who handled disciplinary cases made a good target. Someone at these parties would take the opportunity to harass me when leaving the party. Vince was frequently at these parties.

The most common thing that happened was that my mailbox was knocked off the post. The mailbox was quite a distance from my house, and it was easy to drive by and hit it with a baseball bat or some other object and then flee. This happened so many times, especially after the neighborhood parties, that I attached the mailbox in such a way that it was simple to put it back onto the post. A couple of screws and it was back in place within minutes. However, that didn't lessen the irritation.

Another type of vandalism that happened involved objects being thrown into my yard. One morning I came out to find a rotten turkey lying in the yard. It smelled terrible, and we quickly wrapped it several times to cover the odor and placed it in the trash. Another time my wife and I were hiding behind the bushes as the neighborhood party was breaking up. We were sure we would be vandalized and wanted to catch the culprits. This time someone threw a half-empty whiskey bottle into our yard. It landed just a few feet from my wife. Unfortunately, we couldn't get the license number. This could have done serious damage if it had hit someone. It was pretty good whiskey and my wife, and I had a couple of good drinks that night to stifle our anger.

Finally, in frustration, I openly took down license numbers of all the students who attended the neighbor's unsupervised party. I was obvious about it and made sure they saw me doing so. There was no vandalism that night.

One Halloween night, our whole family went to an away football game. When we returned home, we were shocked to see our daughter's bedroom window knocked in. When we investigated the incident, we found that someone had thrown a pumpkin against the window and knocked the whole frame into her bedroom. This had all of us very upset. It felt like a very personal violation. Of course, there was no way to catch the culprit, but someone knew we would be away from home. This brought me to tears of frustration and anger.

At that time, my sons were occasionally living with us while they were in college. The vandalism became so prevalent that we decided to hide behind a tree across the street and try to catch the vandals. I would take a baseball bat with me, and we would sit in the dark and have some great conversations while drinking a beer and smoking cigars. We seldom caught anyone, but it was good bonding.

One night, near the end of Vince's senior year, my son, Nathan, and I were expecting some action, so we hid out in hopes of catching some vandals. A truck had been cruising the neighborhood, and we were suspicious they were casing the place for another caper. Sure enough, we saw Vince come running from behind some trees. He threw a Molotov cocktail at my pickup sitting in the driveway and then disappeared into the trees. The bottle broke, and the fuel was burning on the driveway underneath the pickup. I ran to smother the flames and told Nathan to chase the culprit. Nathan searched the trees. After extinguishing the fire, I saw the culprit run up the hill and chased him with my bat. Vince was running towards the getaway truck. I was so angry I threw the bat and almost hit the truck, but they got away.

Nathan got in his vehicle and followed them. He got a description of the vehicle and the license number and got a good look at the two in the truck. He followed them for some time as they tried to ditch him. Finally, he decided he had enough information and came back home.

The next day we went to the police department with our information. They identified the owner of the truck, another student named Ben. However, they told me that unless I could positively identify the occupants, there was little they could do. Even if I could identify them, it would be their word against mine. We were frustrated and angry, but there was nothing more we could do so we dropped the case.

Not long after this incident, a bomb threat was called into the school. As we evacuated the students to the lawn, a truck came by with two young people inside, and they threw something onto the lawn. It was the same truck that had been involved in the firebombing. Vince and Ben were mysteriously absent that day, and some students recognized them in the truck. This was before we heard much about school shootings. Later, when school shootings became commonplace, they often began by setting off a fire alarm and then shooting at students as they exited the school.

Vince was relentless in trying to cause as much commotion as possible, but he was smart enough to seldom get caught. This was his senior year, and word got back to me that he was going to disrupt graduation. I met with Vince and his mother, who was always supportive of him, and told them I knew of his plans. I told them that a security guard would be stationed at the end of his row and at the first sign of trouble Vince would be removed. They were angry but rather than deny his plans; they said I had no right to do that.

On graduation day I instructed the guard to stand near his row and watch for any signal from me. I was on the stage with the rest of the administration. About halfway through the ceremony, Vince began to stir and make noise. I made sure he saw me point to the security guard and direct him to go to the end of Vince's row. Suddenly Vince stopped talking and settled down, and we got through the ceremony without incident.

It was a relief to be rid of Vince. I was frustrated with the police department because they had not followed up on my complaint of the firebombing. Sometime later the city attorney's office called me and suggested filing a complaint of harassment against Vince. I didn't think it would do any good because there wasn't enough evidence. I was just glad he was gone and wanted nothing more to do with him. An intern in the office kept pressing the issue and said that he thought this was a winnable case. He finally convinced me to go ahead.

At the trial, Vince and his mother denied everything, and I didn't have enough evidence to the contrary. It became clear to me that the intern had just wanted to get some experience in court. I was angry for letting him talk me into this. As my wife and I walked out of the courthouse, Vince and his mother taunted us. They threatened to sue for harassment.

After his graduation and the trial, I thought we were done with Vince, but he still wasn't finished with his rebellion. It was the custom for the previous Winter Homecoming King and Queen to come back the next year to crown the new royalty. Again, I got word to Vince and his mother that if he didn't follow our rules, he would be denied this privilege. The candidates and the previous year's winners were to be in formal dress. This takes place at halftime of a basketball game. I warned our security guards about the possibility they might have to remove Vince if he didn't follow our rules. True to form he came dressed inappropriately and was already causing a commotion before the ceremony. At my direction, the security guard removed him, and he was not allowed to participate.

That was my last contact with Vince. I have often reflected upon my actions in his regard. My inexperience allowed me to get sucked into a personal vendetta which made the situation worse. I violated my principle of not taking it personally, but that was hard to do after all the personal attacks he made on me. I made a few overtures to try to win him over, but he was determined to fight me every step of the way. The fact that his mother made excuses for him every time just made things worse. She became very hateful towards me and no doubt some of his actions were encouraged by her.

All I can do is hope that Vince eventually came out alright. He was smart enough and talented enough to be successful at just about anything he wanted to do. Some years later I tried to reach out to him via Facebook. He never responded.

Another particularly difficult student in my first experience as an assistant principal was a young man named Miles. He was an outstanding football player who was a good teammate but could be a bully to the rest of the student body. Miles was frequently in my office for minor offenses, mostly having to do with the uniform dress code. However, by his junior year, the offenses were getting more serious. He shoved people in the hallways and was occasionally defiant to teachers, particularly female teachers. Most of the student body was afraid of Miles, so they did not report incidents with him very often.

With the frequency of Miles' visits to my office, I got to know his dad well. At first, we got along well. He acknowledged that Miles could be a handful and said he would work with me. I also tried to work with the football coach to help Miles stay out of trouble. The coach expressed support but seldom enforced any consequences. The coach was one of the few adults Miles respected, so he never saw any of the problems.

As Miles' transgressions became more frequent and more serious, his dad began to take an adversarial position with me. He frequently excused Miles' behavior and accused me of picking on him. Dad had good relationships with some board members and was very close to the football coach. I found out he was using those relationships to undermine my standing with the board.

Finally, on a routine drug dog inspection of vehicles in the parking lot, Miles' vehicle was identified as a positive hit. After receiving permission to search, we found marijuana residue and a knife. Both were serious violations of the school's disciplinary code. A meeting was held with the parents and administration, and it was determined that Miles would be suspended with a very strict contract if he returned to school. The contract stated that any disciplinary referral, no matter how minor, would result in Miles being expelled.

A few weeks after his return to school Miles punched in a locker door in anger about something. Dad again tried to explain it away, but the administration held firm, and he was expelled. By this time dad was in full attack mode on me. He had talked to several board members about firing me. What he did not know was that I already had a contract for the next school year. Miles transferred to a public school and graduated on time. His dad made it a point to tell everyone that his experience in that school was wonderful and no one picked on him.

The situation with Miles would not have escalated if we could have handled things differently. I tried just about everything to save him from getting into serious trouble, including working with the football coach and his dad. Miles was a lot like his dad in that he was stubborn and refused to accept responsibility. I tried to appeal to his dad and felt that if dad had worked with the school, we could have avoided such a negative outcome. Dad had even kicked Miles out of his house because he wouldn't obey house rules. I told dad that if he wouldn't put up with Miles' disrespect at home, what made him think we should put up with it at school. But dad was not willing to support the school in our disciplinary actions.

A few years later, Miles's name appeared in the records section of the newspaper. He had gotten into serious trouble with the law and was arrested. That didn't surprise me at all. About a year after that I saw Miles' dad in a restaurant. He acknowledged me and was friendly. I wanted to ask him how his son was doing but didn't feel it was appropriate in that setting. A couple of years later the football coach went to work for Miles' dad's construction company. That caused me to question the coach's sincerity when I had tried to work with Miles and his dad. Years later, a former teacher who knew Miles informed me that his behavior hadn't changed.

Chris was a young man who came to our school while I was a high school principal. His parents were separated, and he was living with dad until his dad was sent to jail. He then came to live with mom and stepdad. Chris had a chip on his shoulder from the first time I met him, but he told me he wasn't going to turn out like his dad. I knew about his circumstances so never took his actions personally.

Early on, there was little disciplinary trouble. Chris kept to himself, but he was doing poorly academically. It was obvious he was a bright kid, but he didn't care about getting an education. Chris was a very talented wrestler, but because of his poor grades, he was ineligible to compete. I had stressed to him that he needed to get acceptable grades to participate in wrestling but to no avail. He thought we would make some kind of exception for him. When the time came for wrestling season, and he was told he could not participate, things took a downward turn. He lost something he was good at that he enjoyed.

He began to have minor incidents of disrespect toward teachers and had a few conflicts with students. I suspected Chris was also using drugs but had no proof. After a fight with another student, Chris was given an in-school suspension. The suspension room was in the administrative suite next to the bookkeeper's office. She had the responsibility to keep an eye on the suspended student while he was supposed to be doing school work. I visited with him about his behavior, but he expressed no regret for his actions.

The bookkeeper had to leave the office during lunchtime to take payments and tickets. During that time, Chris was unsupervised. When the bookkeeper returned to her office, she counted the lunch money and put $300 in an envelope in a desk drawer. Sometime during the afternoon, she left to use the restroom.

When she returned, she had reason to check on the lunch money and discovered it was gone. She immediately came to tell me what had happened. No one else had been in her office during the afternoon, so we figured that Chris was the only person who could have gone in there during the time she left.

I confronted Chris, and he vehemently denied having anything to do with the missing money. I had him empty his pockets, but nothing was found. The more I questioned him, the more obstinate he became. We knew he had to be responsible because he was the only other person who had access to that room. Finally, I told him we were going to strip search him. Another male teacher, Bill, was brought in as a witness because of concerns about liability. I had just recently read about a school that had done a strip search of a student and was sued when they found nothing on her person.

Chris was asked to remove each article of clothing and then it was searched. Finally, he was down to his underwear and socks. Despair was setting in as I envisioned seeing myself in a lawsuit. I was dreading getting to the point of taking off the underwear. While still in his underwear he was told to remove his socks. He took off one sock and looked at us as if to say,

"OK, you got me."

We then had him remove the other sock. Sure enough, we found $300 hidden in that sock. There wasn't much he could do to deny that. I went to make a call to his parents and left him in the room with Bill. After calling the parent, I returned to the outer office, and Bill asked to talk to me privately. Bill informed me that after I left the room, Chris made the statement,

"I'm going to get a gun and shoot that principal guy."

This was shortly after the Columbine massacre and several other school shootings. School administrators had been advised to take any threat seriously. Bill and I decided that this was a direct threat, so we called the Sheriff's Department and made a report. They came right to the school and arrested Chris for making a 'terroristic threat.'

Later that year, Chris had a hearing before a judge and was convicted for making the threat. Shortly after this the judge called me and asked if I had any recommendations for sentencing. He also wanted to know if we would accept Chris back into school. The judge thought he would only get into more trouble if he were not in school. Chris had been expelled for 365 days which was the guideline in state statute. I told him Chris would be accepted back in school that fall if he went to regular drug counseling, submitted to drug tests and performed community service throughout the summer. The judge made this his sentencing recommendation.

That fall, Chris was accepted because he had followed the judge's requirements. He still had a hostile attitude toward me but had no further trouble in school. He bragged that he would show me that he could make his grades and be eligible for wrestling. He thought I didn't want him to succeed. Once when he had to see me about a minor issue, I told him,

"You are going to be my project. I'm going to see you graduate."

He bristled at that remark and said he hated me. However, he did make his grades and was eligible for wrestling that year. Bill was the wrestling coach and told me Chris was a hard worker and loved wrestling. Every time I saw Chris in the hallways, he gave me a hateful stare, but he stayed out of trouble. The next year he made it to the state tournament in wrestling and graduated on time. I had been promoted to superintendent that year and had little contact with him by then. Bill told me that Chris had remarked several times that he would "show that Schmidt guy he could do it." I couldn't have been more pleased.

After spending 14 years in the superintendency and retiring, the new superintendent asked me if I would fill a sixth-grade teaching position on an interim basis until they could find a full-time teacher. I accepted the position after all those years out of the classroom and returned to daily contact with students. Even in that position, there were still a few who presented serious daily challenges. A couple of students tested my patience and ability not to take their actions personally.

LeBron was a large African American boy who had developed a reputation as defiant and disruptive. Some of the female teachers got along alright with him, but he was particularly difficult with male teachers. I later found out that there were no stable male role models in his life, and he may have been resentful of that fact.

At any rate, LeBron challenged me from the start. He would throw his books on the desk, make loud, sometimes obscene comments and harass other students. When I asked him to stop, he would ignore me. He made it almost impossible to conduct my first-hour class because he was constantly disruptive. It was as if he decided he would be in charge of the classroom. I tried everything I could think of but eventually had to send him out of the room to restore order.

The assistant principal and I decided to call his mom in for a talk. She came willingly and confessed that she had no control over him at home either. He had spent the summer at his dad's house and came back even more defiant. She stated that she was afraid of him. She told us she feared he might kill her some night.

We discussed getting him into a hospital with intense inpatient counseling, but mom was not able to do that. She did have him going to a local counselor regularly. LeBron's behavior continued to deteriorate until he was given an out-of-school suspension. There was some relief on my part that it was because of actions with another teacher and the assistant principal rather than because of my referrals.

After LeBron came back from the suspension, I had a good visit with him. He was a good reader and liked to read library books. He was also above average in intelligence. In our discussion, I indicated he could eventually go to college and make something very productive of his life if he didn't let his behavior get in the way. He enjoyed hearing that, but some mental health issues just kept interfering with any progress.

Eventually, I reached somewhat of an accommodation with LeBron where he didn't become too disruptive in my class. We agreed that he would receive one warning and I would ask him to make a good decision. We also moved him into another homeroom away from some of his partners in crime. By the end of the semester, LeBron and I had a working relationship.

However, LeBron continued to get into serious trouble with other teachers and even with the assistant principal and principal. Things escalated to the point where he was arrested and received a long-term suspension. By the time I left at the end of the semester, he was no longer in school. No one was sure where he was, but I saw him later at the Dr. Martin Luther King, Jr. celebration. As he saw me coming up to greet him, he ducked his head and tried to avoid eye contact. I said hello, and he responded minimally. We never got any further than that.

Another problem child in my final semester of teaching was Libby. Libby was a very social, talkative African American girl. She was used to doing whatever she wanted to do whenever she wanted to do it. She resented my asking her to follow directions and frequently came to class late and was disruptive. I tried to reason with her, but she would become defiant and wouldn't acknowledge my presence. Naturally, this led to some serious confrontations.

Several times, Libby was sent to the office for insubordination. Eventually, she became convinced that I was racist. She believed it was all about the fact that she was black. She saw my problems with LeBron and decided I was just picking on the black kids. She told this to her friends as well, and they soon adopted that attitude.

I visited with the assistant principal about Libby, and he told me that she had always been that way. He had visited with her mom in the past, and mom blamed everything on racism as well. There wasn't much use in bringing mom in to have a conference.

I decided to try to win Libby over with praise when she did

something good. She was not a strong student, but whenever she did something well, I would go out of my way to compliment her. She did a good job on one of the research papers, and I praised her effusively. She began to warm up a bit and at least would look at me when I talked to her. However, her behavior didn't improve appreciably. Libby was in my class for three periods a day, so it was a constant challenge. Dealing with her behavior became an ongoing issue.

There was some success when I explained to her that she would be given one warning and then a referral would be written up. She needed to decide how she wanted it to go. The responsibility was placed on her, and if she did not cooperate, she would get a referral. The assistant principal and I decided he would give her lunchroom detention for referrals which meant she could not eat with her friends. Since socialization was her main motivator, this had some effect. She got a little tired of eating by herself in the office. However, by the end of the semester, there didn't seem to be a lot of progress with Libby. When I took pictures with myself and the students in the last week, she said she didn't want to be in the picture. She must have thought she was hurting my feelings. We went on with the pictures while she stood to the side.

Libby had been the poster child for being late for class, but my warnings had some effect. I heard Libby get on other students for coming to class late when they were occasionally tardy. It did not occur to her how ironic this was.

When I came back to visit several weeks into the new semester, she did greet me warmly. I asked the new teacher how Libby was doing, and she indicated she had not been a problem. Maybe she had learned some self-control.

One of the things I continued to learn throughout my educational career, whether it was as an assistant principal, a principal, a superintendent, or a teacher, was not to take things personally. This is sometimes very hard to do when someone attacks you directly. You just must remind yourself that other factors may be causing their stress and anger, and it does no good to engage personally. When I did that, the outcome was usually much more positive.

There is an old saying in education:

"The kids who are the hardest to love are the ones who need it the most." Anonymous

Another common saying is,

"Be kind, for everyone you meet is fighting a battle you know nothing about." *

Anyone who has been involved in education for any length of time can vouch for the truthfulness of these statements. The adult just must step up and make an effort. Sometimes it works, and sometimes it doesn't, but you can never give up.

*Wendy Mass, The Candymakers

17

BACK TO SCHOOL

After retiring as superintendent, I was contacted by a colleague superintendent who needed an interim business manager. My assignment was to guide her business office staff until she could find a permanent replacement. That job involved a two-hour commute so we worked out an arrangement in which I would arrive two days a week. The superintendent, Sue, began calling me "Two Buck Chuck" because of the two-day arrangement. The work was enjoyable, and it was fun working with a whole new staff.

After that position ended, I ran for the state senate. There had been a strong anti-education contingent in control in the legislature, and I felt it was time for a change. This was a very Republican district, and I ran as the only Democrat. Jeff was the incumbent, and he had joined the ultra-conservative faction that would not increase funding for education. Shortly after my entry, Jeff withdrew, and two Republicans battled for the nomination.

The campaign was time-consuming and difficult, but I learned so much about so many aspects of state government. Some amazing people helped with my campaign and together we worked our tails off. My volunteers and I knocked on 10,000 doors. I received around 10,000 votes, but it was not enough to win. However, the new senator from our district was much more supportive of education funding.

After the campaign, I relaxed and finally began to enjoy retirement. Riding my bike and traveling to see my children and grandchildren made for an enjoyable life. I also began writing this book.

In early August of 2017, the superintendent who had taken my place in Independence called me. He asked if I would be interested in coming back as a teacher. The school district, like many in Kansas, was having a difficult time finding teachers to fill all their openings. They asked me to fill a position as a sixth-grade social studies teacher. The position was only for a semester since they were confident that they could get a newly graduated teacher at the semester break.

Matters were complicated by the fact that Mary and I had put our house up for sale and were planning to move to the Wichita area to be near her new job. She was already working in El Dorado, left on Monday mornings, and returned on Fridays, so I was home alone during the week. When I first contemplated taking the job, we joked that the house would probably sell as soon as I started teaching. To further complicate the issue, we had already scheduled a trip to Scotland in October to see my daughter's family. The superintendent assured me they would find a substitute while I was gone for those two weeks.

Social studies is my area of expertise, so I felt comfortable with that part of the job. However, my teaching experience from 22 years earlier was all at the high school level. It would be a new experience teaching at the sixth-grade level. The sixth-grade curriculum was about world geography and ancient civilizations. I was comfortable with the geography, but not as knowledgeable about ancient history.

I have always gotten along well with kids and was confident that I could do a good job as a sixth-grade teacher. However, there was a concern about how the teachers would take to the idea of their former superintendent returning to the classroom.

Two scenarios concerned me. My first concern was that the teachers who knew me would see this as an arrogant act on my part. They might surmise that I considered teaching easy and I could step right back into the position. The other concern was that I might not do a good job and then they could say,

"See, it's not as easy as you think."

It had been a long time since I was in the classroom and there was a concern that my age might make it difficult to work with such young students. It was going to be a challenge.

When I agreed to take the job, I committed to giving it everything I had. The idea that teachers might see me as a failure in the classroom was not acceptable. I did not want to end my educational career on a sour note. And, as we had suspected, the house sold within a week of my accepting the job.

The position was my third job since formal retirement. My son accused me of just wanting to have lots of retirement parties. After the assignment was completed, he called it my third annual retirement.

While preparing for this semester of teaching, one of the challenges I faced was decorating my classroom with only a few days before students arrived. All the other teachers on my team were women, and they had the most organized, impressive looking classrooms I had ever seen. The classroom I was assigned to had not been in use the previous year, so it had plain walls with no decorations. My classroom was smaller than the others on my team, and I could see that it was going to be crowded. I had to squeeze 22 students into the two-person tables available.

Anxious to keep up with my team, I quickly worked on finding posters to put up in the classroom. There wasn't much time to spare, so I went ahead and ordered some posters online on my credit card. I thought that I could just turn in the receipts and get reimbursed.

When telling the principal what I had done, I noticed a wry grin on Mr. Hayward's face. He informed me that district procedure required that I fill out a purchase order, get it approved, and then wait for the district office to order the materials.

"Who made that stupid rule?" I said. "I don't have time for all that red tape."

"A previous administration developed this process," he smiled. "I'll see if I can work around this by taking it from my building budget."

"Oh, sorry about that," I replied.

Going forward, I followed the district procedure I had previously developed. I was getting a taste of my own policies.

My colleagues had neatly cut out lettering with pithy sayings on them all over the walls of their classrooms. I had a few posters ordered but had to get instructions from Mrs. Hennen to find out how to work the letter cutout in the faculty lounge. I neatly lettered my classroom rules which were summarized into two short sentences. They read 'Respect People' and 'Respect Property.' That seemed to encompass any possible scenario.

I also had to figure out the procedure for laminating paper. Simple but important details like hall passes didn't even cross my mind until I saw the elaborately designed passes of my colleagues. By the end of the first week, Mrs. Carroll took pity on me and provided me with some nicely laminated passes. Hey, I thought I was going to teach social studies and didn't remember all the other necessary details that go along with teaching!

I decided to accept the position for the semester only one week before the start of school. That meant I had to build lesson plans quickly while attending all the requisite meetings that are a staple of the beginning of a school year. I must admit to being somewhat resentful of the superintendent and administration for taking so much of my time. I thought I could have better used it to prepare lesson plans and the classroom itself. Teachers must have thought the same about me when I was superintendent. That was some real payback!

I took some comfort in the fact that much of the material that was covered in these meetings helped orient me to the new position. I dutifully joined all the new teacher training that was offered and participated appropriately. At the meetings attended by all teachers, I could not help but notice a slight smirk in the eyes of some of the experienced teachers. It was as if they were saying:

"He will soon find out how hard this is."

As we prepared for the first day of school, I got to know my fellow sixth-grade teachers on a whole new level. We were in the trenches together. We taught in teams of four and two of the teachers on my team had been there the previous year. Our team leader, Mrs. Carroll, had taught at the school for thirteen years and was extremely helpful. The other new teacher, Mrs. Hennen, was coming back to the classroom after a 20-year absence, which was similar to my situation. The fourth teacher, Mrs. Jackson, was starting her second year at the school.

I was full of questions about rules and procedures. What responsibilities will I have for supervision? What is my classroom schedule? What special events will disrupt my normal classroom routine? I also spent some time asking Mrs. Carroll about classroom activities to keep sixth-graders engaged. If I was successful, a lot of the credit goes to Mrs. Carroll for her guidance and patience with me.

Technology was one of the first hurdles for me to clear. I take pride in being technologically savvy for my age, but there was an entirely new series of programs to learn. There was the program required to submit lesson plans. There was the grade book which was accessible to parents and had to be kept current. There were the SMART boards in the classrooms that I had to learn to operate and program with flip charts. During our complete remodeling of the building under my superintendency, I had insisted on the latest technology. We installed Promethean Boards in every classroom that could accept the latest in audio-visual instruction. At that time, I didn't need to know how to operate them, but now I had to learn. I am comfortable with technology, but I am not patient. Learning all those things in just a few days was almost overwhelming.

I said a quick prayer, "Dear God, give me patience. But hurry up!"

The week of the first day of school I started to have back pains and felt queasy in my stomach. At first, I attributed it to nerves but quickly recognized the signs of a kidney stone. Great! That's all I needed during the first week of school. Poor Mrs. Carroll drove me to the emergency room and watched me puke my guts out as I begged for drugs to relieve the pain. They confirmed a kidney stone, and after an IV I was feeling no pain. With Mrs. Carroll and Kellie, the Director of Learning Services, in the room, I said I felt fine and was ready to teach. They laughed at me and said "You're just high on the drugs. Calm down and pass this thing."

School was to begin on Thursday, and I felt all right on Tuesday. However, by Wednesday afternoon the pain was returning. There was no way I would make it to school on the first day, so arrangements were made for a sub. I felt terrible about missing the first day, but the pain was unbearable, and I made an appointment with my urologist. After checking me over, he scheduled outpatient surgery that afternoon. What a great way to begin the school year. Somebody is going to stick an instrument up my penis and pull out a rock on day one!

Once the stone was removed, I felt great and was ready for my first day on Friday. Twenty-two pairs of sixth grader eyeballs stared at me in first hour, and the new adventure in my life in education began.

With such a short time to prepare for the school year, there were a lot of things I hadn't fully thought out. My first day was spent explaining classroom rules and procedures and expectations for my students. As sixth graders, they were new in the building and fairly compliant during the first week. That first day was easy enough but the next week was a full five days.

That first weekend I spent at least five hours at school working on lesson plans. I was not fully familiar with the program in which we entered our lesson plans but was satisfied that my plans for the first week were successfully entered. When I ran back up to school on Sunday evening to print out my lesson plans, I panicked. The plans that printed out were someone else's, and I had not put my plans in the proper folder. I slept fitfully that night while worrying about what would happen in my classroom the next day.

I went to school on Monday morning gripped by panic. I fumbled around while hurriedly preparing for students. Where were my lesson plans? The computer was fighting me. Suddenly, the plans I had prepared the previous weekend turned up and were printed out. This calmed me down a bit, and I got through the day. That evening I called my wife.

"Mary, I don't think I can do this," I said. "I need to call the principal. At least I can tell him I'll finish the week."

"You can do this," Mary said to me calmly in her level-headed way. "You've been through much worse than this. It's just the first day, Chuck. The first day can be nerve-wracking for anybody."

"I guess I can see how it goes," I finally said.

She had talked me down off the ledge. This time!

On the second day, I was a little better prepared and calmed down a bit. Many of the students were very sweet, remembered me from my superintendent days and made me feel welcomed. Several students drew pictures and presented them to me as their gifts. That softened my heart a bit. By the third day of that week, I was feeling much better and felt that I could make it through the semester as planned. The biggest issue was to get lesson plans put together that would engage the students and help them learn the material.

I spent 6-8 hours on the weekend trying to organize the next week's lesson plans and eventually moved ahead by a couple of weeks. Everything had to be ready up to the week I would leave for Scotland. Then I had to prepare for the two weeks that the substitute would be in my classroom. Also, I wanted to have plans for at least the first week back. It would take several days to adjust to the time change, so I wanted to plan ahead. If I ended up spending my first few nights home burning the midnight oil doing lesson plans, it would be miserable.

The other sixth-grade team had an experienced social studies teacher. I relied on Mrs. Allen to help me with a lot of the preparation and borrowed from her lesson plans. She was a great help, but I didn't want just to copy her lesson plans. I was going to create my own plans that fit my teaching style.

The first few weeks were a review of world geography. Most of the students had received some instruction in the subject in the fifth grade. We learned about the continents and oceans and how to read maps, including the understanding of latitude and longitude.

After the first test, it was a little disappointing that some of the students still couldn't remember the difference between those two imaginary lines. After expressing my disappointment, I asked how we could help them better understand. Some of my students who were involved in sports had mentioned that they frequently run laterals. Laterals are drills in which they slide from side to side in a defensive position. We used that as our memory technique. I had students do laterals in front of the class and then asked them, "Are they moving side to side or are they moving up and down?"

When the obvious response was that they were moving side to side, I said,

"Laterals are like latitude. They go side to side. This is how you can remember them."

This little trick helped a lot of the students, but some still couldn't remember the distinction between latitude and longitude. The only solution was to continue to drill them on the concepts.

After getting through the review of geography concepts, we got into the meat of the subject. We started with Ancient Mesopotamia. I was not that well versed on the topic, so I had to do a lot of research on my own. Our textbook had very little on the topic, so I used outside resources extensively.

We began by understanding that most early civilizations were hunter-gatherers and the Mesopotamians were the first to begin to build civilizations. We learned about the first form of writing, cuneiform, and about how the rivers were essential to life in the earliest civilizations.

To my surprise, the students were very interested in cuneiform. They thought it was cool how the Mesopotamians developed a writing system by carving it into soft clay and then drying the clay. We found a site that translated cuneiform into our alphabet and the students were directed to sign their names in cuneiform. They really enjoyed that little exercise. One student asked if she could bring some clay to make a tablet on which we could inscribe some lettering. We had one student in each class do a model. Again, to my surprise, they were engaged in this exercise. Several began signing their papers in cuneiform. I had to remind them that it still needed to be in English since I could not read cuneiform without a guide.

Ziggurats were another topic that interested the students. These temples to the gods that were erected by Ancient Mesopotamians were intriguing. Several students made model ziggurats out of Legos and egg cartons. I was finding out that anything that involved working with their hands grabbed the interest of most students.

Research on the computer was another area that was engaging for students. If the computers booted up in a timely fashion, most of them stayed engaged. On days when the computers were slow to operate, it was difficult keeping their interest. Eventually, I opened the topics and let students research any area within the subject that interested them. That worked well.

However, one day my seventh-hour class was in the computer

lab doing research when the computers were exceptionally slow. They could not contain their energy and became loud and started goofing around. After a short period, I told them to shut the computers down and return to the classroom. I chewed them out and asked if they had any idea how we could do research productively when there were too many students who just wanted to play around. Several suggested that those who were serious be allowed to do the research while others stayed in the classroom. That sounded good, but I couldn't be in both places at one time, so that wasn't practical. Doing research in our classroom also was not practical because we didn't have enough computers and many of the computers we had were much slower than those in the lab.

I realized that seventh hour was going to be a problem. Students were tired of school by that time and anxious to get out and have their freedom. I would have to conduct that hour differently.

There is a certain amount of terror that grips every new teacher. It is the terror of losing control of a class. That can happen at any time, and there is no foolproof solution. Sometimes it has nothing to do with your technique or planning. It may just be the mood of the students or the time of day. Terror strikes every morning as you hear the students coming to your room. The only antidote is meticulous planning, and sometimes that isn't even enough.

Teachers who have planned for every minute of the period go into the day with much more confidence, but even those plans can go awry if students are uncooperative. Sometimes what you are planning sounds good in theory, but students don't respond like you expect them to. That's why there always needs to be a plan B.

There were many days when I went to school feeling I had a pretty good outline for the day. However, just before the students came in, I questioned if the plan would keep them engaged. Doubt would set in, and panic would threaten to take over. Mrs. Carroll told me she sometimes checks the mood of students in the morning and changes her plans accordingly. If she sees that they are all wound up, she may choose a different schedule. Some days you just can't get much done. The noise level in the cafeteria at breakfast time is a fairly reliable indicator of the mood of students that day. Assistant Principal Moseley told me he was advised by another administrator that a full moon affects student behavior. He didn't believe it at first but said that after a couple of years in that position he is now a believer.

One thing I quickly learned is that students have much shorter attention spans than I remembered from 22 years ago in the classroom. They seem very bright, but if they are not entertained every minute, they get restless and lose interest. I don't know to what to attribute this. Some say it is smartphones and immediate gratification. Others say it's a lack of discipline and yet others say it is video games. It may just be a change in our culture, but it is obvious to me that kids today have much shorter attention spans than I remember from my earlier teaching days. They seem to be smarter, but they seem to care less about learning. I could be wrong, but that was the impression I was left with, at least in that location.

It was terribly frustrating to explain something in detail, and less than fifteen seconds later have students ask me to explain what I had just explained. Frequently, they didn't follow my instructions because they were talking rather than listening, which was terribly annoying. I started using my Dad voice to get their attention. When that didn't work, I would loudly yell "HEY!" That usually quieted them for a minute or two because it scared them, but often they went right back to talking.

After trying several unsuccessful techniques, I finally settled on a widely used management procedure from Kagan Professional Development that worked some of the time. I clapped my hands three times, and the class was then to clap three times and be quiet. It was a signal to listen closely. Over time this technique lost some of its effect, but there were always some students who would clap and ask others to be quiet. It was humorous to see some of the worst offenders get frustrated with their classmates and tell them to "shut up."

I was also concerned about the students' writing skills. I was stunned to see how poorly they wrote on my first assignments. Something as simple as capitalizing the first word in a sentence seemed to be a foreign concept for many, as did writing a full sentence. I decided to insist that they improve their writing skills. My son, Matthew, is a college professor and constantly remarks about how poorly his students write. He makes it his goal to improve their writing. I decided to do the same at a lower level.

I knew that previous teachers taught the concepts. It just didn't seem important enough to the students to take it seriously. After a while, it is easy for a teacher to lower standards out of frustration. I vowed not to do that and made writing skills an important part of my grading process.

Legibility was another problem I encountered. Many of the students had handwriting that was so sloppy it was barely legible. As someone who was taught by a handwriting expert in grade school, this bothered me. Several students' writing was so bad I couldn't even make out their names. None of the students wrote in cursive. It was all printing. I know they were briefly taught cursive, but teachers have said that they just don't have time to properly teach cursive along with all the other things they are required to teach.

I was reminded of a lengthy discussion we had about the topic with the board of education when I was superintendent. Some board members felt it was important to teach cursive writing. Others felt it was no longer critical in our electronic culture. After a lengthy discussion, no real decision was reached except to continue to teach cursive in the limited amount of time that it was already being taught. Some people get very worked up about the teaching of cursive writing. I am ambivalent about the topic. I just want the writing to be legible whichever form it takes.

So, with this backdrop, I settled into my position as a sixth-grade social studies teacher. I was going to learn a lot myself. The team that I worked with was essential because they helped me to keep my expectations realistic yet challenging. Every week was a new adventure for me, but as I got further into the semester, I found my comfort level and settled into it.

Our unit on Mesopotamia went well. Students got engaged in the subject matter and found some topics that deeply interested them. It surprised me how interested the students were in the religious beliefs of ancient civilizations. They loved to learn about the different gods the people believed in and the powers attributed to them. The ancient civilizations credited much of nature to the action of their gods.

I sometimes wondered if my students realized that the gods were legends developed by the people because they didn't understand science. They were enthralled with the purported powers of the gods. Eventually, I realized that the students thought of them as superheroes like they saw in movies and video games. The line was a bit blurry between reality and fantasy. Oh well, it kept them engaged.

I gave the final test on the unit on Mesopotamia and got the tests graded and returned in one day. It was rewarding to see that the students did well on the test. I felt we had covered the subject thoroughly but was uncertain how much the students retained. To my surprise, there were a lot of perfect scores and most students did quite well on the test.

Fridays are always a day of relief for teachers. Whether it was a good or bad week, it is wonderful to get to Friday and know you have a couple of days reprieve from the stress. Frequently, after the kids go home, teachers gather in the hallways and recount the events of the week. Quite often the topic is the few kids that seem to flip everyone's trigger. There is lots of laughter which is our release from the stress of dealing with the difficult kids.

One Friday, our sixth-grade team gathered in the hallway after a particularly difficult week. We had all had trouble with a few of the same kids and were recounting the incidents. We were happily laughing about the antics we had experienced. The FCCLA teacher (Family, Career and Community Leaders of America, formerly known as Home Economics) joined us and told her stories as well. She explained how one particularly difficult student, Deveon, had made pies in her class for a project. The students got to eat their own pies, but when they were finished, there was some left over. The teacher asked the students whom they should share their pies with and Deveon suggested that the principal, Mr. Hayward, should have one. She thought that was very nice of Deveon and gave him permission to take the pie to Mr. Hayward.

When Deveon arrived with a pie and told Mr. Hayward it was for him, he was startled. He thanked Deveon and said it looked very good. Deveon was a frequent flyer in Mr. Hayward's office and had been suspended several times. After Deveon left the office, Mr. Hayward considered the possibility that this pie had been tainted before it got to him. He discreetly wrapped it in a plastic bag and placed it in the trash can.

Later when she heard about this, the FCCLA teacher laughed at herself for not realizing that Mr. Hayward would be skeptical of receiving any food from Deveon because of their frequent adversarial relationship. She didn't think he had contaminated the pie, but she understood Mr. Hayward's reluctance to take the chance. I explained that as a principal I always checked carefully who was working when I went to restaurants. If I saw some of my students, particularly those who had been in trouble, I watched the preparation of my food very attentively.

I told the story of the students' fear of Mrs. Hennen and her math class. Marci was dogged about insisting that students turn in their assignments. Our team frequently had notes to send certain students to see her during homeroom. I began to call her "The Math Nazi." One day there was a note to tell those students who hadn't turned in their assignments that Mrs. Hennen must have them before lunch. One surrendering student came to my desk and said,

"May I take my math assignment to Mrs. Hennen right now? If I don't, she'll just track me down at lunch anyway."

Mr. Kelly and I told our story about being assigned to keep an eye on the boys' bathroom after lunch. Apparently, there had been some incidents in which some kids were filling their hands with liquid soap and throwing it in the faces of other kids. We plotted our strategy, and each took our turn standing by the door. This gave us a view of the sink and soap dispensers. One day while I was watching, a student looked back at me suspiciously as he washed his hands. He soaped them three times and spent a long time washing them off. He kept glancing back hoping I would get bored and leave. However, I diligently held my post and after the third washing urged him to move on. He sauntered out of the bathroom with a disgusted look. Maybe it was just a coincidence, but no soap was thrown that day.

Mr. Kelly was watching during his turn and one of the students, while soaping up at the sink, turned to him and asked why he was there.

"I heard a rumor that there was soap being thrown around in here," he answered. "I'm just here to check it out."

"Oh," the student blurted out and quickly exited the bathroom. No problems were encountered that day.

We all recounted the stories of some of the antics we had dealt with that week. Mrs. Carroll told us about Carl, an ADHD student who simply could not sit still. She caught him feigning masturbation and moved him to the back of the room.

In consideration of the fidgeting of this age of students, Mrs. Carroll had purchased inflatable balls for the kids to sit on. Unfortunately, one of her students had poked a pen into one of her balls and deflated it. Several others were soon punctured, and the inflatable balls were eventually removed, and chairs returned.

Every Friday we remarked to each other that the week was almost over. Even on weeks in which we got out early, we greeted each other with a cheerful "happy Friday." There was visible relief on the faces of teachers on those days. We tried to get as much grading done and entered as possible on Friday afternoon so we would not have to use our weekend for that purpose.

One of the fun things we did with students to create a welcoming atmosphere was hold monthly birthday celebrations. Any students on our team who had a birthday that month were invited to bring one friend and eat lunch in Mrs. Jackson's classroom on a designated day during that month. The teachers took turns bringing a treat, usually cupcakes. It was an opportunity to bond with the students in a relaxed environment. They enjoyed this activity, and the adults sang Happy Birthday to the students.

By early October it was time for my trip to Scotland. Before leaving for my trip, I asked the technology director to set up a microphone and camera on my desktop computer so I could Skype the students while in Scotland. They were excited about the idea and wanted to see the castles and other sites. We had previously discussed time zones, and I showed them there was a six-hour time difference. This meant that when I Skyped the seventh-hour class which began at 2:00, it would be dark in Scotland. They were enthralled with this idea.

I also had to prepare the substitute for the topic he would be teaching. We had just begun Ancient Egypt, and he would have to teach the bulk of that section. Mr. Wilson, who was a full-time substitute, was anxious to teach this class. He was an art teacher by training and planned to do a lot with the magnificent art of Ancient Egypt. I gave him a broad outline and then let him decide how he wanted to handle this topic. I told the kids that Mr. Wilson would do a better job of teaching about Egypt than I could because of his art background.

After finishing all my grading and giving final instructions to Mr. Wilson, I was off to Scotland. It was great being with my daughter's family. My granddaughters, Adelyn and Anna, were ten and eight years old, so Adelyn was just a year younger than most of my students. I had shown my students pictures, and they were especially excited to meet Adelyn through Skype.

On the first day in Scotland, I accompanied my granddaughters to their school. The teachers asked me to talk to the classes about schools in America. I gave them an overview of how schools operate, and they asked very insightful questions. We discussed the different starting times for schools since this school purposely began at 9:00 am to give students more sleep time. We had a great time comparing daily routines, and after visiting with Anna's class, her classmates told her:

"You have the best grandpa ever." That is one of my proudest awards!

After working through the technology and wearing out the patience of my son-in-law Aaron, we finally were able to connect on Skype. The first call was to the sixth-hour class which met at 1:00. My daughter Sarah and I had gotten away together at a local pub, and we decided to make a call to show that it was now dark in Scotland. The students were stunned as I showed them a picture out the window of the darkness while they were sitting in the daylight of 1:00 pm back home. We were in the dark at 7 pm. We were careful to hold the phone in a way that they could not tell we were in a pub.

The following day we all went to see Stirling Castle, a prominent tourist site in Scotland. We made the video call to the students with the castle in the background. After several failed attempts we finally got through to the class and were able to carry on a conversation. Adelyn did most of the talking and introduced her little sister, Anna. The students were captivated by the fact that they were conversing with us halfway across the world. Keep in mind that many of these students had traveled very little, some of them had never been out of Kansas. We were not able to talk very long, but I recorded Adelyn giving tours of different parts of the castle to show when I returned to class.

After a two-week absence, I returned to the classroom with many pictures, videos, and pamphlets. It was gratifying that most of the students were glad to see me back. I received many hugs and warm comments. The unit on Egypt was not yet completed, so after a couple of days of review, we were prepared for the test.

I had instructed Mr. Wilson to make a list of questions on Ancient Egypt that could be used for the unit test. He gave me a good list of things they had covered and those items were added to the test. I also assigned the students a research paper consisting of a minimum of three paragraphs. I insisted the paragraphs be written in full sentences, properly punctuated, and at least one paragraph should give their impression of their topic. They were free to choose any topic associated with Ancient Egypt. Most of the topics were about pyramids, pharaohs, the gods, or ancient weapons of war.

Many of the papers were of surprisingly good quality. Some of the students made very attractive power points with illustrations and explanations. These usually went far beyond the three paragraph minimum. The writing was also getting better. There were still some with poorly written sentences, but it was better than some of the previous assignments. I realized that the students were much more engaged when they could do their own research. There were always a few who were disruptive and played around when we were in the research lab, but even some of those kids became engaged in their topic.

Again, most students did well on the test, and I was relatively pleased with the research papers. I made a point to let Mr. Wilson know that students had performed well and that was a credit to his instruction during those two weeks I was gone. He had enjoyed the time having his own classroom and did a lot of artwork with the students.

The next unit was about Ancient India and the Indian Subcontinent. This did not provide nearly as much interesting material for the students, but again they did well on the final exam. They also did well on the research papers for the area. There were not as many captivating topics as with Egypt, but many of the reports dealt with the sacred Ganges River which was highly polluted, the clothing and foods of the area, and the religions of Hinduism and Buddhism. They also liked to learn about Mt. Everest and the Himalayas. I was able to find a live Google Earth video of climbers on Mt. Everest, and that captured their interest.

In my last several weeks of teaching, the topic was Ancient China and Ancient Japan. Those were topics that garnered more interest among students than usual. There was so much in the history, culture, and art that almost any student could find something that appealed to them. There was added interest because I had visited China six years earlier and had many pictures. Students got excited learning about the Forbidden City, The Great Wall, and the Ancient Samurai Warriors. They also were fascinated by Chinese writing and Buddhism. We learned about Confucius and his wise sayings and studied Japanese Haiku Poetry.

During our study of Confucius, we looked up many of his wise sayings and students were asked to interpret the meaning in their own words. One of my favorites was, "The first step to listening is to stop talking." I reminded my ever talkative students of this admonition frequently. It became a running joke as I repeated this mantra when students were particularly unmanageable.

Another quote that the students liked was, "Real knowledge is to know the extent of one's ignorance."

We discussed the meaning of this at length. Students understood that knowing how much you don't know is a real sign of intelligence. I emphasized that admitting we don't know something and searching for the answers is what intelligent people do. They really got into the wisdom of Confucius.

After studying and analyzing the Confucius quotes, they were given an assignment to make up their own wise quotes and then interpret them. They became very engaged, and some of the students came up with numerous 'brainy quotes.' I was besieged by requests to "Come look at this one, Mr. Schmidt." Many wanted to read them to the class.

That exercise provided what I call 'magical moments' in the classroom. Students are totally engaged in the activity and are enjoying it while they are learning. That was one of my proudest moments during this teaching stint. Other teachers told me they heard students talking about their quotes in the hallways as they worked their way to their next class. It is the ultimate compliment to a teacher when students discuss the topic outside of the classroom. What a great feeling that day!

Following are some of the 'brainy' quotes that students created.

Laney says: *"Friends will break your heart, but real best friends will be right there by your side when it happens."*

Addison says: *"There are no bad people in the world, just people who need a little love."*

Wyatt says: *"Silence is when you hear the most."*

Kenna says: *"Many people will walk in and out of your life, but true friends leave footprints in your heart."*

Abby says: *"Keep calm and dance on."*

The wisdom of these kids was very impressive to me. Sometimes in my frustration with their behavior, I forgot how bright they are.

Another activity that got many students engaged was writing Haiku poetry. This was a form of Japanese poetry that is only three lines with a total of 17 syllables. The general structure is that the first line is 5 syllables, the second is 7 syllables, and the third is 5 syllables. The poem is brief, but it is supposed to paint a vivid mental picture.

Many of the more poetic students became totally engaged in this exercise. They produced several poems that class period and some even came to me with the poems they had done on their own in the ensuing days. We had a handout that helped students organize such poems. They were first to select a topic in which they were interested. Then they were to list some words relevant to that topic and state the number of syllables in each word. Lastly, they were to put these words together in a picturesque, meaningful way to construct the poem. This process helped them get started, and the particularly interested students became quite prolific at producing Haiku poetry. Following are some of the best of the student creations:

Delaney:
Look, leaves falling from trees
Wind a blowing, leaves falling
Looks so colorful

Jayah:
Standing in the cold
Slipping on the freezing ice
Eating cold snowflakes

Delilah:
There are naked trees
Outside the snow is falling
Winter is so fun

Jackson:
Tacos are crunchy
Tacos have good vegetables
Tortillas and meat

Georgia:
Falling white snowflakes
Falling white snow deep today
Melting not today

I felt like the students got engaged in both exercises. There was a lot of creativity, and some quality products were developed. These were the times when the enveloping feeling of success wraps its warm arms around a teacher. It took me back to my earlier days of teaching when I had students writing their own psalms and proverbs. It was a great feeling to see my students creating and knowing that they were working at the highest level of Bloom's Taxonomy, an educational guideline for higher level thinking. Throughout my years as an administrator, I had brought in many experts to train teachers on techniques of engagement and higher order thinking skills. As a new teacher again, it took me several months to be able to apply this knowledge in the classroom.

Because of the engagement of students in the two activities I mentioned above, I had students select what they thought were the best of the quotes and the poems. The selected writings were then posted on a bulletin board for all to see. Fortuitously, Kellie, the district curriculum director was observing my class on the day that we were doing Confucius quotes. I found myself playing to that audience and feeling a deep sense of pride in how engaged the students were. The creativity was flowing, and it was an emotional high for this teacher. I realized I had fully returned to my teacher roots when I found myself trying to impress the administration.

Several students provided unique challenges to this newly minted teacher. Some of the more severe behavioral problems were mentioned in the chapter on difficult students. There were several who tested my patience but could be good students and were somewhat manageable.

Alexandria was a girl who had a very unstable background. From my understanding of her story, her mother was in prison, and there was no biological father in the picture. The father of her half-brother had adopted her and was doing his best to help her be successful. Alexandria had deep-seated anger and would alternate from wanting to please to being totally uncooperative. She had above-average ability but sometimes just refused to do anything.

Our team tried to encourage Alexandria and often kept her after school to finish projects. Her father was cooperative in allowing her to stay after school if he was called and notified. Mrs. Hennen kept her frequently to catch up on mathematics, and I had to keep her after school to guide her through her research paper. She could do the work when she chose to, but frequently just didn't care. I had numerous talks with her, and we got along well. When I mentioned that she sometimes seemed like she didn't care she remarked:

"That's right; I don't."

Finally, our team met with Alexandria and her dad to talk things out. This was when we learned more about her background and why she had this deep-seated anger. She had already been seeing the school counselor, but the counselor told us she had very little to say in their sessions. I asked Alexandria to see the counselor regularly but told her that if she doesn't open up there is nothing the counselor can do for her. She and her dad agreed to this arrangement.

By the time I finished my semester of teaching, it was too early to tell if Alexandria was making any progress. She was seeing the counselor, and we hoped that might eventually make a difference. We told her that even if she gives up on herself, we would never give up on her. Dad was helpful and cooperative. He did not know what to do and was appreciative that we were trying.

Marty was a student who had come from a neighboring state that school year so we knew little about him. His mother had married a local farmer, and he moved with her. It was obvious from the beginning that he was very bright. He was also very loud and could be disruptive. He liked to be the center of attention. I tried to keep him engaged in class, but he frequently became disruptive and just wouldn't be quiet. He was very good with technology, so he was occasionally asked for advice whenever I had trouble with the SMART board or my computer. Eventually, he became hostile to me after I pulled him aside and scolded him a few times. Then his behavior got worse. The rest of the team was having the same problem. Finally, I called his mother and asked her to come in for a visit.

Mom was not at all surprised at what we had to tell her. She told us he had been in serious trouble at his previous school for the same behavior and had been suspended. She said she had not heard from the school this year and hoped that meant he was doing OK. She had heard that one of his teachers was the former superintendent and figured he had probably seen everything and knew how to handle Marty. Wow was she wrong!

Mom stated that he was oppositional at home also and they had little success in getting him to be respectful and compliant. She stated that he usually got worse when he was punished. We discussed several things that we could try and promised to keep in touch. One of the problems we had with Marty is that he was smart enough to know just how far to go with his disrespect. He would take it right to the edge and then back off so that you felt like you didn't want to overreact.

Later that day, Marty made it obvious he was angry that we had met with his mother. He sulked in class and made a few disrespectful remarks toward me. I had kept him from attending Fun Friday activities previously, and he was angry about that also. During lunch, I asked him to come in and have lunch with me so we could talk.

During that discussion, I told him that the teachers would no longer put up with his behavior. I told him he would enjoy school a lot more if he could find a way to be more cooperative and stop being disruptive. I pointed out to him that I would only be here a short time and he would have a chance to reinvent himself with the new teacher, but he needed to start the change now. He listened without much reaction. He was then told that he could go to Fun Friday, but he would have to sit down and talk with me during that time.

Fun Friday was at the end of the day on Friday during Homeroom. Those students who did not have makeup work and had no disciplinary issues were allowed to go outside or to the gym depending on the weather. It was an incentive to get students to be cooperative during the week. When Friday came, and their name wasn't on the list, some students became angry and uncooperative. Marty adopted this attitude frequently. That time, I let him go to the gym but sat him down with me while I supervised. The other kids were running around the gym playing basketball, soccer, or volleyball, or just talking.

I explained to Marty that he was obviously very intelligent and he was also quite hyperactive. He indicated that he is sometimes bored and likes to stay active. I asked if he would like to do little jobs for me which allowed him to get up and move around. He was very enthusiastic about that. I also asked if he would like to help other students who were struggling on assignments and he was interested in that. I told him that he is quickly getting the same reputation that he had at his previous school, and he needed to change that soon.

There were only two more weeks until the end of the semester, so there was not a lot of time to see any change in Marty's behavior. However, in those two weeks, I made a concerted effort to allow him to do little chores around the classroom. His attitude was much better, and although he made it clear he couldn't wait until I left, he was no longer disrespectful. The other teachers reported similar behavior.

Then there was Kierra. She was a likable girl who occasionally gave me hugs and seemed to like being in my class. She could do quite well academically if she tried, but frequently she made no effort. If the topic wasn't of interest, she just shut down and read a book. I would have to physically take the book away sometimes and get her back on the subject matter. She loved art and loved to draw, so I tried to give her opportunities where she could do that. It was a constant struggle to keep her engaged, and she was barely passing the class. The only time she really got involved was when we did the research papers, and she was able to pick her topic. She usually picked something that involved a lot of art.

I visited with her several times and pointed out to her that she reminded me of my daughter, Christine. Christine was intelligent just like Kierra, but if it didn't interest her, she sometimes didn't apply herself. She also liked to draw and was now working on a degree in business marketing. This piqued Kierra's interest, and occasionally she gave me drawings to give to Christine. She was proud of the fact that I likened her to my daughter, but it never really changed her work habits. When I left, she expressed regret that I was leaving, but there had been little change in her behavior.

Kellen was another problem student right from the beginning. He was loud at inappropriate times and oppositional to authority. When I tried to correct him, he immediately pointed to others he claimed were doing the same thing. He argued that he was being picked on. He never admitted anything and always felt he was the victim. That got annoying very quickly. The other teachers complained about the same behavior. He threatened that he would have his mom call me about picking on him. I encouraged him to do so, but of course, she never did.

After a couple of minor disciplinary referrals with no effect, we called the parent for a meeting. Mom was very willing to visit with our team and indicated she had the same problems at home. He never admitted to doing anything wrong and picked on a younger brother mercilessly. She said she would visit with him about our concerns.

The next day Kellen was told I would no longer put up with his disruptions, and his mom agreed. I told him I would simply start writing disciplinary referrals whenever he was disruptive. He was defiant, but he listened. Over the next several weeks, I noticed a distinct difference in his behavior. He began to respond to my requests to be quiet and eventually was urging others to be quiet when I was trying to give some direction to the class. It tickled me to see him becoming irritated with those who were noisy at the wrong times. By the time I left, our relationship was much improved.

During the last week of the semester, we finished our unit on China and Japan and watched the Disney movie Mulan about a Chinese girl who went to war in her elderly father's place. I also took pictures of each class on the front steps of the school. They were told this would help me remember them when I left. We had fun with the pictures as we took serious ones and goofy ones.

It was getting close to Christmas, and many of the students melted my heart with gifts and notes. Some stopped me in the hallway to plead with me not to leave. Of course, there were those who were glad to see me go and one of the most problematic students, Libby, declined to even be in the pictures. It was a bittersweet week. I was glad to be finished with the class but was sad to leave these kids. They were very lovable, especially in that last week.

As I was packing up to leave my rental house the next day, I saw a lady in a wheelchair next door going to her car. I greeted her and apologized for not being a friendlier neighbor. I told her I was seldom home and had only lived there for two months. While talking to her, Abri, one of my students, came running out of the house screaming,

"Mr. Schmidt!"

She ran up and gave me a big hug. The lady who lived next door was her aunt, and she stayed with her occasionally. Abri proudly told her aunt that I was one of her teachers. Again, my heart was warmed by the innocent enthusiasm of my students.

After Christmas break in the second week of January, I went back to Independence for a dental appointment. I made it a point to stop in at school and see the students and my teaching team. What a warm welcome I received. As I poked my head in the door to greet students, they squealed with delight. Even Libby, who had convinced herself that I was a racist, greeted me warmly. Hunter was the first student I saw in the hallway, and she came running to give me a hug. Kierra had an especially warm hug, and Marty went out of his way to shake my hand with a huge smile on his face.

I asked several of them if they were good for their new teacher and they insisted they were. After visiting with the new teacher, Ms. Brunetti, it seemed that things were going quite well. Ms. Brunetti was mature beyond her years and looked to have a solid handle on managing the classroom. Many of the students proudly told me they were studying Ancient Greece and were creating their own Greek Gods. I was reminded of how excited they were when we studied the gods of the early civilizations.

After school, I brought cherry limeades to the teachers (this was a favorite after-school drink) and had lively conversations with them and several students. The whole experience gave me a warm feeling and made me glad that I had taken the opportunity to teach in my last round as an educator. There were even a few tears as I drove home that afternoon. This was finally the end of an exhilarating career.

EPILOGUE

WHAT DOES IT ALL MEAN?

So, what did I learn from my 33-year career in education?

Since I was a teacher and administrator in private and public schools, people frequently want to know my perception about the differences. Generalizing about that topic is difficult. I can only give my impressions from the limited experience I have in both.

My private school experience was all in Catholic Schools. In most cases I found a higher percentage of parents to be more involved than in public schools. They took the effort to enroll their child in a private school for whatever reason, and they were paying for the privilege. This seemed to encourage them to be innately more engaged in their child's education and behavior.

In private schools, the staff has more leverage to enforce rules and behaviors. There are different expectations, and the parents know that when they enroll their child. This doesn't mean that they are always supportive, but they know what they are getting into. If a child does not follow the rules, there is always the threat of expulsion. Students can be expelled much more easily in private schools than in public schools because they are there by choice.

We often hear private schools publicize that their students score higher on achievement tests and college entrance exams. In many cases that is true. However, public schools have very different clientele. They have to take any student that walks in the door. That includes those whose parents are absent, disengaged or even downright hostile. The students of those parents are disadvantaged from the very start. And public schools take those children with every kind of disability. Private schools have the luxury of being selective.

I admit to having used these achievement results to espouse the benefits of the private schools I was associated with. However, after working in public schools, I began to understand that this is an unfair comparison. The teachers that I have been associated with in public schools work just as hard and care just as much as those in private schools. In fact, it seems to me that they have to be more skilled to reach the students that they work with.

I no longer take sides when people argue the relative merits of public or private school. They each have their purpose, and there are good and bad schools in both categories. A parent needs to make that choice on their own. The problem is that so many parents do not have the resources to afford a private school. Many religious based schools provide assistance with the tuition, but it is still a difficult choice for families with severely limited resources.

Taking money from public schools to provide vouchers for private schools is not the answer either. If we strip public schools of resources we leave them short-handed, and they become a repository for the very poor. And if we give public money to private schools, we must demand that they follow the same requirements of allowing any student, regardless of ability or disability, to attend. Many private schools do not have the resources to deal with students with disabilities even though they might wish to do so.

So my answer to the question of which is better; public or private, is an unequivocal, "neither." They serve different purposes, and both have a place in our society.

So, how did my experiences affect me and change my perceptions?

One thing I learned for sure was that, in many ways, kids are different from the early days of my teaching in the 1970s. But in many ways, they are still the same. They are different in that they have much shorter attention spans. Everyone has their theories of why this is so. I don't know the answer to that question, but it was obvious to me that there is a much greater need for today's students to be entertained. I don't mean that in an unproductive way. They can be learning while they are entertained, but many cannot learn if they are not entertained. This is different from my earlier teaching experience. At that time, there seemed to be more interest in learning for the sake of learning.

Today's students seem vastly more knowledgeable than I remember from the '70s to the '90s. They have access to so much information that is easily obtained. They don't always know what to do with that information, but that is a timeless condition. The ease of obtaining information is also a great help to teachers. Gone are the days of going to the encyclopedia or other books to search out facts. Almost any question can be answered in a matter of seconds. Teaching students how to use that information is the primary role of our outstanding teachers today. Putting things in context and learning how to apply facts to real-world situations is what the master teacher focuses on.

Students today come from much more dysfunction than I remember from my early teaching years. In my earliest days of teaching, it was relatively rare to have children from divorced families or single parent homes. Now, it seems to be the norm. Some of the instability that these kids come from makes it hard to focus on school. It is not that there haven't always been disciplinary issues in school, but I believe today's situations are more serious. There is not as much widely held respect for authority and compliance with rules. Students lose their innocence earlier these days. They have seen so much of life that we usually try to shield them from. Today, it is not unusual for middle schoolers to be sexually active. We had a thirteen-year-old middle school girl who was pregnant. Thirty years ago that didn't seem to be as prevalent an issue.

Defiance of authority is much more brazen today in my experience than it was thirty years ago and sometimes with that comes violence. I had 11-year-olds who got physical with the principal and a uniformed police officer.

In my experience, the most glaring difference is in the role of parents. I imagine parents care as much about the success of their child as they ever did. But there seems to be a decline in the guidance and discipline of children. Too many of them come to school today with little or no concept of following direction or respect for others. Our kindergarten teachers spend a good deal of time on these concepts out of necessity. They can easily spot the children who received direction at home or who attended a quality pre-school. Too often I found that when a child got in trouble at school, the parent was quick to blame the school for the problem rather than confront their child's behavior. It is my impression that too many parents are afraid to have their child angry with them. Consequently, they take their side on every altercation.

Teachers today seem much more skilled than in the past. Teachers come out of schools of education better prepared for the classroom. We were given a textbook and keys and told to teach the kids. Today, there are standards and a curriculum to guide the teacher. And today's teacher needs to know so much more about classroom management because they cannot expect students to behave if they are bored. There is great research available to help today's teacher know how to keep students engaged and to understand how learning takes place in the human brain.

I am not implying that things were so great in schools 'back in the day'. Things were different, sometimes for the better and sometimes for the worse. I believe it takes much more skill to be an effective teacher today. In spite of the lackluster pay, the intangible rewards of teaching are as great as ever. When students call you a great teacher or go on to be successful, and you can claim a small part of the credit, that brings an incredible feeling of accomplishment. That is the greatest reward for someone who takes this job because they want to make a difference in students' lives.

If I were to go back to administration again, I would do some things differently. I would be more conscious of the need to give teachers time to prepare lessons and plan for their classrooms. I would also search for the most effective practitioners in education and try to expose my teachers to those techniques. There is so much outstanding research about effective teaching and classroom teachers need that training to add to their toolbox.

I would also do my best to have plenty of support staff for teachers. There is a great need for counselors, social workers, and administrators who can create a better climate so the teacher can teach. Of course, all that costs money, and I would also want to continue to increase teacher pay.

Hey, I can dream, can't I?

These are my impressions from my limited experience. I don't profess to have all the answers, and I'm sure many can legitimately argue against my conclusions. I put it out there to express my feelings and respect anyone who sees it differently.

So what conclusions have I reached personally?

There is no doubt that education was the right profession for me. I have no regrets spending the bulk of my career in this vocation. Sure, I made mistakes that I would like to do over, but I would still spend my career in education as the best place to "make a difference."

During the spring of 2018, I made another trip to Scotland to see my daughter's family. After returning, I emailed Ms. Brunetti to ask if the sixth-grade students might be interested in seeing more pictures and hear about my trip. She replied that they were enthusiastic about having their former teacher come back.

Before returning, I meticulously studied the picture seating chart to remember the students' names. I knew how important that was to the kids and didn't want to disappoint them. When I walked down the hallway I was warmly received by the students and able to remember most of their names. While presenting, I had to ask Marty for help with the SMART Board, and he was happy to comply. I asked several of the kids who were real challenges if they were behaving. They all indicated they were, but when Stetson told me he was being good, one of the girls right behind him said,

"No, he's not!"

Stetson laughingly confirmed, "She's right. I haven't changed." Stetson's candor was refreshing.

Once again, it was a warm feeling to see the students. They were excited to see me. I was much more open to the hugs than I had been when still teaching. It seemed very natural this time around. They indicated they had learned a great deal while I was teaching them. Hearing that is the greatest reward a teacher can receive.

What a way to end my career in education. I had started as a teacher and worked my way up through the chain of command. Ending where I started was a special gift that capped off my career with a bang. I wish every new teacher could have as rewarding a career as mine has been.

THE END

Born in Hays, Kansas, and raised on a dairy farm, Chuck Schmidt graduated from St. Joseph Military Academy, now Thomas More Prep-Marian. He received a BS in education from the University of Kansas, a Master's Degree in Educational Administration from Fort Hays State University and District Certification from Emporia State University. Besides his 33 years in education in Kansas, he also spent nine years in a dairy farm partnership and two years as a Substance Abuse Counselor. He has been a teacher in Topeka, Hays and Independence, Kansas. His administrative positions were in Topeka, Eskridge and Independence. He has five children, five grandchildren and lives with his wife, Mary, in Wichita.

Made in the USA
Columbia, SC
24 July 2019